Anna Aslanyan is a journalist
service interpreter. She grew u
and feels most at home in boc

Praise for *Dancing on Ropes*

'Translation is a matter of life and death – and not only
because it is poorly paid. That's the thrilling, rather
chilling, message of this wonderful history by translator
and interpreter Anna Aslanyan, who blesses jaw-dropping
and entertaining tales with an insider's insight' Rosie
Goldsmith, *Financial Times*

'Full of lively stories … leaves the reader with an awed
respect for the translator's task' *Economist*

'Wide-angled and reader-friendly … Aslanyan covers huge
swathes of territory with a pleasantly light touch … A
singular achievement' Boyd Tonkin, *Spectator*

'Engaging … Aslanyan's compendium of tales of
interpreters at work spans not just the globe but historical
experience … [She] doesn't merely pay homage to her
forebears in this honourable profession. Her deeper
purpose is to get us to consider the future: to drive home
the point that while this may be an era of machine-
learning, it's too soon to dispense with the human
professionals' Bridget Kendall, *Literary Review*

'Ranges engagingly across period, geography and media
… Illumine[s] both the complexities of the craft and the
thorny question of the translator's agency' Sarah Watling,
Times Literary Supplement

'Joyous ... A real treat' Robert Fox, Reaction

'Anna Aslanyan compellingly recounts ... verbal exploits [and] miscommunications ... weaving in anecdotes from her experience as a Russian–English interpreter and translator' Emily Lawford, *Prospect*

'Language both connects and divides us, and translators are the bridges between us: if ever there were a time when we needed to remember that we don't all think the same way, that concepts and idioms are different in different languages, it is surely now. And Anna Aslanyan is the perfect guide for this journey. She has produced a wonderful compendium of stories from the world of translation, which turn out to be stories of the world' Natalie Haynes, author of *Pandora's Jar*

'This richly stocked treasure-house of stories about the amazing exploits of translators introduces us to a huge cast of heroes. With engaging lucidity, Anna Aslanyan explains the complexities and conundrums that language professionals have grappled with over the ages, showing just how much skill, courage, ingenuity and wit they have deployed to keep the peace, spread the word and foster conversation among the peoples of the world' David Bellos, author of *Is That a Fish In Your Ear?*

'A colourful tribute to the translators and interpreters slogging away throughout history, oiling – or clogging – the wheels of diplomacy and culture. Flitting from saints to cheats, drudges to adventurers, pedants to geniuses, Aslanyan sketches a lively history of an underrated art. Highly enjoyable' Gaston Dorren, author of *Lingo*

DANCING
ON ROPES

Translators and the Balance of History

ANNA ASLANYAN

P

PROFILE BOOKS

This paperback edition first published in 2022

First published in Great Britain in 2021 by
Profile Books Ltd
29 Cloth Fair
London
EC1A 7JQ

www.profilebooks.com

1 3 5 7 9 10 8 6 4 2

Printed and bound in Great Britain by
CPI Group (UK) Ltd, Croydon, CR0 4YY

A CIP catalogue record for this book is available from the British Library.

ISBN 978 1 78816 264 7
eISBN 978 1 78283 552 3

Contents

Introduction		1
1	Shaking the World	8
2	Comic Effects	22
3	The Arts of Flattery	33
4	Observation and Analysis	48
5	Treasures of the Tongue	64
6	The Sublime Porte	74
7	Infidelities	87
8	Precision Was Not a Strong Point of Hitler's	97
9	Little Nothing	109
10	The Last Two Dragomans	120
11	As Oriental as Possible	131
12	Fifty Per Cent of Borges	145
13	Word-worship	158
14	Journalation	172
15	Dealing with the Natives	184
16	Rectify the Names	193
17	The Obligation of the Competent Authorities	208
18	Alogical Elements	220
Notes on Sources		237
Acknowledgements		249
Index		251

Introduction

On 26 July 1945, the Office of War Information in Washington issued the Potsdam Proclamation, an ultimatum demanding that Japan, still at war with the Allies, surrender. On learning of it the next morning, the Japanese foreign minister Shigenori Togo did not see it as a command to surrender unconditionally, and instead proposed negotiations with the Allies, urging the government to treat the matter 'with the utmost circumspection, both domestically and internationally'. One of the cabinet members disagreed, proposing instead to reply that they regard the proclamation as absurd, but Prime Minister Kantaro Suzuki supported Togo, and it was decided to publish the text in the press without comment. The papers, however, couldn't help remarking on the ultimatum, which they considered a 'Laughable Matter', to quote one headline. Another compromise was found: the prime minister would read a statement making light of the proclamation without rejecting its terms. At the press conference, Suzuki said that the government did not think the document very important, adding, 'We must *mokusatsu* it.'

The Japanese word literally translates as 'kill with silence', though Suzuki later told his son he had intended it to convey 'no comment', an expression for which Japanese has no direct equivalent. The Americans translated it as 'ignore' and 'treat with silent contempt'. On 30 July, the *New York Times* front page announced, 'Japan Officially Turns Down Allied Surrender Ultimatum'. The fate of Hiroshima was sealed.

Historians are quite right to point out that the tragedy wasn't caused by translation difficulties alone. Yet debates around the translator's role, as old as the profession itself, always revolve around the question of their agency. In our multilingual world the balance of history, unstable as it is at the best of times, hinges on different interpretations of words. Some translators believe themselves to be a mere conduit, ideally an invisible filter through which meaning flows; others argue that it's far less straightforward: in the end, they use their own words, accents and inflections, and so they inevitably influence things. Can translators take liberties? Should they? The nature of the job, as we are about to see, means that interventions are hard to avoid.

When Donald Trump referred to certain states as 'shithole countries' in 2018, translators the world over took the trouble to mitigate this definition. The most polite version, used in Taiwan, was 'countries where birds don't lay eggs'; Japan went for 'countries that are dirty like toilets'; in Germany they said 'garbage dump'. The same year, the international media interpreted the word used by Jair Bolsonaro during the Brazilian presidential campaign, *limpeza*, as 'clean-up'. What did the candidate really mean? Did this translation underplay the predicament of his enemies, who might have actually been threatened with 'cleansing'? However broad the spectrum of meanings hidden in the original message, a translator's choice of words can have immense consequences. When the literal phrase 'Death to

America' – widely used in Iran since the 1979 revolution – is rendered as 'Down with America', the world begins to make a bit more sense.

My own work as a freelance translator and interpreter has never, to the best of my knowledge, tipped the scales of history. But it has given me ample food for thought, allowing me to see more vividly the figure of the translator surrounded by precarious events in which they cannot help intervening. It is this image that I would like to outline in these pages.

Human communication, even in one language, always comes with the proviso that we understand and are understood much less than we hope. Early in my interpreting career, a court case made this especially clear to me. The woman I was interpreting for sat there with her head buried in her hands throughout the hearing, which concerned the custody of her child. I didn't realise at first, and she wouldn't say when asked, how little the legal formulae (which I did my best to translate, showing off my recently learned legalese) meant to her, when all she wanted to know was whether she would be reunited with her son. When the judge got to 'It would be my intention to allow this appeal' she still didn't react to the good news. Afterwards, as her lawyer explained the judgement in plain English, I duly interpreted it, feeling the dead weight of dictionaries falling off my shoulders as she looked up and nodded. This time she understood it all.

Anyone who has ever tried translating anything will be especially interested in gaps between languages: gaps created by conceptual differences and cultural assumptions. It is in these often overlooked spaces that translators must make decisions, often relying solely on their own judgement. What else are you to do when you are the one holding all the cards? What informs this decision-making process is your belief in the translatability of human experience.

The Spanish philosopher José Ortega y Gasset opens his famous 1937 essay 'The Misery and Splendour of Translation' with the claim that translation is a utopian enterprise. He argues that humans think in concepts rather than words, and that no dictionary is able to provide equivalents between any two given languages as no two words conventionally regarded as translations of each other can ever refer to the same objects. Others have made a similar point by talking of the language of thought, or mentalese, a non-verbal code processed by the human brain.

According to this theory, to be able to translate accurately you need a thesaurus with a comprehensive list of synonyms for each entry, as well as examples of each word's use in every context imaginable. Then, provided the other party has a similar reference book containing not merely words but experiences, you might be able to find the exact correspondence between the two. Unless such compendiums are available, perfect translation is a fantasy (and so, by the same logic, are writing, reading, speaking and indeed all intellectual endeavours). In this light, translation may appear to be an unsolvable problem, yet it's worth tackling, especially given the evidence that communication in more than one language is, after all, possible. It can be effected in infinite ways, though word-for-word translation is seldom one of them. Things would be different in the ideal world, where every word would have the perfect match in every dictionary, every sentence would be clearly written and every message carefully enunciated. Our world is not like that – and so much the better.

The translator's real concern is not words but sense. To preserve it, you can smooth the original's strange features to make the meaning more accessible, or you can retain some foreign notes in your translation, ensuring that it comes across as such. Do these approaches have to be mutually exclusive? A hint lies in the way translation as a practice is defined. It can be considered an art, a craft, a pastime, a hobby, a necessity, depending on what motivates those engaged in it. It can be as creative as you make it, but it is also a secondary activity: the original has to be there first. It can be a vocation, a calling, a main occupation, but also a sideline, something to fall back on when you need a break from your other job, when you are desperate for some new experience or just desperate. Translators have often doubled as poets, slaves, doctors, apprentices, lawyers, spies, preachers, diplomats, soldiers, and so on. 'So let us say that translation is a trade, like cabinet-making or baking or masonry,' the writer and translator Eliot Weinberger proposes. 'It is a trade that any amateur can do, but professionals do better.'

Translation, therefore, is a job like any other, driven by supply and demand; something you can be inspired by or simply do for a living, taking things on as they come: a divorce case or an experimental novel, a car manual or a holiday brochure. As you go about your task, your actions can change the world around you in more ways than you expect. This book will talk about translators doing things that, while not being part of their official remit, shape the way they approach their job. It will talk about the quality of translators' work, an elusive concept, and look into the relationships between translators and those who need them, something made especially complex by inevitable gaps in mutual comprehension. Finally, it will give a glimpse of the future – not too distant it seems – when translators may have to grow even more versatile in order to compete with machines.

The stories collected here show translators at work, describe what they do and what happens next: concrete actions and their consequences, momentous or otherwise. As for theory, it's the province of the translation police (as the more dogmatic among translation studies scholars are known in the trade), who see it as their task to enforce rules, from linguistic to ethical to political. These people are part of the translation ecosystem but not of this book. It is about those who, rather than lurching between abstractions, take the plunge, hoping to solve a problem that may or may not have a solution. What keeps them awake at night is not the thought of how feasible translation is, but the question of how to translate a particular idiom, treatise, poem, address, novel, judgement, joke; to make it intelligible while preserving both the letter and the spirit; to get at its meaning; to make it work.

If translation is about finding a space between gaps, or a compromise between meanings, how best to perform this balancing act? 'It is almost impossible to translate verbally, and well, at the same time,' John Dryden wrote in 1680 in the preface to his translation of Ovid's *Epistles*.

In short, the verbal copier is encumbered with so many difficulties at once, that he can never disentangle himself from all. He is to consider at the same time the thought of his author, and his words, and to find out the counterpart to each in another language; and besides this, he is to confine himself to the compass of numbers, and the slavery of rhyme.

After giving the matter careful thought, Dryden delivers his verdict, still valid today:

> It is much like dancing on ropes with fettered legs: a man may shun a fall by using caution, but the gracefulness of motion is not to be expected; and when we have said the best of it, it is but a foolish task; for no sober man would put himself into a danger for the applause of escaping without breaking his neck.

A figure dancing on a rope, with its joyful as well as sinister connotations, is an apt image for the profession. Translators must simultaneously work towards several goals: to get the message across and not to break certain constraints, to stay upright and to maintain flexibility. To keep everything in balance, they constantly move between these near impossibilities, and the world moves with them.

1

Shaking the World

If you want peace, prepare for war. As the USA and the USSR clashed in the Cold War, each striving to prove the supremacy of their ideology, both claimed to be acting in the name of peace. Along with a range of technological innovations, a new vocabulary was deployed: 'computer', 'cybernetics' and suchlike became ubiquitous; 'sputnik', the Russian for 'companion', was adopted to denote a satellite on the other side of the Iron Curtain; 'capitalism' and 'socialism' needed little translation, although their definitions varied between the rival camps. The conflict – as much a war of meanings as of beliefs – often had the opponents sound vague: sometimes genuinely unsure of what to say; sometimes trying to achieve something; sometimes falling into traps set by their own language of propaganda. Verbal exchanges between the two superpowers, refracted through translation, would occasionally spiral into a stand-off or culminate in a real showdown.

As Richard Nixon and Nikita Khrushchev prepared for their first meeting in 1959, everyone expected a duel of proverbs. Given the Soviet premier's penchant for idiomatic expressions, the vice president was advised to brush up on American sayings. Having done so, he didn't pull his punches in their 'verbal slugfest', to quote Khrushchev's biographer

William Taubman. When a discussion about the Captive Nations Resolution, recently passed by the US Congress in support of the 'Soviet-dominated nations' (the Soviets, for some reason, preferred a less specific adjective, 'enslaved'), reached an impasse, Nixon ventured to say, 'We have beaten this horse to death, let's change to another.' Khrushchev hit back: 'This resolution stinks. It stinks like fresh horse shit, and nothing smells worse than that.' Nixon had his reply ready: 'I am afraid the chairman is mistaken. There is something that smells worse than horse shit, and that is pig shit.' Perhaps hoping to clear the air, Khrushchev's interpreter replaced 'shit' with the Russian word for 'manure', duly registered by the note-takers but later ignored by commentators in favour of the direct translation.

It was on this occasion, at the American National Exhibition in Moscow, that Khrushchev famously claimed the USSR would soon 'catch up with and overtake' or, in another translation, 'overtake and surpass' America. Nixon riposted by suggesting that his hosts might be leading in the development of rockets, but 'there may be some instances – for example, colour television – where we're ahead of you'. With these words, he gestured to the camera recording them on what must have been the first videotape to have travelled that far east. 'Nyet, nyet,' Khrushchev interrupted. 'We've overtaken you in that technology too.' The 'kitchen debate' continued in the Miracle Kitchen, full of shiny state-of-the-art gadgets, which Khrushchev found ridiculous. 'Do you have a machine that puts food in your mouth and pushes it down?' he asked. Shown the IBM 305, he similarly waved it away, saying that the Soviets had computers too, in abundance, just as powerful but much bigger.

Nixon was impressed with Khrushchev's boisterous delivery style as well as with his body language, which included 'a repertoire of gestures that a conductor of a brass band would envy'. Not that it made his improvisations any easier to translate. The shit exchange was followed by more colourful boasts and threats from Khrushchev, yet it was his extemporaneous forays into Russian folk wisdom that made the aides' job especially difficult. Unlike literary translators, diplomatic interpreters tend to stick to word-for-word rendition as much as possible, even at the expense of losing a bit of atmosphere or fluency. So when Khrushchev promised to show the Americans 'Kuzma's mother', the proverb – an unspecified threat meaning, roughly, 'We'll show you what's what' – was translated literally, and subsequent explanations didn't make it much clearer.

The mysterious mother continued to puzzle the Americans for a while. At another meeting later the same year, when Khrushchev repeated, 'We'll show you Kuzma's mother,' his interpreter, Viktor Sukhodrev, chose to translate it as a teasing remark. Everyone braced themselves for an argument, but then Khrushchev turned to Sukhodrev: 'Did it go wrong with Kuzma's mum again? Listen, just explain to them, it's simple. What it means is, "something they've never seen before".' The penny dropped: Khrushchev had never intended to intimidate anyone (at least not with this expression); he had merely been misusing the Russian idiom all the while.

Literalism in translation can reduce the risk of what's known in the trade as 'extending a metaphor': a situation when a seemingly innocuous saying loses its figurative quality. Numerous examples of this have been passed down the ages as true stories, albeit varying in detail and not always traceable back to a concrete occasion. Apocryphal or not, they illustrate well the treacherous nature of proverbs. One such incident is reported to have occurred at a major international conference when a Soviet delegate used a proverb approximating to 'mixing apples and oranges', and the interpreter went all in: 'Something is rotten in the state of Denmark.' When a Danish representative grabbed the mike to protest against this 'unwarranted slur', the dumbfounded speaker condemned what he assumed to be a provocation. On another occasion, an interpreter enlivened an EU meeting by translating 'Some prefer not to use liquid manure' as 'Liquid manure is not everyone's cup of tea.'

The uncertainty that permeated Cold War discourse, while often deliberate, could also stem from insecurity. If in doubt, the strategy seemed to be, crack a joke. Sometimes this approach worked; sometimes it backfired. Meeting Hubert Humphrey, an American senator, in Moscow in 1958, Khrushchev asked him about his home town, and when Humphrey pointed out Minneapolis on a map, Khrushchev circled it with a blue pencil, explaining, 'That's so I remember to give instructions to spare this city when the rockets fly.' The senator, on confirming that Khrushchev lived in Moscow, said, 'I am sorry, Mr Chairman, but I cannot return your kindness.' Although the exchange amused everyone present, it was not at all clear who was going to have the last laugh. The USSR was enjoying rapid economic growth and advances in space exploration, with the launch of Sputnik I in 1957 followed two years later by the first mission to the moon. Khrushchev was on a 'peace offensive', which culminated in a trip to the

US in 1959, a high point in his love–hate relationship with the West. He was accompanied by aides-cum-interpreters, among them Oleg Troyanovsky, soon to become his chief foreign policy assistant, and Sukhodrev, an accomplished linguist well respected in both camps. The pair draw on the visit in their respective memoirs.

Visiting America for the first time, Khrushchev was determined not to show how impressed he was. His interpreters were instructed to convey his reactions in an appropriate catch-up-and-overtake spirit. Things that required interpretation in more than one sense of the word emerged immediately upon their arrival when, on the way to Washington, they saw people lining the route: of an estimated 200,000, a few smiled and waved, but the majority stood there, as Taubman relates it, 'stone-faced and strangely silent'. The *Washington Post*'s George Dixon wrote of the mood in the crowd: 'I didn't know whether to cheer wildly, applaud perfunctorily or just stand there emitting little sounds that could be translated as anything.' Whatever sounds were emitted, the Soviet press translated them unequivocally: 'shouts rolling up like waves', 'outbursts of applause', 'joyous cheers', 'gladness, warmth and cordiality' all featured in their reports. Sukhodrev did notice some enthusiastic faces – the Soviet embassy had strategically placed its staff and their families along the route.

To break the ice at their first meeting, Khrushchev presented Dwight D. Eisenhower with a box containing a model of the space capsule that had recently reached the moon. He was as talkative as ever: Sukhodrev remembers his 'irrepressible volubility', while William Hayter, the British ambassador in Moscow in the 1950s, describes him as 'rumbustious,

impetuous, loquacious, free-wheeling, alarmingly igno-
rant of foreign affairs'. He 'spoke in short sentences, in an
emphatic voice and with great conviction', even though he
often 'stumbled in his choice of words' and 'said the wrong
thing'. When that happened, his interpreters usually corrected him discreetly. There are no hard and fast rules on
whether an interpreter should preserve errors or remedy
them. Sukhodrev's basic principle was: if a speaker makes a
mistake that's clearly a slip, correct it without drawing their
attention to it. Not all interpreters are of the same school.

As his American hosts went to great lengths to impress
Khrushchev, he wallowed in his insecurities, throwing
tantrum after tantrum, taking many things as insults, and
when his aides tried to explain that a number of more controversial questions reflected 'American pluralism', he still
wasn't having any of it. Visiting IBM in California, in a
reversal of his position on kitchens, he liked their cafeteria
better than their computers (self-service catering facilities
soon appeared in some Soviet cities, whereas computers
took longer to arrive). Dismissing advances in information
technology, Khrushchev said that he hasn't been 'converted
to your capitalist faith' because, as a Russian proverb has it,
'Every *kulik* praises its own bog.' Sukhodrev – who'd heard
of the bird called *kulik* but, like most city-dwellers, had no
idea what it looked like – didn't know the English word for
it. He extricated himself with the impromptu 'Every duck
praises its own pond;' one of his American colleagues used
the dictionary definition, 'snipe'; a newspaper report offered
another variant, featuring 'snake' and 'swamp'. The next
day, another paper ran a story headlined 'Cold War Between
Interpreters'.

At one of the events in New York, when someone brought up Stalin's terror, Khrushchev, who had three years earlier denounced the personality cult of his predecessor, went red in the face and once again tapped into folk wisdom: 'A lie, however long its legs, can never keep pace with the truth.' Some of his utterances were so confusing, it was as if he had rejected Stalin's chilling clarity along with the rest of the dictator's legacy. In fact, Khrushchev's idiomatic outbursts were a curious product of preparation (like Nixon, he had been encouraged to bone up on things) and improvisation. Although most of his speeches were carefully rehearsed, he was never one to watch his tongue. On a memorable occasion in 1956, he snapped at Western diplomats, 'Whether you like it or not, history is on our side. We will bury you.' As he explained later, he meant that the USSR would outlast the West economically and politically; moreover, his words had a basis in Marxist theory: capitalism was fated to die a natural death, and since someone had to bury its corpse, the job naturally fell to socialism. But that's not how the remark was understood on the spot. *The Times* reported the phrase literally; the coverage in *Pravda* omitted it along with 'fascists' and 'bandits', words used by Khrushchev in reference to Britain, France and Israel earlier the same day.

During the 1959 US trip, at a reception in Los Angeles, the mayor reminded the Soviet premier of his now-notorious prediction: 'You can't bury us, Mr Khrushchev, so don't try. If challenged we shall fight to the death.' The guest was beside himself: he had come to offer the hand of friendship to America, 'and if you don't accept it, that's fine'. Afterwards Khrushchev pretended he had been driven by 'cold calculation' rather than rage. Whatever the truth, the incident, like most of the visit, was reported in wildly different ways, sometimes for ideological reasons, sometimes because of language discrepancies. In any case, translator-enabled communication, by its very nature, tends to generate stories that are hard to verify or disprove: whatever facts might be standing in the way, they usually leave plenty of room for interpretation.

In Los Angeles, Khrushchev planned to make a 'very short and unemotional speech', but then he couldn't help flinging his humble origins into the faces of the Hollywood crowd (which included Marilyn Monroe wearing, as instructed, her 'tightest, sexiest dress'), and so he held forth: 'Here we are now, in your city, where you have the cream of the artistic world film stars, as you say in your country.' Watching a cancan performance, he castigated it for immorality: 'In the Soviet Union, we are in the habit of admiring the faces of our actors, rather than their backsides.' The Soviets portrayed the show as positively indecent, in line with the then standard Russian dictionary definition of the cancan: 'a dance involving immodest movements'. The next day, Khrushchev was still thinking about it: 'This is what you call freedom – freedom for the girls to show their backsides.'

Not that he was a prude in his own speeches. Published as *Khrushchev in America*, they contain some fruity, and mostly unfunny, jokes, a typical opening line being 'It sometimes happens that too choosy a girl lets time slip, stays a spinster too long, and is left empty-handed.' The collection was translated from a Russian edition (the translators are not credited), which came with inevitable cuts, such as heckles from the audience and the speaker's irritated responses ('You think you've pinned me to the mat,' he snapped at one point). Called by the Soviet press 'thirteen days that shook the world', the trip was partly successful, with some progress made on the Berlin question, but Khrushchev's personality proved too awkward for the delicate diplomatic tasks he faced. A loquacious, short-tempered, foul-mouthed politician given to going off-script, militantly monolingual and not overly concerned about how he would be perceived in other languages, he might have fared better had he visited America today.

Tales of Khrushchev's humour on his first foray into the enemy camp include one about an unsigned note passed to him at an event: 'What were you doing when Stalin was committing these crimes?' He asked the author to identify themselves, and when no one came forward, he said, 'Well, comrades, now you know what I was doing then.' A good joke, especially in comparison with his other attempts, but it turns out to have been fake news, which leaves us with a single funny contribution from the Soviet premier during that visit. Seeing a woman with a placard inscribed 'Death to Khrushchev, the Butcher of Hungary' on a street corner, he lost it again. Did Eisenhower invite him here to have him insulted? When told that the president hadn't arranged it, Khrushchev said, 'In the Soviet Union, she wouldn't be here unless I had given the order.' A true bon mot, albeit unintended.

The US–USSR proverb race continued on Khrushchev's next visit to New York, in 1960, when he was interviewed by David Susskind on TV. After Khrushchev urged America to embrace the idea of peace, it was Susskind who used an idiomatic expression, asking his guest if he might be 'baying at the moon'. Sukhodrev later thought he could have translated

Susskind's words as 'breaking down an open door', but at the time, doing it live on TV, he rendered it word for word. 'I did add, "as we say", though,' he recalls in his memoir, 'to indicate that it's idiomatic.' But it was too late. Khrushchev exploded, telling Susskind that he was the leader of a great socialist state, not a dog come here to bark. Still, the interview ended peacefully.

Meanwhile, the space race was in full swing. When another American journalist asked Khrushchev if the Soviets were going to send a man to the moon, Troyanovsky interpreted 'send' as *zabrosit'*, a word often used in the sense of 'deploy', but also meaning 'throw'. Once again, Khrushchev grew indignant. 'What do you mean, "throw"? As in, "throw out"?' Raising his voice, he assured everyone that the Soviet state valued its men and would never chuck them around. On 12 April 1961, Yuri Gagarin was indeed sent into space; a few weeks later, in June, Khrushchev and John F. Kennedy had their first summit in Vienna.

'Roughest thing in my life,' Kennedy said after two days of talks. At one of the meetings, discussing West Berlin, which Khrushchev wished to incorporate into the Soviet bloc, Kennedy expressed his concern about a possible 'miscalculation'. The record of their exchange has Khrushchev describing miscalculation as 'a very vague term' and wondering whether the US wanted the USSR 'to sit like a schoolboy with his hands on his desk', but the American stenographer might have downplayed the Russian's response. According to Kennedy, 'Khrushchev went berserk. He started yelling, "Miscalculation! Miscalculation! Miscalculation! All I ever hear from your people and your news correspondents is that damned word, miscalculation! ... I'm sick of it!"'

The next day, Khrushchev continued his peace offensive, saying that if America wanted a war over Germany, 'let it begin now'. The Soviet note-taker toned this down to 'let the US assume the entire responsibility for doing so', while their American counterpart wrote down 'let it be so'.

Nuclear war was one of Khrushchev's favourite topics. On his 1959 visit to the US, he talked about it so often that one of the American interpreters, Alex Akalovsky, started using a shorthand symbol in his notes – a little mushroom cloud. Speaking at the UN General Assembly, Khrushchev proposed that 'all states should effect complete disarmament' within a space of four years. The Soviet media was ecstatic, praising 'the indefatigable fighter against the powers of darkness' and his 'profound, strictly scientific analysis' delivered in the most powerful oration 'in the history of the United Nations'. The West saw it differently, calling Khrushchev's speech 'so absurd and impractical as to be insulting'.

In his heart, Sukhodrev agreed with the latter assessment. It's just as well he didn't have to interpret the speech (that honour fell to a UN interpreter); like any professional, however, he often had to translate all sorts of rubbish without batting an eyelid. In his memoirs he recalls a ride through New York when Khrushchev noticed some building work going on and launched into a lengthy tirade about the merits of the Soviet construction industry. Listening to this popular lecture on how to build houses, the interpreter was glad there were no Americans present. 'Otherwise I would still stand by him and interpret this nonsense,' he writes. 'Any sensible person would see that it's nonsense. And yet interpret it I would!' Reminiscing years later, Sukhodrev doesn't dwell on his own political beliefs, implying that the party line had to be toed, but his true loyalty was to language.

Disarmament, the hottest topic during the Cold War days, seemed an easy notion to define – quite simply, a state of affairs when countries 'no longer possess any means of waging war' – but such glib phrases meant so little that, when translated, they caused more disagreement than the proverbs. In 1961, Khrushchev invited John J. McCloy, Kennedy's adviser on arms control, to his dacha. McCloy and his Soviet counterpart, Valerian Zorin, worked on a bilateral disarmament agreement – or, as McCloy's biographer Kai Bird describes it, 'argued over language, mechanically reading prepared speeches to each other. Zorin continued to insist on the phrase "general and complete disarmament" while McCloy held to his own formulation of "total and universal disarmament".' The two phrases being identical in Russian, 'the argument seemed rather nonsensical', as indeed did the idea of completely avoiding war as 'an instrument for settling international problems'. The UN passed the agreement (with Zorin's wording) the same year; ten months later, the world found itself on the brink of destruction.

The events of October 1962 – when the future of humankind, despite earlier peacemaking efforts, looked less certain than ever – are variously referred to in different languages as the Caribbean, October and Cuban missile crisis. After the US attempted to invade Cuba in 1961, Khrushchev and Fidel Castro got it into their heads that the best way of deterring the imperialist aggressor would be to bring Soviet nuclear missiles to the island. In reply, having considered two options, an air strike against the missile bases and a naval blockade of Cuba, the US fixed on the latter and notified the USSR. A message sent from Washington to the Kremlin on 22 October sounded rather oblique. 'I hope that your Government will refrain from any action which would widen or deepen this already grave crisis,' Kennedy wrote, 'and that we can agree to resume the path of peaceful negotiations.'

The next day, the president sent another telegram, using the term 'quarantine' rather than 'blockade', which further blurred the situation: the Russian word *karantin* has less threatening, mostly epidemiological connotations, while *blokada* brings to any Russian-speaker's mind the siege of Leningrad. During the 1959 American trip, when told he couldn't go to Disneyland, Khrushchev quipped, 'Why? Do you have rocket-launching pads there? Or is it in quarantine?' Coming from the White House, the word, while not exactly conciliatory, didn't set off any alarm bells. However, the sense of calm it created was short-lived. Over the next few days, the confrontation escalated, and when the Kremlin received yet another letter from Kennedy, dated 27 October and signed with the president's name alone, without the usual 'Sincerely', they realised that the time of vague talk was over.

The same evening, Khrushchev dictated a reply to Kennedy, thanking him for his 'sense of proportion' and promising 'to dismantle the arms which you described as offensive'. The Soviets avoided the word 'missiles' all along, feigning incomprehension, and ended up being hoist by their own 'offensive arms'. It was this ambiguous wording that later allowed the Americans to extend their demands from missiles to bombers, which eventually, after protracted negotiations, also had to be evacuated from Cuba. But in October

1962, there were far more important things to worry about. Once Khrushchev's aides translated his letter and went over it several times to bring it up to the mark, it was delivered to the US embassy. Although it was delayed by demonstrators picketing the building, chanting 'Hands off Cuba' (were they there on someone's orders?), the text reached Radio Moscow in time for the evening news broadcast. Whoever translated the letter into English got the message across all right.

In these stories of the world at the edge of the abyss, the act of translation itself emerges as a culture clash where infinite variations of meaning are capable of tipping the balance of events. We'll never know if a catastrophe would have occurred had any of the above communications been translated differently. What's evident is that the Cold War was fought not just through but also by translators. The two sides might not have always had a clear idea of what they wanted to say, but everyone knew what they never wanted to happen: a nuclear war. Better a lean peace, as the saying goes, than a fat victory.

2

Comic Effects

Ivan Melkumjan didn't envisage a career in languages for himself. An Armenian from Baku, he trained as an opera singer in Leningrad, married an Italian who fell for his baritone, moved to Italy in 1986 and began looking for work. His dulcet tones secured him a radio job translating and presenting a Russian-language programme. One day it so happened that the Italian diplomatic service was short of staff, and they approached him. 'I hardly slept the night before,' he remembers, telling me the story. 'And the whole time I was interpreting, one of the principal's aides, who knew Russian, kept looking at me, nodding his head. I thought I must've made some mistake, and he's just trying to cheer me up.' It turned out to be genuine approval, and soon Melkumjan found himself working for Silvio Berlusconi, the prime minister of Italy. That was a lucky turn, at least for one of them.

'Working with Berlusconi was difficult and easy at the same time,' Melkumjan says. 'He's a real character, he's got this artistic streak to him.' One problem with Berlusconi was his tendency to improvise, indulging in light-hearted deviations and quips, the sort of humour that, funny or not, could catch an interpreter unawares. 'When he was with friends, with people who evidently found him likeable, I went the full monty translating his flourishes, but at protocol events I usually toned them down a bit.' The only thing that seemed to stop Berlusconi from telling jokes was concern that his audience wouldn't get them. Often, however, the temptation proved too strong. On Melkumjan's first day, the official part went well, and then, as everyone was sitting down to dinner, Berlusconi pulled the interpreter towards him and whispered, 'So, shall we tell a joke?' It was a rhetorical question, but Melkumjan still felt he had to respond, and so he said, 'Well, let's try.' He gave it his all, changing some details, zeroing in on the punchline. Everyone laughed on cue, and Berlusconi immediately suggested, 'Shall we tell another?' When it was over, he turned to one of his entourage and said, 'This guy is going to work with us.'

Asking an interpreter – or indeed a humorist – how they work is like asking a centipede how it walks. Like most interpreters, Melkumjan has a good short-term memory, but at the end of a long assignment he remembers little of what was said – a professional hazard or perhaps a blessing in disguise. It was his quick-wittedness that helped him to make his name as a diplomatic interpreter in a short time. Despite being unable to understand Melkumjan's renditions of his speeches, Berlusconi thought them good; what mattered to this experienced showman was the reaction the interpreter got from audiences. After all, the main thing about translating a humorous utterance is to make sure it comes out funny, if necessary sacrificing accuracy. So what if you can't translate jokes literally? You don't need to; what's important is to get the punchline across.

Melkumjan's ability to paraphrase often came in handy. In his own words:

There's a series of jokes about *pidocchio*, a louse, popular in Italy. I know they don't like the creature in Russia: there it's a symbol of poor hygiene. So Berlusconi is telling one of those jokes, the one that ends with the husband discovering his wife's lover in the wardrobe and crying out, 'What, have we got lice here?' Naturally, I change the punchline, going for a Russian-friendly version, 'Look, there's a moth!' It works just the same – who cares what exactly they've got there.

In theory Melkumjan could have got away with random jokes from his own repertoire, picking those most likely to lighten the mood (if anything, he might have improved on the originals), but the actor in him wouldn't have been satisfied with that. Instead he raised the art of translating humour to new heights, doing it live, thinking on his feet. That was one of the main requirements with Berlusconi, who, unlike most politicians, never provided a brief beforehand. Begging his aides for reference materials was no use; the prime minister would always go off-script anyway. Melkumjan would spend the night before each important meeting reading the latest news, trying to guess what might crop up.

This wasn't always easy to predict. When Barack Obama was elected president in 2008, Berlusconi, speaking at a press conference, described him as 'giovane, bello, abbronzato'. Translated into various languages as 'young, handsome, suntanned' (to use the English equivalent), the phrase went viral: in some countries it was taken as a joke, in some as a faux pas. In Italy it caused a scandal. Melkumjan was standing next to Berlusconi at the press conference, interpreting for Russian-speaking audiences. This is how he remembers it.

I realised it was a joke and I just translated it as it was. Italian channels, reporting it, made a lot of fuss about Berlusconi's drift, and when my mum saw it on TV and heard my voice in the background, she thought it was all my fault. When I called her back she was crying: 'What did you say just now? They're all up in arms here!'

In Russia the remark went down a storm. Melkumjan's artistic talent must have played a part in it. Then again, the entertainment value of most jokes in translation needs to be converted into the local currency, and faced with the appearance of the first black American president, the rouble proved typically weak. In a nation that often regards racism as a laughing matter, the 'suntanned' bit would never have failed to provoke amusement.

Another memorable occasion when Melkumjan needed all the sense of humour he could muster while keeping a straight face was an interview Berlusconi gave for a documentary about the Russian president Vladimir Putin. 'So he's sitting there by the fireplace, relaxed, telling anecdotes about his partner and good old friend – it's all improvised,' Melkumjan begins.

At one point the presenter asks, 'Where do you both get your endless energy from?' I see Berlusconi smile, and my heart sinks because I know there's something coming up. And sure enough, he goes, 'Oh, we just use these special suppositories before work.' It's actually quite common in Italy, I mean suppositories, but I know the Russians might have a bit of a problem with that, and so I take a plunge: 'Oh, we just take three special magic pills before work.' Incidentally, this version wouldn't work in Italy: here pills are usually associated with junkies.

Anyway, everyone loved the sanitised joke, and it generated a lot of comments, so much so that journalists began asking Putin, 'Is it true that you've got some magic pills?' On hearing that, Melkumjan went cold, but luckily Putin laughed it off. 'And I just kept thinking to myself, Ivan, where would we all be now without those pills of yours?'

Humour is just one of Melkumjan's tools. His special talent seems to be his ability to explore gaps between meanings, where things tend to get especially interesting. No matter how small, these spaces can be filled with just enough nuance to convey a message accurately and, if need be, with a twist. Ambiguity, one of the hardest things for an interpreter to deal with, is, like almost everything else in human speech, culture-specific; it's also difficult to identify with certainty. 'When it's used on purpose – Berlusconi, for instance, loved doing it; he'd say something vague and give that make-of-that-what-you-will smile – then I keep it, giving the same signal, inviting the audience to interpret the hidden message themselves,' Melkumjan explains. 'But that's only when I know the speaker and their ways well enough. Otherwise, when I'm not sure if a phrase is really meant to sound ambiguous, I'll translate it as it is, so that the question itself – whether or not the message is clear – remains unclear.' Interpreting at negotiations, he often feels that if he were to translate everything exactly the way the parties put it, that wouldn't get them very far. 'Then I follow my intuition: tweak the structure of a sentence, shift an emphasis, that kind of thing. Without changing the meaning, I quietly drop or downplay things that might lead to a dead end.'

One of Melkumjan's best stories didn't result from an effort to amuse. Some Russo-Italian celebrations were being planned, he recalls. 'So the Russians said to their Italian partners, as a special gesture of our friendship, we'd like to start by performing an Italian song, say, "Bella ciao", your favourite – it would mean so much to the entire nation. Whatever gave them the idea?' This song, the anthem of the Italian partisans during the war, is now essentially seen as a leftist piece and is in fact a long way from topping Italy's music charts. Melkumjan, translating, took the liberty of modifying the suggestion: 'We'd like to perform some Italian song, one of your favourites, something that would mean to the entire nation as much as "Bella ciao" used to mean to the partisans.' Otherwise, he knew, some tension would be inevitable. The Italians liked the idea and proposed a few other songs, eventually fixing on 'O sole mio', and everyone was happy.

To translate someone well you have to understand not only what they are saying but also why. This applies to jokes (which, as we have seen, don't have to be rendered literally to produce the desired effect) and serious utterances in equal measure. 'When my client wants to achieve something, I'll make that my priority. I'll do my best to help them get there, using my skills, my delivery style,' Melkumjan says. 'I know a lot of people who just want to translate everything accurately and don't really care about the rest. I'm not like that: I work towards whatever goal the speaker has in mind.' And it appears to pay off.

The fees I charge these days are quite high, so I often ask myself, why do you think you're able to do that? I think it's because my clients come to meetings with high expectations, they have some complicated agendas, and they know I can help them realise these agendas. My aim is to allow the discussion to move forward for as long as possible. It's only when I feel it's definitely come to an end that I stop trying.

On one occasion, this attitude allowed him to turn things around completely. A large company based in one of the former Soviet countries was having problems with financing; they had spoken to a number of international banks with a view to getting a loan, but their prospects looked grim. A lot of money was at stake. Eventually they approached an Italian bank in a last-ditch attempt to save themselves from collapse. When Melkumjan, called at a short notice, arrived to interpret for them, the company representative was resigned to failure.

He was pretty sure they'd never get anything from the bank. Still, he put a lot of effort into it, speaking eloquently, addressing the bankers not on behalf of the management but personally, telling them how bad he felt about many people losing their jobs. But he clearly believed he'd already lost. At one point I said to him, why don't you try and use shorter sentences, and I'll see if I can convey what you've got to say in a more immediate way. Then I started tweaking his monologue, naturally without changing any of the meaning: a little laugh here, a stress there, always trying to give it a bit

28

more human touch. I wanted the bankers to feel exactly how he felt, to imagine the consequences exactly as he imagined them. I was nudging them towards a possibility of moving forward. I highlighted every nice thing he said; I introduced apologetic tones, rejigging his sentences a bit; I made it sound like he was asking a favour, which he'd never have done himself. And guess what: after half an hour (the whole thing was only supposed to last fifteen minutes) they parted friends, with the bank promising him to consider another loan.

The situations Melkumjan describes are the opposite of those occasions where the interpreter has to say, 'The distinguished speaker is telling a joke.' This always brings about laughter, if not of the kind the speaker is hoping for. Besides, translation can make people laugh even despite the original intention. Meeting in New York in 1995, Bill Clinton and Boris Yeltsin came outside after a session to speak to journalists. 'You wrote in your reports that our meeting was going to end in disaster,' Yeltsin said to them. 'Now I'm telling you, it's you who have ended in disaster.' It didn't sound particularly strong in Russian – Yeltsin just wanted to tease the hacks a bit and certainly didn't mean to say anything hilarious – but the American interpreter Peter Afanasenko rendered his remark as: 'Now I can tell you that *you* are a disaster!' It wasn't just what he said but also how he said it.

Well loved by colleagues for his talents, which included translating jokes, Afanasenko might have overdone it slightly, underestimating how neutral Yeltsin's words were meant to be, forgetting that no Western politician would ever attack the press like that. Anyhow, the two leaders being on the same wavelength made for an encouraging sight and an iconic photo, in which everyone is laughing their heads off. Clinton especially: he's doubled over.

In speech and in writing alike, humour, like any special effect, often requires paraphrasing. In *Is That a Fish in Your Ear?* David Bellos talks about two types of jokes: those universally understood and those exploiting the metalinguistic function of language. To illustrate the latter, he cites an example from Georges Perec's novel *Life A User's Manual*: a visiting card that reads 'Adolf Hitler, Fourreur'. The last word means 'furrier' and in French sounds similar to 'führer'. Bellos translated the inscription as 'Adolf Hitler, German Lieder', proving that a pun unique to a given language shouldn't automatically be dismissed as untranslatable.

In fact, the activities of Perec and his fellow members of Oulipo – a group exploring various constrained genres, such as homophonic translation, which involves puns based on similar-sounding constructions, for instance, 'ABCDEFG' rendered as 'Hay, be seedy! Effigy!' – are proof that translators, if given carte blanche, can do anything. 'In conjuring up faithful simulacra of works, it's thought ordinarily that translators should vanish; good translators would simply morph into shadows or ghosts of a work's author,' Derek Schilling writes (omitting the letter 'e', as dictated by another rule, in this lipogram). 'But can this invisibility fully obtain for Oulipian works born of constraint, works that call out for a forward-looking, if not brash approach to translation, and for linguistic acrobatics to boot?' When allowed to crank up the humour, a translator can actually outdo the author: those familiar with the 1935 Hungarian translation of *Winnie the Pooh* by the humorist Karinthy Frigyes believe it to be even funnier than the original.

That humour implies interaction is obvious; what every translator decides for themselves is the degree to which they are prepared to interact with it. Some choose to leave room for imagination, allowing the reader to grow into a joke; others prefer to play it safe. Umberto Eco in *Experiences in Translation* quotes a joke from his novel *Foucault's Pendulum*. The dialogue in which it features literally translates as follows:

> 'God created the world by speaking. He didn't send a telegram.'
> 'Fiat lux, stop. Letter follows.'
> 'To the Thessalonians, I guess.'

William Weaver tweaked the key phrase into 'Epistle follows' with Eco's approval. In fact, he would have probably got away without this change: in English, as in Italian, 'letter' can also be used in the implied context, and for what it's worth, at the time of writing 'Letter to the Thessalonians' produces more Google search results than 'Epistle to the Thessalonians'.

Still, such subtleties can easily kill humour and therefore need to be fine-tuned. Sometimes it's easier to rework a joke completely, especially when its premise is universal. If it uses an idiomatic expression with no direct equivalent in the target language, in many cases a similar one can be found or invented. The French author Laurent Binet, confronted with the saying 'six of one, half a dozen of the other' in a story he was translating, created an analogue for it, 'deux demis et une pinte', based on the simple fact that two halves make a pint anywhere on earth. When everything else fails, an arbitrary variation on a related theme can sometimes do the trick. Years ago, translating Penelope Fitzgerald's novel *At Freddie's* into Russian, I wrestled 'A cut above the rest' (a hairdresser's sign) into 'Don't cry for your hair', in a nod to the proverb 'When it's off with your head, don't cry for your hair.' It may not sound like the perfect recipe for business success, but it has raised a few chuckles.

Anyhow, one of the most solemn tableaux I've ever witnessed was a row of passengers on the Moscow Metro, each reading their copy of a certain Russian periodical dedicated to jokes, entitled, approximately, *Fun for Everyone*. Watching the readers silently turn the pages, I didn't spot a single smile; a philosophical treatise might have generated more mirth. The absurdity of the spectacle provoked two thoughts. First, humour often falls flat on the page, and when it's put in writing twice, its chances of survival are further diminished. Perhaps even a successful joke sometimes needs to be killed before it can be resurrected in another language. The other thought was that humour is rarely designed for individual consumption. At least two people have to share a joke for it to come alive, and if one of them happens to be the joke's author and the other wants to translate it, laughing at it together is the first step towards making it funny the second time round.

3

The Arts of Flattery

Now as the High in rank, the Possessor of genius and understanding, the Endowed with sagacity and judgment, the Prop of the learned among the followers of Messiah, the Chief among the wise people of Christendom, the English Padré Wolff, has the intention of proceeding in that direction, urged by the sincere friendship which exists between us, and in order to promote the unanimity of Islam, we are induced to issue this auspicious friendship-denoting letter, the love-increasing zephyrs of affection being reflected towards your benevolent mind, and the opportunity being favourable for announcing the ties of friendship which of old and now bind us.

Thus begins a letter the shah of Persia sent to the emir of Bokhara in February 1844. Translated by the Reverend Joseph Wolff himself, it appears in his *Narrative of a Mission to Bokhara in the Years 1843–1845, to Ascertain the Fate of Colonel Stoddart and Captain Conolly.* Over the course of his journey, he translated parts of the Koran from Arabic into Persian, conversed with Jews, Turks and Armenians, and preached in English, German and Italian.

Wolff's knowledge of these languages, however, would have been less use to him had he not adopted the motto 'When in Rome do as the Romans do.'

In July 1843, Wolff wrote to the British military 'in behalf of two of your fellow-officers, Captain Conolly and Colonel Stoddart, who are at present captives in the great city of Bokhara; but having been myself two months at Bokhara; and knowing, as I do, the character of the inhabitants of Bokhara, I am fully convinced that the report of their having been put to death is exceedingly doubtful'. A committee was formed, funds raised, and Wolff, volunteering to undertake the mission for expenses only, set off in October for the holiest city in Muslim Central Asia. Bokhara the Noble, also known as Bocara, Boghar and Bukhara, was proof that toponyms are the traveller's nightmare (translators, too, struggle with them all the time), and so Wolff prudently stocked up on maps annotated in Arabic characters. His baggage also contained a clergyman's attire, copies of the Bible, silver watches and three dozen copies of *Robinson Crusoe* in an Arabic translation. 'On reading the book which I gave them,' he recalls, 'the Arabs exclaimed, "Oh, that Robinson Crusoe must have been a great prophet!"'

And so Wolff – 'a brave but highly eccentric clergyman', to quote Peter Hopkirk's *The Great Game*; 'a splendid and quixotic Victorian original, unprepossessing, small of stature, with a flat homely face', as Karl E. Meyer and Shareen Blair Brysac describe him in *Tournament of Shadows* – proceeded on his journey. Along the way, visiting numerous legations and missions and attending meetings between British, Russian, Turkish and Persian officials, he enlisted their help, not so much linguistic as

34

administrative. For a European, travelling in Central Asia was impossible without letters of introduction. Originals usually sufficed for the polyglot Wolff; only occasionally did he rely on someone else's translation: 'His Excellency Count de Medem promised me a letter of recommendation in Russian, and I requested him also to have my doctor's diplomas and ordination-papers translated into Russian, for they have Russian interpreters at Bokhara.'

Equipped with references, Wolff commenced the last leg of his mission. He was

> dressed in full canonicals the entire distance from Mowr to Bokhara, being determined never to lose sight of my position as mullah, on which alone I soon perceived my safety depended. I also kept the Bible open in my hand; I felt my power was in the Book, and that its might would sustain me. The uncommon character of these proceedings attracted crowds ... all which was favourable to me.

Wolff's willingness to observe local customs proved as important as his command of Bokhara Persian, the language of the court. Before his first audience with the emir, asked by one of the courtiers if he would be prepared to submit 'to the mode of Selaam', Wolff said he'd gladly perform the ritual thirty times, let alone the prescribed three. 'I bowed repeatedly, and exclaimed unceasingly, "Peace to the King," until his Majesty burst into a fit of laughter, and of course all the rest standing around us. His Majesty said, "Enough, enough, enough."'

What might have seemed an embarrassment later turned out to be a lifesaver. Soon the worst suspicions of Wolff's

associates were confirmed: Colonel Charles Stoddart and
Captain Arthur Conolly had been executed on the orders
of Emir Nasrullah. The officers had paid with their lives for
their part in the Great Game. In the confrontation between
Britain and Russia over Central Asia, both parties had to
translate not only between languages but, crucially, between
cultures. Stoddart, for all his knowledge of Persian, had
failed to make himself understood on his arrival in Bokhara
in December 1838. A brave soldier but a poor diplomat,
the British envoy rode in full regimentals to the emir's
palace instead of respectfully dismounting, as was custom.
During the audience with Nasrullah, he broke every rule in
the book. Unlike Wolff, who tended to go the extra mile to
observe ceremony, Stoddart comported himself as if on a
working visit to a minor official, and as a result was thrown
into a dungeon beneath the citadel, where for many months
his sole companions were rats and other vermin. Jailers
communicated with him by lowering a rope into the pit,
although by this means he was able to smuggle out letters
to his family.

Presumed, not unjustifiably, to be a spy rather than
an emissary, Stoddart knew his fortune depended on the
success of the British in the region. 'My release will not
probably take place until our forces have approached very
near to Bokhara,' he wrote in one of his letters. Once an
executioner climbed down the rope with a death warrant,
telling the prisoner he must convert to Islam or die. Stoddart chose the former, and had to undergo circumcision (he
later declared the forced conversion invalid). Released from
the dungeon into the custody of the emir's chief of police,
he remained Nasrullah's prisoner. 'I apprehend nothing

now from the Ameer,' he wrote in another letter home, 'and the chances of his cruelly treating me diminish as his fears increase.' The authorities in London and Calcutta did try to get Stoddart out, but the emir complained that their notes appeared to have no meaning. Nasrullah's capricious despotism and the fact that the British had more important worries than the loss of a single pawn in their game didn't help either.

Stoddart's fortunes followed those of the British military in Afghanistan more generally. In January 1841, his position somewhat improved, he wrote: 'My employment for the last two months and hereafter is to translate from my books ... what I think useful for this country; and, besides this, the Ameer called for an account of European armies.' (The note doesn't say which books piqued the despot's curiosity.) The colonel's hopes were further raised in November, when Captain Conolly, a veteran of the Great Game, arrived in Bokhara on a rescue mission. Nasrullah received him politely at first, but soon the emir's mood darkened, possibly because he got no reply to a friendly letter he had sent to Queen Victoria. Ultimately, the fate of Stoddart and Conolly was sealed when the news came from Kabul that the British were losing control in Afghanistan. In June 1842, the emir put the pair back in prison, and one day the officers were taken out into a square and made to dig their own graves. Stoddart was the first to be beheaded; Conolly, offered a chance to convert to Islam, refused, and then it was game over for him too.

Of the two victims, Conolly was the more adept at reading the East. He had been travelling on official government business for years, and when in Central Asia he would sometimes adopt Persian disguise, despite acknowledging in his journals that 'however well a European spoke the native tongue ... his mode of delivery, his manner of sitting, walking or riding ... is different from that of the Asiatic'. It was easier for an Englishman to pretend to be a French or Italian physician, or a merchant en route from India, a trick Conolly occasionally used to his advantage. In 1830 he posed as a doctor in Afghanistan, 'secretly observing and noting down everything of significance'.

Others employed similar tricks too, with varying degrees of success. Around the same time, Lieutenant Eldred Pottinger, fluent in Persian and Pushtu, travelled to Kabul impersonating a horse trader. The disguise worked there, but on the way back he fell into the hands of Uzbek robbers. They were suspicious of his pale skin, his shaky knowledge of Islam and the papers and books he carried. Pottinger explained that he was a recent convert from 'the land of many mountains' south of Hindustan, and the Uzbeks, apparently convinced by his colloquial Persian, let him go. In 1837, he came to Herat on a reconnaissance mission posing as a Muslim holy man, his skin darkened with dye. As he wandered around, someone stopped him in the bazaar, whispering, 'You are an Englishman!' Luckily, the man turned out to be a friend of Conolly's. It took one Westerner to spot another – or at least to reveal as much in a language both understood straight away.

Russian explorers were as conspicuous as their English rivals, and as inventive in their efforts at assimilation. In 1819, sending Captain Nikolay Muravyov on an expedition to the city of Khiva, the capital of a powerful Central Asian khanate, his commander told him, 'Your capacity for making yourself liked, together with your acquaintance with the Tartar language, can be turned to great advantage. Do not regard the arts of flattery from a European point of view. They are constantly used by the Asiatics, and you need never fear of being too lavish in this respect.' To protect himself against slave traders and robbers, Muravyov travelled through the Karakum Desert disguised as a Turkoman, although his guides knew he was a Russian carrying gifts and messages for the khan of Khiva. Five days short of their destination, they came across another caravan, and someone pointed at Muravyov. His men had the presence of mind to tell the others he was a captured Russian and that they were taking him to Khiva to sell. They were congratulated and allowed to proceed.

On reaching the city, Muravyov was imprisoned: his notebook may have betrayed him as a spy. After toying with the idea of burying him alive in the desert, the khan deigned to receive him. Muravyov went in full-dress uniform but without his sword, as he had been advised. Hesitating over how to approach the khan, he was suddenly grabbed from behind and prepared to fight for his life, but someone explained that it was an ancient Khivan custom for any envoy to be dragged before the ruler. Muravyov submitted to the ritual and then saluted the khan in the local fashion, telling him that the tsar had sent him 'to express his deep respect' and to deliver a letter. 'I am also commanded to make certain verbal representations to thee,' he added, 'and only await thy order to discharge myself of the message now, or at any time that may be suitable.' He then proposed to establish mutually beneficial relations and assured the khan, 'Sire, if thou wilt but ally thyself to us, thy enemies shall also be our enemies.' The khan was open to negotiations: 'I myself desire that firm and sincere friendship may grow between our two countries.' Although successful, Muravyov's mission didn't result in anything politically significant. After reading his reports, his superiors gave him promotion and sent him on another assignment, ignoring his proposal for the annexation of Khiva and the liberation of its slaves. He went on to have an illustrious military career and a distinguished, if somewhat uneven, administrative one (among his own, he would occasionally ruffle too many feathers). Still, Muravyov's journey to Khiva, to quote Hopkirk again, 'was destined to mark the beginning of the end of the independent khanates of Central Asia'.

Going native was a survival tactic in the Great Game, and if period documents are full of horror stories, that's often because its players failed to blend sufficiently into their surroundings. Lieutenant Alexander Burnes, an officer in the Indian army, came to Bokhara in June 1832 with a florid letter to the grand vizier, which he had composed himself, calling the recipient 'the Tower of Islam' and 'the Gem of the Faith'. When summoned before the vizier at the emir's palace, Burnes changed into local costume and went there on foot, knowing that non-Muslims were forbidden to ride in the holy city. The vizier questioned Burnes for two hours, enquiring about his religion (Burnes had to bare his chest to show that, unlike his fellow Christians from Russia, he wasn't wearing a crucifix) and whether Christians ate pork. When asked what it tasted like, Burnes diplomatically replied, 'I *have heard* it is like beef.' He told some stories of life in Europe and gave the host one of his only two compasses.

They parted friends, with the vizier asking Burnes to bring
him a pair of English spectacles next time.

'My dress is purely Asiatic,' Burnes wrote home in 1832.

My head is shaved of its brown locks, and my beard,
dyed black, grieves – as the Persian poets have it – for the
departed beauty of my youth. I now eat my meals with
my hands, and greasy digits they are ... I never conceal
that I am a European ... The people know me by the
name of a Sekunder, which is Persian for Alexander, and
a magnanimous name it is.

In his native country he was nicknamed Bokhara Burnes
for his pioneering explorations, described in his bestselling
Travels into Bokhara.

The same year, Burnes found himself in Kabul, where he
met Wolff. The latter came there, according to one source,
'emerging from Central Asia in a state of nudity after having
been plundered and compelled to march six hundred miles
without clothing'. Describing the Christian preacher as 'the
missionary of the Jews' and someone who had 'entered
Tartary as a Jew, which is the best travelling character in
a Mahommedan country', Burnes noted that Wolff's 'mis-
fortunes had originated from his denominating himself a
Hajee'. The reverend, it seems, was too keen on going native;
his language skills, however, were still limited at the time.

On their visit to the ruler of Kabul, Burnes acted as
Wolff's interpreter in a theological debate between him and
'several Mahommedan doctors'. Reticent at first 'on the
grounds of being no moollah', Burnes soon went beyond
his brief and proceeded to confound the learned gentlemen

with tricky questions about the Koran and to entertain them with European anecdotes. The ruler enjoyed the spectacle and promised the guests every assistance in their travels.

In 1841, Burnes was in Kabul again. The First Anglo-Afghan War had led to growing resentment of British rule, and although our adventurer was quite sure the Afghans would never do him any harm, one day a fanatical mob surrounded his house and set it on fire. As one version of events goes, a traitor offered to lead him and his brother to safety if they disguised themselves in native dress, but as soon as they appeared, he cried out, 'This is Sekunder Burnes!' and the pair were hacked to death.

Burnes' end had a precedent in another tragic tale of oriental tongues and treachery, which unfolded in January 1829, when Alexander Griboedov, the Russian ambassador to Persia, arrived in Tehran. The two countries had recently been at war. Russia's declaration of war, prepared in 1826 by an official trained in Kazan, presumably in Tatar, had been written in such bad Persian that the Persians returned it and asked for a text they could understand. As a result the Russian attack was unexpected and undoubtedly proved even more effective. It was Griboedov who in 1828 had negotiated the terms of the Treaty of Turkmenchay (extremely humiliating for Persia), and now he had to make sure they were fully carried out. With his excellent knowledge of Persia, its language and customs, he had premonitions about the trip: for one thing, he knew that his sojourn in the capital would coincide with the holy month of Muharram. Never the less, he left his pregnant teenage wife in Tebriz, promising to return soon.

Getting ready for his audience with Fath Ali Shah, putting

on his gold-embroidered monkey suit and tricorne hat, Griboedov felt as if he was dressing for some silly masquerade. A polymath whose real passions were music and poetry, he despised the pomp his role entailed. His comedy *Woe from Wit* (*Chatsky, or The Importance of Being Stupid* in Anthony Burgess' punny translation) had recently become a sensation in St Petersburg, banned by the censors but widely read. Still, here he was, far from the literary salons, theatres and his beloved piano, no longer the author Alexander Griboedov, just a vizier mukhtar in a peacocky uniform. He had no choice but to go through with it. The shah received him with much ceremony. The audience, filled with silences that were heavier than words, lasted nearly an hour as the victors continued to dictate their will to the defeated.

And yet it was no easy task to ensure full compliance with the terms of the peace treaty. Griboedov tended to be rather peremptory in his dealings with the Persians: he would, for instance, use only half of the shah's official titles in a note, to stress that its demands were non-negotiable. One of the treaty's clauses gave Armenians living in Persia the right to return to their homeland, now part of the Russian empire. Wishing to take advantage of this provision, three people – a eunuch from the shah's harem and two wives of the shah's son-in-law – sought and were given asylum in the Russian legation. The shah demanded that all three be handed back to him, but Griboedov refused, insisting that it was his duty to protect his emperor's subjects. He anticipated that his decision might cost him dearly, but he also knew what would happen to the fugitives otherwise.

Word of this new insolence, committed by the loathed infidel in the holy month, soon spread through the city. The

mullahs incited the people to march on the Russian legation and seize the refugees. Several thousand stormed the
compound. The ambassador and a handful of his men held
out until the end and were torn to pieces by the mob. A
kebab seller cut off Griboedov's head and displayed it to
the crowd's delight. The mutilated body of the ambassador
was later found on a rubbish heap, identified by a deformed
hand, the result of a duel, and what little was left of his
monkey suit. Fearful for the consequences of this atrocity,
Fath Ali Shah sent his grandson to St Petersburg with lavish
gifts. The young prince reportedly offered to kill himself
with his own sword before the eyes of Nicholas I, by way
of atonement. However, the tsar, for whom such diplomatic
spills were just another day at the office, urged him not to
overreact, concluding, 'I consign the ill-fated Tehran incident to eternal oblivion.'

The value of assimilating into the culture of a people whose
language you are trying to speak, manifest in these stories,
is best illustrated by the Reverend Joseph Wolff. Throughout
his stay in Bokhara, Emir Nasrullah kept him on a short
lead, often sending a *makhram*, or chamberlain, to him
with various questions. When the emir wished to know 'the
names of the four grand Viziers, and twelve little Viziers of
England, and the forty-two Elders', Wolff supplied a list,
but 'the Makhram returned in a fury, and said that his Majesty had found me out to be a *liar*'. Apparently his account
differed from the one the moody despot had received from
Stoddart. Brought before the emir, Wolff rescued the situation by giving him 'a complete idea of the Constitution
of England'. 'Though his Majesty could not understand it

fully,' he reported, 'I yet convinced him that my list might be true also.' These exchanges were not getting Wolff anywhere, and he was preparing to share the fate of Stoddart and Conolly when the emir received another letter from the shah. 'Well, I will make you a present of Joseph Wolff,' he said to the messenger who brought it. 'He may go with you.'

On his way home, Wolff met 'an interesting and unfortunate young gentleman at Tabreez, whose name is Edward Burgess, well acquainted with the Persian language'. Employed by a local prince to translate English newspapers for him, Burgess found himself in trouble when his brother, sent by the Persian government to England with a substantial sum of money, disappeared. Now essentially a hostage, Burgess got on with his work, which included translating a letter from his employer to Wolff. 'I hope the translation will please you,' he wrote to the reverend.

> I have made it as near the Persian as possible to make sense of it, and I endeavoured, as much as our language will allow, to preserve the idiom of the Persian; you, who are acquainted with the latter language, know how difficult that is. The title 'Excellency,' which is given to you in the letter, may appear strange in Europe, but it is the only translation I could give to the word *Jenaub*. In this country it is only used to priests of high rank and ambassadors, and has always been translated as I have done.

Thus it was that Wolff briefly enjoyed a title that might have been too grand for him, but which helped him return to England safely and publish an account of his travels.

Nowadays, getting a name or a title wrong is less likely to result in a beheading, but cultural markers are still vital in translation. My own mission to Bokhara took the form of several asylum cases I worked on as an interpreter. In one of them, a sex worker trafficked to Britain from Uzbekistan kept addressing everyone – the lawyers, the judge, myself – in the matey second person singular, *ty*, instead of using the formal Russian *vy*. I frowned at such overfamiliarity at first, but then it occurred to me that in the woman's culture this form of address is a token of trust, not a sign of impudence. Translating, I made sure she sounded as respectful in my rendition as she actually meant to be. Her asylum application was granted, and we said goodbye to each other in a way that no longer struck me as too familiar.

Making a cultural faux pas in a more relaxed setting can be just as bad. At a meeting with Azeri businessmen, their host told a self-deprecating joke, calling himself fat. (He was indeed on the bigger side, as were some of his guests.) I translated it literally, not thinking it necessary to resort to the euphemistic 'full-bodied' or 'well-rounded'. The guests were visibly shocked: a word deemed perfectly ordinary in my native Moscow sounded rude to people accustomed to the more courteous form of Russian spoken in Baku. One of them gently corrected me, replacing 'fat' with 'portly', and I apologised.

However, not every failure to play by local rules ends in embarrassment. The most memorable form of address I've ever had to translate came from a court witness who began each of his answers with 'Mister Judge, sir'. Perhaps he was channelling some TV drama or trying to fit into the unfamiliar surroundings of an English crown court, using what he thought was the standard formula. Looking at the woman judge in a wig who presided over the proceedings, I took the liberty of changing his opening to 'Your Honour'.

4

Observation and Analysis

In August 1877, the Italian astronomer Giovanni Virginio Schiaparelli turned his telescope towards Mars. The director of the Brera Observatory in Milan had installed an eight-inch Merz refractor on the roof of the Brera Palace, initially to observe double stars. Pleased with its performance on that task, he wanted to see if it 'possessed the necessary qualities to allow also for the studies of the surfaces of the planets'. With Mars due to be in opposition with Earth in early September, Schiaparelli decided to seize the opportunity.

The observations he made over the next two months transformed our image of the Red Planet. In addition to previously noted brighter and darker areas, referred to as *terrae* (lands) and *maria* (seas), he could now distinguish, at first 'in a very vague and indeterminate manner', dark lines connecting the seas. Schiaparelli produced a new map of Mars, on which he dubbed these markings *canali*.

When Schiaparelli's findings were reported in English, translators rendered *canali* as 'canals', ignoring another possibility, 'channels'. This caused a stir. In 1882, J. T. Slugg, an English chemist and member of the Royal Astronomical Society, summarised the reaction of the international scientific community in a letter to the *Manchester Guardian*: 'The first thought that will enter every one's mind after reading this account will be the question, "If these canals are real, are they natural or artificial?" The great French astronomer Flammarion says "if these canals are authentic they do not seem natural, and appear ... to represent the industrial work of the inhabitants of the planet."' Camille Flammarion, whose *La Planète Mars et ses conditions d'habitabilité* was to prove influential, used the French word *canaux*, which, like 'canals', suggests artificial origins. The existence of artifice implying the presence of intelligent beings, he further speculated that, thanks to the planet's low gravity, 'the inhabitants of Mars are of a different form from us, and fly in its atmosphere'. Many theorists followed him into the clouds.

Among the most ardent proponents of the intelligent-life theory was the American astronomer Percival Lowell, who founded an observatory in Flagstaff, Arizona and threw himself into studying what he termed the planet's 'non-natural features'. His books – *Mars, Mars and Its Canals* and *Mars as the Abode of Life* – inspired many discussions and a whole subgenre of sci-fi from H. G. Wells' *The War of the Worlds* onwards. There were, of course, those who took Lowell's enthusiastic claims with a pinch of salt; yet his conviction proved infectious. In his article 'Giovanni Schiaparelli: Visions of a Colour Blind Astronomer', William Sheehan, one of today's leading Mars scholars, remarks that in the last decade of the nineteenth century the obsession with the idea that there was intelligent life on Mars reached the level of mass hysteria. In 1899 Théodore Flournoy, a psychologist from Geneva, described the case of a woman who, under hypnosis, visited Mars and produced illustrated accounts of its landscapes and its inhabitants, their language and alphabet.

The question arises: how differently might the course of history have run if, confronted with the word *canali*, Schiaparelli's anonymous first translator had chosen 'channels' instead of 'canals'? The latter may sound more like the original, but the former is arguably more valid, and certainly less startling. Here we have an example of polysemy, or the coexistence of multiple meanings, as well as so-called false friends: words that sound similar in two languages but mean different things. (They often trip people up, as happened to the French president Emmanuel Macron, who, on a state visit to Australia in May 2018, thanked Prime Minister Malcolm Turnbull and his 'delicious wife' – clearly a calque of *délicieuse*, which in French can mean simply 'charming'.)

Before blaming the translator for all the confusion that followed, we need to know what Schiaparelli himself meant by *canali*. One can imagine training some kind of mind-reading telescope on his brain, zooming in on the thought in his head and bringing the intended feature into perfect focus. But this is not how translation works (yet). Just when the most minute discrimination seems called for, the translator must paradoxically widen the field of investigation, go abroad and gather intelligence, less astronomer than sleuth. To understand Schiaparelli, in other words, one must first *understand Schiaparelli*.

So the detective gets to work. What kind of man was he? Although nearsighted and partially colour-blind, Schiaparelli was a good draughtsman, able to quickly capture his observations on paper. Presenting his Martian discoveries to various officials in Rome in 1878, he stressed that he could achieve even better results with more powerful equipment. He assured them 'that Mars appears to be a world little different from our own; and by employing a little the Flam-marionesque style, I managed the affair rather well'. This 'very exciting phantasmagory' was a success: the Italian government, keen to support the country's scientists in the post-unification nationalistic climate, agreed to the purchase of a new, eighteen-inch telescope: expensive, state of the art, perfect for interpreting optical signals from Mars.

Schiaparelli knew that even good telescopes magnify distortions caused by atmospheric conditions – much as a translation, even one done in good faith, can increase the amount of random noise already present in the original. 'In the actual state of things,' he wrote, 'it would be pre-mature to put forth conjectures as to the nature of these *canali*. As to their existence, I have no need to declare that I have taken every precaution for avoiding all suspicion of illusion. I am absolutely sure of that which I have observed.' In his less buttoned-up moments he went as far as speculat-ing about an irrigation system built by enlightened states to distribute Martian water in a just and efficient manner. In 'Life on the Planet Mars' he imagined a utopian socialist society in which 'the interests of all are not distinguished from the other; [sciences] are developed to a high degree of perfection; international conflicts and wars are unknown; all the intellectual efforts [are] unanimously directed against the common enemy, the difficulty which penurious nature opposes at each step'. This widely read article, translated into a number of languages, was probably his most fanciful work. A lapse in scientific rigour, it might have been inspired by the contemporary canal age on Earth. With the Suez completed in 1869 and the Panama under construction, the prospect of discovering canals on our planetary neighbour must have been extremely alluring; another engineering feat, another step towards modernity.

Schiaparelli crossed the line between fact and fancy with great care: 'I myself would guard against combatting this supposition, which does not include anything impossible … One can nevertheless hypothesize such activities … as, for instance, extended agricultural works and irrigation on a large scale.' Here we find both a scrupulous reticence about his own opinions and a willingness to indulge the more exotic speculations of his peers. It's not the decisive evidence we might have hoped for, but we are getting somewhere with our inquiry. Had the early English-language commentators asked him to elaborate, would he have told them what exactly he had in mind? Were it not for 'canals', would our knowledge of Mars, enriched by the early interest in the false conjecture, be poorer today? Would NASA have launched its Mariner programme? Would the search for water on Mars have continued, leading to the much-trumpeted announcement of its discovery in 2015, followed two years later by the more tentative claim that the 'recurring slope lineae' are more likely to be flows of dry sand?

We may never be able to answer these questions with certainty. However, they prompt further, broader ones, about translation and the plurality of meanings. Whoever took it upon themselves to communicate Schiaparelli's message to the English-speaking world had to interfere with the original, to expand on it, perhaps inadvertently and apparently without bothering to justify their choice. It is odd that this attracted so little notice, while other aspects of the affair received close scrutiny. The pictures themselves, for example. Some contemporaries doubted Schiaparelli's drawing skills. The artist Nathaniel Green remarked that his 'hard and sharp lines' must be the result of his style of representation. The astronomer Edward Emerson Barnard wrote to him in 1893, 'In your published drawings of Mars the canals are shown very strongly marked. The drawings in your notebook do not show these lines so heavy. Is it an accident of the reproduction that they are so heavy and dark in the engraving?' Schiaparelli replied, 'The reproductions of my drawings unfortunately can mislead the reader. I cannot find artists who reproduce them well.'

The use of 'canals', however, remained mostly unchallenged by the scientific community and the general public, although one of the word's opponents, the English astrophysicist J. Norman Lockyer, insisted on 'true water channels'. To appreciate the challenges Schiaparelli's translators faced, it's useful to consider his other writings, where a great interstellar space of possible miscommunication opens up. He formulated a whole new vocabulary to describe the features of Mars. 'In general,' he explained,

> the configurations seen represented such a clear analogy to those of the terrestrial map that it is doubtful whether any class of names would have been more suitable. Do not brevity and clarity induce us to use such words as 'island', 'isthmus', 'strait', 'channel', 'peninsula', 'cape', etc.? Each of which provides a description and notation which otherwise could not be expressed but by means of a lengthy paraphrase, and one having to be repeated each time one spoke about the corresponding object.

His suggestion that these terms 'may be regarded as a mere artifice to assist the memory and to abbreviate the descriptions' would have been generally approved by translators, who often employ such tricks (in the best cases, sparingly and advisedly). But the point remains: Schiaparelli's watery vocabulary was – at least to some degree – metaphorical.

Then again, metaphors have a way of taking on a life of their own, intelligent or not. Even the flamboyant Percival Lowell was cautious to start with. 'I have adopted his nomenclature,' he wrote twenty years after Schiaparelli's early observations, 'and in the naming of the newly found features have selected names conformable to his scheme, which commends itself both on practical and on poetic grounds.' Initially, he did try to exercise some reserve: 'At this point in our inquiry, when direct deduction from the general physics phenomena observable on the planet's surface shows that, were there inhabitants there, a system of irrigation would be an all-essential of their existence, the telescope presents us with perhaps the most startling discovery of our times, – the so-called canals of Mars.' The qualifier was soon dropped.

In *Mars*, Lowell developed Schiaparelli's metaphors to highlight the artificial nature of the system: 'Dotted all over the reddish-ochre ground of the desert stretches of the planet … are an innumerable number of dark circular or oval spots. They appear, furthermore, always in intimate association with the canals. They constitute so many hubs to which the canals make spokes.' He discussed 'an end and object for the existence of canals, and the most natural one in the world, namely, that the canals are constructed for the express purpose of fertilizing the oases', before concluding,

'All this, of course, may be a set of coincidences, signifying nothing; but the probability points the other way.'

Lowell's *Mars and Its Canals* was dedicated to Schiaparelli, whom he called 'cher Maître Martien'. They corresponded extensively, mainly in French, which at the time was more popular than English in many fields, including the natural sciences. Schiaparelli also published in German and was able to read English – as suggested by some of Lowell's missives, such as the telegram he sent to the Maître Martien on 17 August 1896: 'Ganges is double.' If in 1895 Lowell had accepted the feature could be 'a set of coincidences', by 1906 he was adamant: 'No natural force propels [the water], and the inference is forthright and inevitable that it is artificially helped to its end. There seems to be no escape from this deduction.' At first he relied on drawings, then switched to photography, and, as Abbot Lawrence Lowell, the astronomer's brother, says in his biography, 'finally in 1905 upon the plates canals appeared, thirty-eight in all and one of them double. On learning of the success Schiaparelli wrote in wonder to Percival: "I should never have believed it possible."'

He had his reasons to be sceptical. In the late 1890s, another Italian astronomer, Vincenzo Cerulli, whom Schiaparelli saw as his successor, claimed that the canals of Mars were an optical illusion and that when more powerful refractors became available, they 'will lose that linear form that presently makes them so mysterious and interesting'. In 1909, the Greek astronomer Eugène Michel Antoniadi supported this view, demonstrating that neither Schiaparelli's nor Lowell's telescopes provided sufficient resolution to distinguish straight lines. Cerulli and Antoniadi, with their better-adjusted devices, acted as translators revising someone else's version in the belief that the more iterations it undergoes the more accurate it becomes, a principle that doesn't always extend beyond the ideal world. Flammarion's reaction to the new theory was refreshingly dialectical: 'Has each astronomer, then, in physics as in moral matters, a "manner of seeing"?'

Schiaparelli's manner of seeing is summarised in Sheehan's article. 'Clearly he had channels rather than canals in mind (with its connotation of artificial construction). Indeed … he tends to use the terms *canale* and *fiume* (or river) rather indiscriminately.' It is true that *fiume* and *canale* are interchangeable in Schiaparelli's writings; the Nile and the Ganges, for instance, are called by either name. What's really interesting, however, is not how *canale* should have been translated back then, but how many aspects of translation the story reveals: the importance of naming things; emotional aspects of communication, including persuasion and trust; the tendency to abbreviate in the hope of still being understood; the necessity of having a clearly worded source; and most crucially, the fact that although communication is always fraught with error, it doesn't mean we should stop attempting to understand things, including situations that involve more than one language. If Schiaparelli's story teaches us anything, it's that there is always an element of seeing through a glass darkly, even with one eye glued to the eyepiece. A translator doesn't work like a telescope, rendering what was previously invisible, visible. But then again, what does?

Scientific texts are often assumed to be easier to translate than literary works, the latter's potential for ambiguity forcing the translator to improvise. However, when I first began to translate for academic journals to earn some money as a student, I soon realised that the supposed clarity of science was, like the Martian canals, an illusion. For one thing, the language of AI or laser optics or operator theory is usually only spoken by a few specialists who don't need too many words to understand each other. 'If you can't explain it to a six-year-old,' Albert Einstein may or may not have said, 'you don't understand it yourself' – but not every scientist pitches their ideas to children, however entertaining a child might find them. One of the first articles I had to translate from English into Russian was proof of that. The editor, who knew both languages but not physics, had changed every instance of *dyrka* (hole) to what she thought a more appropriate synonym. ('Electron hole', or simply 'hole', is an established term for a place where an atom lacks an electron. Both the English word and its Russian equivalent have other, non-scientific uses, a common problem with technical vocabularies, which tend to adopt everyday words with no regard for the difficulties that might create for potential translations.) Featured in nearly every sentence, the term had been replaced throughout with *otverstie* (opening), the editor wishing to sound more refined.

The act of translation inevitably distorts the original, though that in itself doesn't obliterate the intended meaning, as long as the drift is calculable. As a translator with a mathematical background, I searched for a metaphor to set against Schiaparelli's telescope and found it in a place that could hardly have been more satisfying. Three decades before the *canali* controversy, another Italian scientist, Luigi Federico Menabrea, met the English mathematician Charles

Babbage, who had been busy inventing machines that would revolutionise the world. In August 1840, Babbage came to Turin to give a lecture at the Accademia delle Scienze on the Analytical Engine – a computer in the modern sense of the word, the first mechanical device ever envisaged which could, in theory, perform programmed operations.

It was the mathematician and astronomer Giovanni Plana who had invited Babbage to the 'meeting of Italian Philosophers', where, according to Babbage, 'M. Plana had at first planned to make notes, in order to write an outline of the principles of the engine. But his own laborious pursuits induced him to give up this plan, and to transfer this task to a younger friend of his, M. Menabrea, who had already established his reputation as a profound analyst.' Babbage spent several days talking to his Italian colleagues; it is reasonable to assume that they conversed mostly in French. Menabrea transcribed his notes, added some explanations and later the same year published the paper under the title 'Notions sur la machine analytique de M. Charles Babbage'.

An English translation of the article appeared in 1843. 'Sketch of the Analytical Engine Invented by Charles Babbage Esq. By L. F. Menabrea, of Turin, Officer of the Military Engineers' was signed simply 'A. A. L.' but didn't go down in the annals of history as an example of self-effacement; nor was it noted for any mistranslations. The person who translated it and added extensive notes – nearly twice the length of the original work, including a table often described as the first computer program – is today well known in both literary and scientific circles.

Ada Lovelace's early education was broad if somewhat patchy. One of her governesses, Miss Lamont, wrote of 'lessons in the morning in arithmetic, grammar, spelling, reading, music, each no more than a quarter of an hour long – after dinner, geography, drawing, French, music, reading, all performed with alacrity and docility'. Lovelace also studied Italian, but sciences interested her more than languages. It was her mother who introduced mathematics, an unusual subject for a girl at the time, into Ada's curriculum (she hoped to neutralise whatever hereditary madness Ada might have picked up from her father, Lord Byron). Lovelace was seventeen when she met Babbage, who showed her a part of what was to become a steam-powered computer.

The home lessons Lovelace had taken provided her with merely a basic level of maths, and in 1840–41 she took a correspondence course with Augustus De Morgan, a prominent logician and professor of mathematics at what is now University College London. Their letters, kept at the Bodleian Library, show that Lovelace had a keen eye for detail: she would often spot errors or typos in the books she was reading. Another of her strengths was her persistence in getting to the bottom of each statement until she fully understood it. These qualities, useful in any mathematician, also turn out to be valuable in translation, not least when one has to tackle such an extravagant proposition as Babbage's machine.

'The imagination is at first astounded at the idea of such an undertaking,' Menabrea, in Lovelace's rendition, says of the Analytical Engine. The design 'is based on two principles: the first, consisting in the fact that every arithmetical calculation ultimately depends on four principal operations – addition, subtraction, multiplication, and division; the second, in the possibility of reducing every analytical calculation to that of the coefficients of the several terms of a series. If that last principle be true, all the operations of analysis come within the domain of the engine.' In other words, the computer would be able to deal with formulae as well as numbers. A list of its potential advantages follows: 'First, rigid accuracy ... Secondly, economy of time ... Thirdly, economy of intelligence.' While hopeful about the machine's power, Menabrea also observes prophetically that 'such machines ... require the continual intervention of a human agent to regulate their movements, and thence arises a source of errors'.

Lovelace, however, could have given the machine a run for its money. One of her footnotes reads:

> This remark seems to require further comment, since it is in some degree calculated to strike the mind as being at variance with the subsequent passage. The apparent discrepancy is stronger too in the translation than in the original, owing to its being impossible to render precisely into the English tongue all the niceties of distinction which the French idiom happens to admit of in the phrases used for the two passages we refer to.

Another note reads, 'This must not be understood in too unqualified a manner.' Yet another warns, 'This sentence has been slightly altered in the translation in order to express more exactly the present state of the engine.' Working through the text, A. A. L. exercises more initiative than a translator would usually be expected to. 'I considered that I ought myself to supply the deficiency,' she writes, 'conceiving that this paper would have been imperfect if I had omitted to point out one means that might be employed for resolving this essential part of the problem in question.' It's as if the translator in her gives way to the author, someone with more to say than what's offered by the source text. Let us not forget her close collaboration with Babbage, which suggests that the English translation may have had his approval.

A translator who may have no intention of actively intervening yet fails to stay neutral is a good example of what the profession involves in our imperfect world, where few things have clear-cut definitions. What made Lovelace exemplary was that she, unlike those responsible for the *canali* confusion, wanted to be as true as possible to her source as she understood it, not just in letter but also, most importantly, in spirit. Although able to achieve a good degree of transparency – that desirable feature – she didn't want to rely exclusively on the text. Hence her decision to move from being a passive conduit to making her own inquiries before expressing her views on the subject. She managed to do so without compromising the accuracy of her translation, partly thanks to the qualities inherent in the subject itself, but also to her informed approach. In fact, her success demonstrated that maths and translation are related more closely than it might appear at first glance. The Analytical Engine, with its binary logic, is the opposite of the telescope, which requires constant fine-tuning. A good translator is able to work in both modes: they focus and refocus the optics again and again as they ponder their choices – until that crucial moment when they put the glass aside and switch on the engine. Rather than being afraid of the formulaic nature of this device, they use it to strip the text of seeming ambiguities and, with any luck, finally put the right words in the right order.

After Lovelace's death, an unsigned obituary published in *The Examiner* on 4 December 1852 drew attention to her scientific achievements. 'The Countess of Lovelace was thoroughly original,' it read, 'and the poet's temperament was all that was hers in common with her father. Her genius, for genius she possessed, was not poetic, but metaphysical and mathematical, her mind having been in the constant practice of investigation, and with rigour and exactness.'

Over the next century and a half, scholars who concerned themselves with her work oscillated between giving her too much credit for her mathematical research and dismissing it as full of schoolboy errors. In *Ada: A Life and a Legacy*, Dorothy Stein seems to find Lovelace something of an intellectual disappointment. Trained as a psychologist, Stein is never the less able to conclude, on the basis of her subject's letters, that simple algebraic manipulations were beyond her competence and that Babbage himself must have worked on the notes to the 'Sketch'. In a series of recent works, the science historians Christopher Hollings, Ursula Martin and Adrian Rice challenge 'earlier judgements impugning [Lovelace's] competence to contribute to the 1843 paper, and her potential, in time, for mathematical research', giving a number of examples to support their view. Betty Toole in *Ada, The Enchantress of Numbers* cites Lovelace's phrase 'poetical science', calling her 'a synthesizer and a visionary' who 'saw the need for a mathematical and scientific language which was more expressive and which incorporated imagination'. Here, as in the Martian mythology, the power of poetics allows the spirit to triumph over the letter.

Lovelace was, among other things, a gambler, a wife, a mother, a thinker of broad vision, a researcher and a translator. The latter role wasn't what she was most proud of; her ambitions went much further than practising a skill possessed by many at the time. 'I do not believe that my father was (or ever could have been) such a Poet as I shall be an Analyst,' she boasted. One might argue that, even as a translator, Byron – notorious for the liberties he took with Dante – is better known than Lovelace the mathematician. She died at thirty-six, the same age as her father, but while his early death served to cement his legend, Lovelace's cut her off in the middle of her work.

Babbage's engines all remained unrealised in his lifetime. There were plans to implement his design for one of the Analytical Engine's predecessors, the Difference Engine, but the funding fell through. The Difference Engine No. 2, an upgrade on the original one, was created by London's Science Museum to mark Babbage's bicentenary in 1991; it took seventeen years to complete and worked just as its creator had intended. The Analytical Engine was never built, but Lovelace's prophecy that it 'might compose elaborate and scientific pieces of music' came true in another world: the very imperfect one we live in.

The tales of the glass and the engine are emblematic of translation. Here we have it all: the translator's tendency to stay in the background or to step forward; the impact their initiative can have; their ability to make others trust their words; the leaps of faith required of them to see through the original, no matter how opaque; and finally, the importance of inquiry for their success. It is these facets of translation that take us to the spaces where the most interesting – linguistically and otherwise – verbal interactions occur.

5

Treasures of the Tongue

Born in 1553 in London to an Italian father and English mother, John Florio grew up in Europe and, upon his return to England as a young man, became a teacher of Italian. The language and Italian culture in general were in vogue in Elizabethan England, despite the suspicion with which foreigners were traditionally treated. In the preface to *Florio His Firste Fruites*, a textbook published in 1578, Florio mentions those 'yl manered' Englishmen who neglect languages; still, he was never short of work.

Consisting of a grammar and forty-four dialogues, printed in English and Italian side by side, *Firste Fruites* was not just a phrase book but also a style manual of sorts, featuring proverbs for various occasions, which Florio often rephrased. He loved idioms and used every opportunity to sneak them into his writings. A bill he sent to one of his pupils in 1600 (written in Italian, presumably with pedagogical aims), demanding a fee for lessons, has two: 'The priest gets his living from the altar' and 'Hunger drives the wolf from the wood.' Freelance translators often have to chase invoices, but I've never seen one as colourful as Florio's. Alas, no record of payment from this pupil survives.

In 1583 Florio was hired by the French embassy in

London and spent the next two years teaching the ambassador's daughter, acting as an interpreter, running errands and, most probably, spying. His duties included taking messages to 'Monsieur de Raglay' (to all appearances, Sir Walter Raleigh), bribing officials to get the ambassador's butler out of trouble, dealing with an angry mob gathered outside the embassy, and settling the ambassador's debts after his departure from England. During this time, he made friends with the Italian philosopher Giordano Bruno, who appears in his next textbook, *Florios Second Frutes*. The largest published collection of proverbs at the time, it contains a list of 6,000, many of them woven into dialogues. 'I aplie my selfe to all, and am like to a millers sack, and not as some, who sometimes make it a matter of conscience to spitt in the Church, and at another time they will beray the altar.' These words, put in the mouth of a character based on Bruno, were likely intended to defend the philosopher from the charges of atheism and blasphemy which eventually led him to the stake. Frances A. Yates in her life of Florio points out that her subject must have been criticised for his Italian sympathies. In the preface to *Second Frutes*, Florio mocks his detractors, snatching his own weapon back from them – 'Vn Inglese Italianato è vn Diauolo incarnato. Now, who the Diuell taught thee so much Italian?' – before signing for the first time with an adjective that will be for ever associated with his name, 'Resolute I. F.'.

While working for the French, as well as translating dispatches from Rome, printed to satisfy the high demand for news in Elizabethan England before the emergence of newspapers, Florio was also compiling a 'most copious, and exact Dictionarie in Italian and English'. *A Worlde of Wordes*, published in 1598, contains 44,000 entries (its only predecessor had 6,000); its revised editions provided the main reference material for Italian scholarship throughout the seventeenth century and served as a basis for subsequent dictionaries. The majority of its entries cover a remarkable range of meanings and contexts. To pick a random example, *parare* has twenty-four definitions, including 'to adorne', 'to make readie', 'to set foorth' and 'to teach a horse to stop and staie orderly'. There are regional Italian words; there is slang, marked as 'gibbrish or rogues language'; there are all kinds of English, from formal to vulgar. Florio himself was impressed with his discoveries, which put the two languages on an equal footing: 'And for English-gentlemen me thinks it must needs be a pleasure to them, to see so rich a toong out-vide by their mother-speech, as by the manie-folde Englishes of manie wordes in this is manifest.'

How did translators manage before dictionaries? They had no option but to consult ordinary books instead. Along with its obvious disadvantages this had at least one extremely important benefit: words came complete with contexts, ready to be used in a concrete situation, with no danger of picking a wrong definition from a list. Today, with a wealth of sources at our disposal, we mustn't dismiss that artisan method completely. In fact, most translators use dictionaries as a starting point before further researching specific usages of words and expressions. Back in the sixteenth century, when bilingual dictionaries first appeared in Europe, the need for monolingual ones was already evident, partly thanks to the mutual penetration of cultures in the Renaissance era. For example, the number of words in English, as estimated from surviving texts, more than doubled between 1500 and 1650 as it absorbed foreign vocabulary.

An influx of specialised terminology was also transforming Europe's early-modern linguistic landscape. For instance, the Dutch scholar Adriaan Koerbagh published a legal dictionary in 1664. One of the most radical thinkers of his era, Koerbagh sought to demystify the arcane language that allowed lawyers to take advantage of their clients. In 1668, continuing his campaign against abuses perpetrated by the professional classes, he compiled another dictionary, explaining for the common man a further swarm of technical terms, legal and medical, as well as the language of scripture, also deliberately obscure in his view. It was this last addition that caused an uproar in Amsterdam. Koerbagh left the city but was soon arrested and jailed for blasphemy; he died in prison a few months later. Most of his published works were destroyed as incendiary.

Specialised language presents somewhat different challenges for translators and for interpreters. If you need to translate a technical document, resorting to glossaries is a straightforward step: here, compared to general-purpose dictionaries, terms are more likely to have unique standard definitions. To give a basic example, the word 'set' will typically be univocal in a mathematical paper, while elsewhere it may evoke associations with anything from china to tennis. Translating for specialists, you don't have to worry about tuning into their mentalese first, as they are already largely on the same page as each other. Interpreters, too, look things up in advance when preparing for an assignment. However, unlike translators, who can safely assume that concepts discussed in their source text will be familiar to its intended reader, interpreters sometimes have to assess their audience as they go along. Sticking to technical jargon is fine at a conference, but when a professional is talking to a lay person, you need to gauge reactions and play the same interpretative role as Koerbagh took upon himself.

Thankfully, present-day doctors go easy on Latin when talking to their patients. Lawyers, on the other hand, are notoriously attached to legalese, and it can fall to the interpreter to bring their register a notch down for the benefit of a client. Having passed my interpreting exam, I was at first keen on all those recondite words I had learned from reference books and, crucially, from transcripts of court proceedings: put into context, they made a lot more sense. Then I began practising, and situations where I had to translate from legalese into plain Russian – replacing 'affray' with 'fight', 'perjury' with 'lie', 'malicious communication' with 'dirty message' – made me appreciate both the usefulness of dictionaries and their limitations.

After finishing his dictionary, Florio put his rich vocabulary to good use when he embarked on a project that brought him lasting fame. *The Essayes*, translated from Montaigne's celebrated work first published in France in 1580, was printed in England in 1603. Subtitled *Morall, Politike, and Millitarie Discourses*, it begins with an address 'To the Curteous Reader'. 'Shall I apologize translation?' Florio asks, before enunciating what has always been every translator's predicament: 'The sense may keepe forme; the sentence is disfigured; the fineness, fitnesse, featnesse diminished, as much as artes nature is short of natures art, a picture of a body, a shadow of a substance.' This rather fanciful arrangement of metaphors and alliterations sets the style for the main text.

'I desire therein to be delineated in mine owne genuine,

simple and ordinarie fashion, without contention, art or study; for it is my selfe I pourtray,' Montaigne says in his preface, and Florio follows him closely, but not for long. 'It is somewhat ironical that Montaigne, who was one of the first great writers in a modern tongue to write in a modern manner, should have had as his translator one to whom elaborate rhetorical word-pattern was an instinctive necessity and a habit,' Yates remarks. Examples of Florio's euphuism can be found nearly on every page. He adds flourishes for effect; he doubles and trebles words and phrases; he introduces qualifiers. Under his pen, 'nous ne travaillons' grows into 'we labour, and toyle, and plod', and 'l'entendement' becomes 'understanding and conscience'. Sometimes these changes are made for the sake of alliteration alone (another hobby horse of Florio's), for instance when 'une estude profonde' is rendered as 'a deepe study and dumpish'. 'Le parler que j'ayme,' Montaigne writes, 'c'est un parler simple et naif ... esloigné d'affectation et d'artifice.' 'It is a naturall, simple, and unaffected speech that I love,' Florio obliges – and then, in a volte-face, proceeds to embroider the text as he fancies, throwing in 'these boistrous billowes' in place of 'ces flots' and extending 'cette renommée' to read 'this transitorie renowne'.

Florio's interventions predated by nearly a century John Dryden's reflections on the mode of work 'where the translator (if now he has not lost that name) assumes the liberty not only to vary from the words and sense, but to forsake them both as he sees occasion: and taking only some general hints from the original, to run division on the ground-work, as he pleases'. Do such liberties characterise Florio as a vain *homme de lettres* whose compulsive meddling does

Montaigne no favours, or as an experienced stylist who understands that for the French thinker to be appreciated in England, by readers conditioned to associate simple speech with a simple mind, he has to be embellished? To quote Dryden again, 'a translator is to make his author appear as charming as possibly he can, provided he maintains his character, and makes him not unlike himself'. Reading *The Essayes*, I was occasionally tempted to dismiss Florio's floridity as unnecessary (and contagious), but in the end it proved too charming to annoy. In a more practical vein, F. O. Matthiessen, in *Translation, an Elizabethan Art*, points out that Florio sometimes used synonymic repetition 'to naturalise an unusual word by pairing it with one well known'. This is especially true in light of Florio's experimentation whereby he introduced new words, phrases and grammatical constructions that he thought the English language might 'well beare'. They include 'entraine, conscientious, endeare, tarnish, comporte, efface, facilitate, ammusing, debauching, regret, effort, emotion, and such like', as well as the pronoun 'its'.

Can these neologisms 'apologize' the inaccuracies? Yates believes so, writing that despite all his affectations and exaggerations, 'Florio was genuinely an artist' who 'loved words with an aesthetic delight in their strength' and had a 'noble sense of rhythm'. T. S. Eliot, too, thought *The Essayes* a great translation, putting it second only to the King James Bible. It was an important influence on many writers, most famously Shakespeare, whose debt to Florio includes such borrowings as the verbs 'rough-hew' and 'outstare', as well as an entire passage used in *The Tempest* with some modifications. That Shakespeare read *The Essayes* is beyond doubt:

scholars have identified in his works about a hundred close correspondences and another hundred passages showing some similarities with Florio's work. A copy of its first edition kept in the British Library has 'Willm Shakspere' on the flyleaf, although its provenance has been debated. Never the less, Yates concludes, Shakespeare owed Florio much, 'as indeed do all Englishmen who value the rich treasure of their tongue'.

'Translating means not only leading the reader to understand the language and culture of the original but also enriching one's own,' Umberto Eco once said in a lecture. This function of translation includes creating neologisms, a game many translators like to play. Not every novelty is adopted: for instance, 'netify' as a version of 'wash', tried by Florio, never caught on. Still, the early-modern era was quite receptive to new notions brought forth by advances in sciences and arts, travel and commerce, which naturally required new words. John Shute, who in 1562 translated Andrea Cambini's history of the Ottoman empire, introduced 'aga', 'cadi', 'seraglio' and 'vizier' into English.

Changes generated by translation are not limited to new words; nor do they belong exclusively to the distant past. Translations of Martin Heidegger's works into French from 1931 onwards have changed the style of French philosophical discourse (some existentialists might argue for the better); Elio Vittorini, who translated American writers, contributed to the flourishing of a new Italian realism after the Second World War. But neologisms emerging from translation seem easier to coin for novelties, especially tangible ones, immaterial notions being more resistant to external influences. Vladimir Nabokov noted that the Russian word *toska*, whose meaning shades from 'great spiritual anguish' to 'yearning' to 'boredom', cannot be fully rendered by any single word in English, and although translators have tried to transplant it into English soil, it didn't take root.

One of the hardest things in translation is voice. It's difficult enough to sustain a chosen register, avoiding shifts from demotic to elevated through various degrees of formality, but at least these characteristics, once identified, can be more or less accurately matched in many languages. But what if a text contains a local dialect or some other idiosyncrasy? Various solutions have been tried. In another lecture, Eco gives two examples from *Foucault's Pendulum*: its French translator used Provençal as an analogue of the 'Frenchified' Italian spoken by one of the characters; in the German version, German inflections in the voice of another were replaced with archaic speech. When trying to trade like for like, however, you have to take extra care, as a splash of local colour may prove either too unfamiliar or too distinctive to allow for any new connotations. Collaborating on a book partly set during the 1930s famine in Ukraine, Robert Chandler and I were trying to find a suitable analogue for its regional Russian peppered with Ukrainian. Scots, I suggested, might do the trick. 'Famine in Scotland?' Chandler said. The image seemed so incongruous that the idea was dropped by mutual consent. Using Irish cadences seemed less appropriate still, so we ended up with the odd West Country phrase.

Finding the right register is even more important in live speech. Eco asks what would happen if 'Bonne journée' at the end of a conversation was translated as 'I hope you will have good and enjoyable experiences for the rest of the day,' or if the exclamation 'Attento allo scalino' was turned into 'I advise you to pay attention to the step whose presence may perhaps have escaped your notice.' Formally speaking, the meanings would be the same, but the point is that greetings and warnings should be brief. Interpreters, who have to keep up the tempo all the time, are especially sensitive to lengthy passages. They also watch out for any peculiarities, so as not to throw listeners off balance. Thus, UN interpreters are not supposed to highlight what little colour might be present in speeches: essentially, they work into UN-ese, a conventional language they learn as part of their training. When I asked Stephen Pearl, who spent several decades at the UN before retiring as chief of the English Interpretation Section, if their approach might be too formulaic, he disagreed. 'All the speakers usually want is to get it on the record, preferably in two minutes,' he said. 'Things are really decided by arm-twisting behind the scenes.'

6

The Sublime Porte

Until the beginning of the nineteenth century, few Muslims in the Ottoman empire knew any languages other than Ottoman, Persian and Arabic. 'With its elaborate sentence structure and complex vocabulary,' the historian Philip Mansel writes in *Constantinople*, 'the Ottoman language erected a wall between the empire and the outside world.' The Ottomans communicated with foreigners through dragomans, as translators used to be called in the Near East. Their job involved much more than conveying ready messages. They translated, orally and in writing, but also drafted notes and negotiated deals, ran errands and sold secrets. When translating, they intervened, adding and cutting, sometimes changing the meaning, often reframing the source, glossing cultural aspects or contextualising political demands, rephrasing the author's wording or rewriting their introduction. Why didn't they restrict themselves to getting things across in a neutral and accurate fashion? Were they too scared to repeat certain utterances? Too self-important not to put in their twopenn'orth? Wise enough to know better than to stick to the original?

In the sixteenth and seventeenth centuries, Italian served as a lingua franca in the Mediterranean. One of the

Ottoman empire's most important trading partners was the Republic of Venice, which, beginning as early as in the sixteenth century, would send its subjects to Constantinople to train as translators. Young men were recruited into the household of the Venetian representative – the *bailo* – to serve as *giovani di lingua* (language boys). These apprentices learned Ottoman while going about their tasks, and the best of them were eventually promoted to dragomans.

The Ottoman government, known as the Sublime Porte, used its own dragomans, found among slaves and refugees, merchants and sailors. Their ranks included Jews from Europe; Christian-born converts to Islam, or renegades; Armenians and Greeks who travelled abroad; and starting from the seventeenth century, the offspring of Christian families – mostly affluent Greeks from Constantinople, known as Phanariots – who studied in Europe and came back with knowledge of Western languages and traditions. Finally, European embassies and consulates hired their own interpreters, relying on Levantines. These last – the descendants of Europeans, often Italians or Greeks, who had settled in the empire – escape clear categorisation: to quote the orientalist Bernard Lewis, they were 'European but not really European', with 'a smattering of European ways and education'. The majority of that era's dragomans were, as the historian E. Natalie Rothman puts it, 'trans-imperial subjects', intermediaries crossing cultural, religious, ethnic, political and, of course, linguistic boundaries between the East and the West. And over time, that liberty brought some of them real power.

Alexander Mavrocordato was once described by a French diplomat as 'one of the best actors in Europe'. Portraits of dragomans, commissioned by themselves or by Europeans interested in oriental customs, were a popular genre in the seventeenth century, and although I have never seen an image believed to be of Mavrocordato, I find it easy to imagine him at work: a solemn bearded man in a fur hat and crimson cape (worn on official duty; daily attire was blue), equipped with his stamp and a belt of writing implements, he sits there listening closely, processing someone's words before speaking himself.

Born in 1641 into a family of Greek merchants, Mavrocordato was among the first citizens of Constantinople to be educated in the West, studying at the Greek college in Rome and then at the universities of Padua and Bologna, where he wrote a thesis on blood circulation. What circulated through his life, professional, political and private, was another kind of stream: a fast-flowing stream of information. After returning home and serving as a physician to several local rulers, in 1671 he became the secretary of Panagiotis Nikousios, the grand dragoman of the Porte. This high post, established a decade earlier, combined the duties of chief government interpreter and deputy foreign minister. On Nicousios' death in 1673, Mavrocordato took the top job. His career was interrupted by the Great Turkish War, or the War of the Holy League, and in 1683, following the Ottoman defeat at Vienna, he was taken to prison in chains and fined an enormous sum. Still, his knowledge of European languages and customs made him indispensable, and he was soon reinstated.

In 1699, Mavrocordato helped to negotiate the Peace of Carlowitz between the Ottomans and the Habsburgs, succeeding in making each party believe that the initiative came from the other. His contemporary Dimitrie Cantemir writes that the chief Ottoman official at Carlowitz 'was but a mere tool to Maurocordatus, by whose secret persuasion and advice he did many things; which Maurocordatus, as being a Christian, could not propose in publick; and therefore many things are falsely ascribed to his skill and penetration, which none but a man of Maurocordatus' discernment and capacity could have invented'. For his success in this mission Mavrocordato was appointed *mahremi esrar*, or, as Cantemir's English translator N. Tindal has it, one 'to whom secrets are discovered'. Cantemir says that he 'invented this new name for his office, which was never used before, nor has been since his death granted to any other'. It was perhaps a natural progression from his earlier job as a court doctor, which gave him access to what was going on behind closed doors. Modern historians usually render this unique title as 'minister of the secrets' or, more intriguingly, *secretaire intime*. This is the term used in Nestor Camariano's *Alexandre Mavrocordato, le grand drogman*, in which the subject's associates are quoted as awarding him various epithets, from 'un bel homme fort discret et civil' to 'instruit en tout et sage et pratique' to 'Judas'.

In his correspondence with William Paget, the English ambassador, Mavrocordato comes across as exceedingly silver-tongued, though perhaps not so much by the standards of his time. 'Our desires are equally strong, but whereas Your Excellency's is born out of your infinite goodness, mine comes from my increased urge to find your generous auspices nearer,' begins a letter dated 20 April 1699, written in Italian. For all his grandiloquence, Mavrocordato also used textspeak in his missives, for instance, '7bre' for *settembre*. His handwriting became even more ornate when he switched to Latin (or did he choose to dictate on those occasions?), his flourishes truly fanciful. More than three centuries on, they are still encrusted with the sand he used instead of blotting paper.

As I sat in the archive sifting through the bundle of letters, those grains and splotches of sealing wax stuck to the parchment pleased me almost as much as my ability to understand Mavrocordato's Italian, archaic but fairly comprehensible. 'So great is the attraction of Your Excellency that staying so long deprived of your sweetest ways and gentlest features is almost unbearable,' he goes on, showering gems of oriental eloquence upon Paget. His relationship with the French ambassador Charles de Ferriol was, according to Camariano, less cordial; yet, whenever there was trouble in Constantinople, Mavrocordato took refuge in the French embassy.

A polymath and corrupt politician, a grandee and a schemer, a scholar 'celebrated by the learned World on many accounts', a rich man whose private library was famous across Europe, a confidant of the great and the powerful, a polyglot who knew Ottoman, Persian, Arabic, Greek, Latin, French, Italian and probably also German and Romanian, a prince of the Holy Roman empire, 'Professor of Philosophy, Divinity and Physic', an eminent figure in Eastern and Western politics, Alexander Mavrocordato was also the founder of a dynasty of dragomans. Their story reflects in many ways the history of Greeks in the Ottoman empire. Christians in the midst of Islamic civilisation, they retained their religious and ethnic identity while being part of that culture, a feat achieved partly through language. It was the dragomans' official status that brought them and their families a number of privileges denied to other non-Muslims, including the right to be judged by the grand vizier's supreme court and to enjoy certain tax exemptions, to ride on horseback and to be accompanied by armed guards, to grow beards and to wear fur hats.

The Mavrocordatos and the other Phanariot families that came to prominence in a similar way, with their minority status linked to their ability to communicate with the West, were both builders of the empire and its beneficiaries, insiders with an outsider's perspective, a unique position they exploited to the full. 'Far from being prisoners of one identity,' Mansel writes, 'they regarded a nationality as a career,' and although it is difficult to tell where their real allegiances lay, they 'believed that, while the Ottoman empire existed, they and their fellow Greeks might as well benefit from it'.

Alexander Mavrocordato took bribes and traded information, though 'his corruption and indiscretion were by no means exceptional', and it is possible that he acted on the grand vizier's instructions or with his knowledge. The advantages of being the grand dragoman of the Porte were so great, they might well have outweighed whatever he secured from his foreign associates. His son Nicholas, born in 1680, knew as many languages as Mavrocordato *père*, all learned in Constantinople rather than abroad. After succeeding his father as the grand dragoman, in 1709 he was elevated to the throne of Wallachia, paving the way for his descendants. A 'Man well vers'd in the Oriental and Occidental Learning', to quote Cantemir again, he wrote the first modern Greek novel, *The Leisure of Philotheus*, set in Constantinople. Its narrator might be speaking for the entire dynasty when he says, 'We were as Greek as it is possible to be.'

Predating the Phanariots, there existed another category of translators finding themselves in a role they probably never expected to play: Europeans who shed their identity and reinvented themselves according to their new circumstances. Here, briefly, are the stories of three sixteenth-century renegades who didn't end up in the Ottoman lands by their own free will but never the less found purpose in their situation. Yunus Bey, originally a Venetian subject from the Peloponnese, was captured as a young man and became a dragoman, assisting with the Ottoman–Venetian peace negotiations in 1539. He co-wrote a guide to the Ottoman administration, introducing Italian-speakers to the Turkish words for 'minister', 'head of the imperial guards', 'palace steward' and 'head cook', among others. The first known work by Ottoman authors writing for a European readership, it was a useful piece of public information with elements of propaganda.

Another renegade, Mahmud Bey, born in Vienna, was also captured by the Ottomans and, with his native German and good Latin, began serving the empire in the 1540s. His magnum opus, *History of Hungary*, billed as a translation from Latin of a book found in a Hungarian fortress conquered by Sultan Süleyman, in fact deals mainly with Alexander the Great. The source has been identified as *Historiae Philippicae*, a work by the Roman historian Pompeius Trogus. The translator follows the original fairly closely but with substantial glossing, ascribing to Alexander several of the sultan's titles, including 'ruler of the seven climes'.

Mahmud hoped to present the monarch with this book, which portrays his conquest as the highest point in the history of Hungary, but it is unlikely that Süleyman ever saw it. The book remained relatively unknown and wasn't published until 1859. Still, it was a clever move: opting for the immunity of a mere translator in a bid to rewrite history, or at least to smuggle in a few unorthodox ideas.

And then there was Murad Bey, born in Transylvania, who spent two and a half years in captivity. After converting to Islam, he was appointed an imperial dragoman in 1553. Murad, who knew Ottoman, Hungarian, Latin, German and possibly Arabic and Persian too, believed in the importance of translation for the promotion and subversion of religious ideas. An author in his own right, he wrote *Guide for One's Turning Towards God*, a polemical treatise with an account of his conversion added to it; he also translated a number of religious and historical works, including his own, into different languages. One of his sources was Cicero's *De senectute*, retold in Ottoman as *In Praise of Old Age* with various deviations. Some historians believe it was not a translation at all but a pastiche of Cicero written under commission, while the introduction claims the original to be a recorded conversation between Sultan Murad II and his son. In his criticism of foreigners with limited Arabic embarking on translations of the Koran, inevitably producing versions full of omissions and blasphemies, Murad remarks that 'for every word in one language there are many synonyms, so that to understand it when it is translated into the final language, one cannot help but infer a different meaning'.

Whether speaking for themselves or on someone else's behalf, dragomans usually resorted to a deferential and florid mode of expression. A 'severe message' would be passed on to an official as a 'humble supplication'. When one of the locals working for the British consulate in Constantinople was imprisoned, he begged the authorities for leniency in a characteristically worded letter:

> Having bowed my head in submission, and rubbed my slavish brow in utter humility and complete abjection and supplication to the beneficent dust beneath the feet of my mighty, gracious, condescending, compassionate, merciful benefactor, my most generous and open-handed master, I pray that the peerless and almighty provider of remedies may bless your lofty person, the extremity of benefit, protect my benefactor from the vicissitudes and afflictions of time, prolong the days of his life, his might and his splendour and perpetuate the shadow of his pity and mercy upon this slave.

Were dragomans excessively subservient or merely prudent in their politeness? Their tendency to avoid forceful statements was well known. The Venetian envoy Antonio Tiepolo wrote in 1576 that 'the dragoman, who is often impeded by the difficulty of interpreting, and even more by failing to apprehend not only the issues, but also the *bailo*'s mode of impressing these issues, weakens the arguments and exhibits that timidity which is never the *bailo*'s share'. There were certainly reasons for them to be timid, especially when they were locals with no diplomatic status, while their foreign employers rebuked them all the same for being too scared of the Ottoman authorities to deliver unpleasant news.

That, according to Lewis, is just one of the many complaints about Levantine dragomans to be found in the European documents of that time. Others concerned their incompetence (unjustified in Lewis' view, although many commentators note that the Levantines were not as well educated as their higher-standing Phanariot colleagues) and disloyalty, their masters accusing them of 'selling their services to the highest bidder', European or Ottoman. They were mostly related to each other, which made it easy for them to pass one embassy's secrets on to another. The British ambassador James Porter wrote in the eighteenth century of

> a great perplexity to zealous ministers, for if they entrust their secret to interpreters, who with large families live upon a small salary, and are used to Oriental luxury, the temptation of money from others is with difficulty withstood by them and even exclusive of any considerations of gain, they are often excited by mere vanity to discover the secret they are entrusted with in order to show their own importance.

Never the less, another historian, Alexander de Groot, remarks that Levantines 'in Frankish dress' were among the best mediators, indispensable in relations between the European powers and the Porte. Whatever inaccuracies dragomans allowed in their translations, mistakes of other kinds were more dangerous for them to make, no matter what side they were on. Even the most respected of them, Mavrocordato and his descendants, oscillated between the court, prison and the French embassy. To quote de Groot, dragomans 'never put all their eggs in one basket', moving from one protector to another, now relying on their Western friends, now reverting to the Ottoman state. The Phanariots continued to benefit from their loyalty to the empire, as well as to have a monopoly on the office of grand dragoman, until the nineteenth century, when they were suspected of supporting the Greek War of Independence. In 1821, Stavrachi Aristarchi, the last Phanariot dragoman, was accused of high treason, exiled and killed.

Some of the linguistic problems early-modern translators had to solve are described by Rothman in her paper 'Interpreting Dragomans', which cites two interesting examples of their interventions in texts they were given to work on. She compares two versions of a letter sent by Sultan Murad III to Doge Pasquale Cicogna in 1594, in response to protests voiced by the Venetians after one of their galleys was attacked by North African corsairs in the Adriatic. The translations were done independently: one in Constantinople by Girolamo Alberti, brought there from his native Venice as an apprentice and then made a dragoman; the other in Venice by Giacomo de Nores, who was born in Cyprus and spent his childhood and youth as a slave in an Ottoman household before becoming a dragoman for the Venetian Board of Trade. The differences between these documents exemplify the main questions that divide the translation community to this day: to remain invisible or to take the initiative; to paraphrase or not.

Alberti, taught more systematically, is more literal in his work, while de Nores uses a highly interpretive style. Many of de Nores' choices, such as Italianised titles, legal terms and calendar dates, show his penchant for cultural glossing.

He introduces and frames the document – 'through a petition just presented to my elevated seat'; 'it is further added in that petition that' – distancing himself from it, much as UN interpreters nowadays insert the red flag 'The distinguished speaker says' to stress who is responsible for any potential blunders. In the same vein, de Nores often avoids the first-person pronouns used by the author: where Alberti faithfully refers to peace 'which obtains between us', de Nores writes 'between the two parties'; 'friends of our friends' become 'friends of the friends of this Sublime Porte'; 'do not lend help to our enemies' is changed to 'do not give their enemies any sort of help'.

Rothman notes that de Nores' version 'suggests an effort to extricate the translator from any complicity in the sultan's perspective and to position himself in a supposedly more "neutral" intermediary space'; it also seems that de Nores lacks training and so has to guess at the meaning of unfamiliar terms, often elaborating on them as if trying to compensate for any inaccuracies. Were the two of them to sit an exam to qualify as a translator today – in which candidates are typically required to produce accurate translations of general and specialised texts – Alberti would have fared better than de Nores.

Not that standards are set particularly high in the twenty-first-century translation market, where the lowest bidder takes all. Concerns over the quality of translation and interpreting in certain fields stem from the you-get-what-you-pay-for attitude, and the perception of being undervalued has led some in the trade to talk of 'slave labour'. The meaning of this term has certainly changed since the Ottoman days, as has the status of the translator. The éminence grise of old enjoyed power and recognition that have no analogues in the profession today. Alongside such figures of influence toiled rank-and-file translators, little noticed unless their efforts resulted in something undesirable, and yet holding in their hands more than mere words. For all of them, knowledge of languages was no use without such qualities as prudence, discretion, versatility, interpersonal skills and acting flair. When his son became the prince of Wallachia, the old Alexander Mavrocordato 'beat his head and tore his hair, proclaiming that it was the ruin of his family', Mansel writes. 'He was practising Talleyrand's maxim, that words are given us to hide our meaning.'

7

Infidelities

ATTORNEY GENERAL: Describe what happened afterwards.
KING'S INTERPRETER: She asks, is it on the same evening?
LORD CHANCELLOR: Translate her answers direct as she
gives them, in the first person; when she says 'I', do not
you say 'she'.

This exchange took place during an 'important and eventful trial' held in Parliament in 1820. In fact, it wasn't a trial
in the ordinary sense. The proceedings were brought by
King George IV, who accused his wife, Queen Caroline, of
adultery. Their marriage had been troubled from the start:
George was drunk at the wedding ceremony in 1795; when
their daughter was born the year after, he made a new will,
leaving everything to his mistress; his disgust towards Caroline was common knowledge; the couple lived separately,
both, it was rumoured, having affairs. George's excesses
made him unpopular with the public, while Caroline was
widely seen as the injured party. In 1814, under establishment pressure, she agreed to leave Britain and settled in Italy.

One of the servants she hired there was a former army
officer called Bartolomeo Bergami. Over the following
years, according to some accounts, Caroline raised the man

'from obscurity to distinction', allowing him access to her bedroom. When the news reached George, he set up an investigation into his wife's behaviour, hoping to divorce her on the grounds of infidelity. By 1820, his spies had dug up enough dirt to fill a large green bag, and George applied for the dissolution of their marriage by bringing the so-called Pains and Penalties Bill before Parliament. The reading of this bill in the House of Lords, which Caroline attended, was staged as a trial to prove her adultery.

Most of the prosecution witnesses were foreign – Italian, French and German – and required an interpreter. The first to be sworn in, the Marquis di Spineto, had received instructions from representatives of the Foreign Office and the Treasury, so the queen's legal adviser, Henry Brougham, was compelled to call in another interpreter, Benedetto Cohen, to ensure fair treatment of his client. Brougham's own impartiality, however, was somewhat compromised. Before the witnesses were called, he warned everyone present that these foreigners could not be trusted, launching an attack so vicious that the attorney general had to come to their defence. 'Would their lordships listen to such an argument as this?' a record of the proceedings reads. 'Let them pride themselves on the superiority of the English character, but let them not by a sweeping condemnation declare that all foreigners are unworthy of credit.' Many found this suggestion hard to follow.

When the first witness, Theodore Majocchi, was summoned, the sight of her former servant made Caroline cry out, 'Theodore, oh no!' Questioned at length about sleeping arrangements in the queen's household, he reported that Bergami's bedroom was close to Caroline's, and that creaking noises and whispers were occasionally heard from the royal chamber. During cross-examination by Brougham, however, the witness sounded less convincing. As the queen's counsel grilled him on various details related to his earlier evidence, he repeatedly answered, 'Non mi ricordo,' a phrase Brougham made a song and dance about. He asked Spineto for an exact translation and was told that it could mean 'I do not remember' or 'I do not know.' He then turned to Cohen, who gave just one version: 'I do not recollect.' Pressed to expand, Majocchi did his best: 'When I say "non mi ricordo" I mean that I have not in my head to have received the money, for if I had received the money I would say yes; but I do not remember it now, but I do not recollect the contrary.'

Soon the interpreters were no longer waiting for requests to elaborate on Majocchi's words and volunteered explanations straight away. When asked if he was asleep at a certain time, the witness replied, 'As I am now asleep,' prompting the interpreter to clarify, 'He means that he was awake.' As the cross-examination went on, Majocchi was compelled to satisfy their lordships' great interest in the queen's dresses and bathroom habits, as well as in his own family circumstances. Possibly as a result, his answers grew as devious as the questions put to him: 'I can swear and I do swear ...' The general antipathy towards the slippery foreigner increased, both in and outside the Lords. To add insult to injury, one of the interpreters complained that he couldn't properly communicate 'with such a stupid fellow'. By the end of his ordeal, Majocchi was 'frightened out of his wits'. When allegations of bribery reached him, he asked one of the interpreters to assure everyone of his honesty, and the message was duly passed on.

Other witnesses were met with the same suspicion. Brougham claimed that 'if their evidence was to be believed then the Queen was worse than Messalina, or as bad as Marie Antoinette', and made far-fetched generalisations about Italians. The interpreters, in their turn, became more and more alert to potential misunderstandings, now flagging anything ambiguous on their own initiative. When a witness mentioned Bergami sleeping 'together' with Caroline, Spineto explained that the word he used, *insieme*, could also mean 'likewise', and the witness corroborated this by adding, 'in two different beds'. The questioning turned to an occasion when Caroline was seen in the garden with Bergami, and another witness specified the time as 'about one or half-past one'. Spineto translated this literally (perhaps to prevent other Italian-speakers present from interrupting him, as they often did, not always helpfully) before remarking, 'The Italian and the English time is reckoned by a different manner.' He explained that the phrase meant an hour and a half after dusk, and Cohen confirmed this: 'My lords, I was born in Lombardy myself, and I know this is the mode of reckoning.'

The Italian drama over, the prosecution called another witness, Barbara Kress, a chambermaid, and a German interpreter, Georg William Kolmanter, took over from Spineto and Cohen. Someone pointed out errors in his translation, and after some bickering it was decided to bring in another German-speaker. Consequently, Brougham asked for an adjournment, and when criticised for being unprepared, he enquired whether next he 'would, on the spur of the moment, be called upon for a Tunisian, a Turkish, a Greek, or an Egyptian interpreter; for in all these countries the Queen had been'. The next day Charles Karsten was sworn in, and the examination of Kress resumed. As the hunt for the queen's dirty laundry continued, the poor maid had to describe in detail the state of Caroline's bedsheets on a certain morning. 'The word she has used cannot be inter-preted in English,' Karsten claimed, and so Kolmanter was invited to step in again. The pair discussed such possibili-ties as 'disorder' and 'waste' until Kress was prevailed upon to utter another word, univocally translated as 'stains'. The house asked whether she was married herself. She answered in the affirmative, then burst into tears.

Outside the Lords, the public and the press were even more hostile towards the venal foreigners giving evidence against the poor wronged queen. Majocchi's testimony alone gave rise to a great many xenophobic outbursts, including various comic songs in this vein:

> What chambermaid, what valet,
> Came running to the bell O?
> What footman brought the dinner up?
> Non mi ricordo quello,
> Indeed I cannot tell O –
> A d—d convenient fellow!

Periodicals carried caricatures mocking the king, as well as songs of support for the queen. Printed in *Satirical Songs, and Miscellaneous Papers, Connected with the Trial of Queen Caroline*, these included some charged verses:

> Then let England and Ireland, and Scotland aloud,
> For the rights of the women declare.

The whole sordid spectacle eventually ended with the bill being abandoned. Despite her popularity with the masses, a year later Caroline was prevented from attending George's coronation. She fell ill and died not long after the ditty 'The Italian Witness (England's Lament)' fell out of fashion.

One of the earliest examples of a royal affair turned into tabloid fodder, the trial also highlighted a number of issues familiar to present-day interpreters. One thing their lordships took seriously was the quality of interpretation, hence their insistence on having interpreters work in pairs, an obvious step that regrettably is often dismissed as impracticable. Despite formally representing opposing camps, the interpreters cooperated with each other, filling in gaps when needed. Concerns about potential conflicts of interest would rule out such an arrangement in most settings today, though it's hard to see why a professional shouldn't be able to maintain impartiality regardless of whose payroll they are on. A more serious obstacle to quality control is, of course, the ubiquitous scarcity of funds.

Another aspect manifest in the 1820 proceedings that hasn't lost its relevance today is the importance of cultural glossing. The court interpreter's oath used in English and Welsh courts includes the promise to 'explanations necessary make' so as to ensure full comprehension. Details peculiar to a speaker's culture, from domestic habits to religious traditions, need to be spelled out. And then there is the basic principle that requires interpreters to convey the original account in the first person, except when referring to themselves ('The interpreter would like to clarify ...'), which, as the opening of this chapter reminds us, has been acknowledged for a long time. Sticking to this rule is the only way to avoid confusion, and yet surprisingly many people instinctively perceive the interpreter as the actual speaker rather than a conduit. Curiously, this inability to distinguish between the medium and the message becomes especially acute when one doesn't get what one wants. Some responses – such as 'I don't know what you mean' or 'You must be fucking kidding me' – can easily make people forget who they are really talking to. They roll their eyes in exasperation – not at their interlocutor but at the person who uttered the offending words. Such situations bring to mind the *Blackadder* episode in which another royal marriage gets off to a bad start as the Spanish infanta woos Rowan Atkinson's Prince Edmund with the help of her interpreter, Don Speekingleesh. When the latter translates, 'I am the infanta,' Edmund shrieks, 'What? No one told me you had a beard!'

Stories like these, invariably rooted in mistaken identity, repeat themselves for every generation of interpreters both in and out of court. Swearing – a fairly common occurrence in the witness box – is a case in point. While some of my colleagues worry about what the court might think of them if they start emitting profanities, I always delight in translating swear words, mainly for linguistic reasons, since obscene language highlights a number of inherent differences between Russian and English. Once, when a witness refused to repeat what exactly had been said in the course of a heated argument, I struggled to conceal my disappointment. Another time I got luckier with a defendant who didn't mind his language: when I translated one of his general-purpose Russian expletives as 'shit', he corrected me, saying that he meant a stronger four-letter word, which I willingly supplied.

Another perennial source of confusion are non-verbal messages coming from the interpreter, sometimes preventing listeners from focusing on the speaker. In October 2019, at a meeting between Donald Trump and the Italian president Sergio Mattarella, an interpreter was caught on camera at an awkward moment. She was probably just concentrating on the discussion, which concerned military action in Syria, but some took her expression as a painful reaction to what she was hearing. The video went viral, accompanied by misguided speculations about whether or not it was professional for an interpreter to look horrified at Trump's ramblings. In focusing on this minor detail, the commentators overlooked real examples of unprofessional behaviour: the interpreter had been repeatedly interrupted by journalists and by Mattarella himself. Even those determined to be polite to their interlocutor tend to be less bothered about cutting short the translator, at the same time expecting them to get the message across and look photogenic to boot.

Appearances also played a part in the 1820 parliamentary farce. One Italian witness was described in the official record as having a 'most stupid and clownish appearance'; another, when questioned about an exotic performance attended by Caroline, had to demonstrate the dancer's movements. While the interpreters were generally treated with respect, those who gave evidence were mocked throughout the hearing. This attitude, appalling on all counts, never the less has one encouraging implication: it suggests that the audience were, after all, able to separate the identity of the speaker from that of the translator.

Meanwhile, the interpreters, the record suggests, showed little emotion unless they saw the parties struggle to understand each other, which made them anxious to offer clarifications. In *The Trial of Queen Caroline*, painted by George Hayter from life, the scene is animated: most of the sitters listen attentively, some leaning forward; the leader of the Whigs, Lord Grey, stretches his arm towards Spineto, trying to stop him mid-sentence; the interpreter, however, remains calm, counting something off on his fingers as he translates Majocchi's evidence. Was Grey trying to challenge Spineto on some perceived inaccuracy, as several of the peers did in the course of the hearing? Sometimes the interrupters had a point, but often it was just nitpicking. While their clients made much ado about nothing (the die was cast when they agreed to treat a divorce case as a parliamentary matter), the interpreters took it all in their stride. Faced with high expectations – unsurprisingly, given the significance of the event – they did their utmost to accommodate everyone.

'The first great leap forward in the history of translation,' to quote David Bellos, 'must have been when some two communities found a way of agreeing that the speech of the translator was to be taken as having the same force as the immediately prior speech of the principal.' I often wish my clients could make a leap in the opposite direction, stop taking my first-person sentences as my own and address each other directly. Such occasions remind me of another piece of drama: *Translations*, a 1980 play by Brian Friel. Set in rural Ireland in the 1830s, it is a reflection on language as a form of oppression, resistance and self-determination. In one telling scene, when a British army captain talks to a group of Irish-speaking villagers in English, he speaks 'as if he were addressing children – a shade too loudly and enunciating excessively', despite having an interpreter at his side. The listeners snigger, and the interpreter is embarrassed for everyone. His role as a translator – a mediator between two sides – costs him his identity; he is doomed to remain stuck between 'us' and 'them', neither the Irishman he once was nor the Englishman he aspires to be. His name is Owen but his employers call him Roland and he doesn't have the nerve to correct them.

The translator's anonymity can take different forms. Although the Queen Caroline trial was well documented, the interpreters' names were spelled variously, which makes it hard to trace them. The only exception here is Spineto, who taught at Cambridge and published *Lectures on the Elements of Hieroglyphics and Egyptian Antiquities*. As for the others, I drew a blank. Did they have careers in humanities, law or some other field? Specialising in a particular area can prepare a translator for a more active role in it, so it's not unusual to see facilitators becoming practitioners – making it after a period of faking it, so to speak. In another scenario, translators juggle a variety of subjects and tasks, their general knowledge growing broader if not necessarily deeper. Such versatility can be conducive to career U-turns, when after a stint in translation one restyles oneself as a revolutionary or a businessman, a bureaucrat or a therapist. Until that happens, in the course of performing their duties translators must continue to refer to themselves in the third person for the sake of those who rely on their voice.

8

Precision Was Not a Strong Point of Hitler's

'I woke up one morning,' Eugen Dollmann recalled in his
memoirs, 'to find myself in the SS.' Remembering the events
in question three decades later, he says that his 'motives were
a mixed bunch – a compound of thoughtlessness, guileless-
ness, and, above all, a desire not to see my sojourn in Rome
and Italy placed in jeopardy'. The son of a Bavarian bar-
oness, a product of the last days of the Austro-Hungarian
empire, Dollmann studied in Munich before going to Italy
for his research, to read Michelangelo's manuscripts and
look for traces of the sixteenth-century cardinal Alessandro
Farnese. Asked to interpret at a banquet attended by Hein-
rich Himmler and Arturo Bocchini, the German and Italian
chiefs of police, he did so well that his career path was set
for the next decade. 'If it had been the European ministers
of education or agriculture,' he muses, 'things would probably have turned out otherwise.' As it was, he soon met 'the
two corporals' (the rank of both Hitler and Mussolini in the
First World War) and facilitated their communications for
as long as his services were required.

'Personal impressions and experiences are all I have to
add to the whole libraries that have been written about the
Munich Conference.' So begins Dollmann's account of the

97

international gathering in September 1938 that resulted in an agreement allowing Germany to annex the Sudetenland, then part of Czechoslovakia, and hence dominate Central Europe. Dollmann was there as Mussolini's interpreter, but his boss was keen to practise his language skills, no matter how imperfect. 'Thanks to the fact that Benito Mussolini was acting as interpreter-general,' Dollmann writes, 'I did not find myself overworked.' For his German counterpart, 'the indefatigable Dr Schmidt', the conference 'lasted without respite for nearly thirteen hours' since he constantly had to assist Hitler. During conversations involving Neville Chamberlain and Édouard Daladier, Paul Schmidt 'had to translate everything that was said continuously into three languages ... and so spoke literally twice as many words as the Big Four put together'. As if that was not enough, he was often interrupted by the person addressed. He always asked to be allowed to finish, knowing from experience how confusing such gaps could be. People watching the session through glass doors later told Schmidt that when he demanded everyone's attention, he looked 'like a schoolmaster trying to keep an unruly class in order'.

Schmidt began working for the German government in 1924, became Hitler's interpreter in 1935 and continued to work for the Third Reich until the end, also joining the SS. Throughout his memoirs, first published in 1958, he mentions his prescience regarding the future of Germany under the Nazis, giving the impression of someone who knew how it would turn out but could do nothing about it for obvious reasons. From 'the fateful year 1939', it was clear to him that 'the day of reckoning could not be long delayed'. His 'awareness of Hitler's intentions' runs through the book, although it has been said that long after the war he still talked about the führer with admiration. It's impossible to know what his feelings were at the time. Still, when it comes to linguistic matters, his professional remarks come across as sincere. In one episode prior to the Munich Conference, Hitler meets Chamberlain to discuss the fate of the Sudetenland and, assuring the British prime minister he would never resort to force, says, 'I shall settle this question in one way or another.' Schmidt duly translates the phrase (which later came to be used often) without realising that it actually means, 'Either the other side gives in, or a solution will be found by means of the application of force, invasion, or war.'

If Schmidt portrays himself as a decent man in the service of an evil regime, Dollmann merely mentions in passing his fascination with 'the game of toy soldiers in which the two dictators engaged'. Take, for instance, his account of a trip to occupied Ukraine in August 1941, when he accompanied Hitler and Mussolini on a trip to inspect their armies. As they drove across the ravaged country, the führer released a 'torrent of verbiage' about the conquest of Asia. Mussolini's reply made even less sense than his interlocutor's spiel, and Dollmann hesitated for a moment before translating: 'What then? Shall we weep for the moon like Alexander the Great?' Hitler asked what this meant and was treated to a poem. 'This was more difficult,' Dollmann recalls, 'but the Duce helped me with it, hardly giving me time to explain that it was the opening of Giovanni Pascoli's famous poem on Alexander.' With this, the cheered Mussolini and the annoyed Hitler proceeded to greet their troops among the smoking ruins, attended by their amused interpreter.

Dollmann works hard to give his stories a veneer of

humour and self-deprecation, doing his best to downplay his own complicity in the dictators' deeds. One example of his whitewashing is a 'Goering-size affair lasting nearly two hours, throughout which time I had to translate statistics and technical points of which I understood nothing in German, let alone Italian'. Schmidt, by contrast, is always serious. In July 1940, when Hitler made his 'very magnanimous peace offer to England', Schmidt was determined to translate the speech into English as well as possible: to combat the enemies who 'often translated German statements very inaccurately and capriciously', as well as to give everyone the chance to prevent bloodshed. While Hitler addressed the Reichstag, Schmidt sat in a broadcasting studio with the English text; as a colleague indicated with a pencil where the speaker was, he read it, switching his mike on and off at intervals to let listeners hear Hitler's voice. 'Many newspapers marvelled at my achievement,' he writes (they assumed that he had translated live). Happy with his own performance, he was never the less 'profoundly disappointed in the content of the speech' and surprised that Hitler 'should believe that such a meaningless, purely rhetorical, observation would have any effect upon the sober British'. Further on, the criticism is even more explicit: 'I had often noticed at negotiations that precision was not a strong point of Hitler's.'

Meanwhile, Dollmann, a self-styled art lover and bon vivant, sees his work as a mere nuisance, but at least it leaves him enough time to flit nonchalantly from one social engagement to another: 'there was virtually nothing for me to do as an interpreter … so I decided to improve my sadly neglected mind by spending more time at the opera'. A world-weary aesthete who by a twist of fate finds himself in the company of people he wouldn't normally mix with, he looks upon the situation with a wry smile. 'I took advantage of the lunch at Hitler's rather grisly private apartment,' he writes about one of his assignments, 'to savour the bad taste of the devoted Party members, male and female, who had paid homage to their idol by presenting him with frightful specimens of home-handiwork and countless other souvenirs and tributes of every description.' While Dollmann's artistic sensibilities suffered, 'Mussolini, who was not overburdened with an aesthetic sense, found the sight quite undaunting'. Unimpressed by the two corporals, the retired interpreter often indulges in gossip about their private lives, including Hitler's 'peculiarly diffident attitude towards the countless women who later competed for his favours'. On the rare occasions when he does talk shop, he positions himself as a 'star interpreter' able to 'evade some of the less agreeable assignments', so that he is 'left victorious on the battlefield of the Italo-German crusades'.

Both memoirists are apparently above the fray, although in different ways. Dollmann turns up his nose at 'this bazaar of human emotions, most of them rather primitive', while Schmidt is interested in the high-level political games played by the Nazi regime rather than in the minutiae of its crimes. 'My growing indispensability to the success of the Italo-German love affair still puzzles me to this day,' Dollmann writes, admitting that there must have been many interpreters better than himself, 'who was generally regarded as anything but an exponent of literal translation'. Schmidt is more proud of his skills. After the war, his testimony and notes were used at the Nuremberg trials. He spent 'three years being moved from prisons to concentration camps and even to hotels, at times as a prisoner and at others as an employed linguist, but always as an interpreter', before becoming director of the Munich Institute of Languages and Interpreting in 1952. Dollmann, too, got off lightly, despite the fact that, as a Nazi official in Rome in 1944, he was responsible for the slaughter of 335 Italians in reprisal for the death of 32 German soldiers killed by Italian partisans, an episode omitted in his book. It is thought that the Allies helped him to escape trial for the massacre in exchange for his assistance in the negotiations that had led to the Nazi surrender in Italy.

As Hitler and Mussolini, assisted by their interpreters, plotted what they hoped would deliver 'a mortal blow' to 'the dying democracies', the Allied leaders discussed possible ways to stop them. Coming to Tehran in November 1943, each of the Big Three brought his own interpreter. Charles Bohlen, an experienced diplomat, not only translated for Franklin D. Roosevelt but also acted as the president's adviser, political and otherwise – for instance, suggesting that he divide his speech into two- to three-minute-long portions to hold the audience's attention. To quote Bohlen, Roosevelt 'was an excellent speaker to interpret for … showing consideration for my travails'. Arthur Birse, who worked for Winston Churchill, also thought highly of his employer, whose speeches were 'always clear and to the point'. There were occasions, however, when the prime minister wouldn't let Birse finish taking notes, asking him impatiently, 'What is he saying?' When speaking himself, Churchill 'preferred not to be interrupted by the translation until he finished'. In that he was worse than his Soviet ally, Stalin, who, by Bohlen's recollection, was 'considerate of his interpreter and ... meticulous in observing the length of time that he spoke'. According to Birse, he had a 'slow, simple manner of expressing himself'. Unlike his two colleagues, Vladimir Pavlov, Stalin's interpreter, left no memoirs, so we don't know how it felt to work for the dictator.

'Nothing could upset his calm, deliberate manner,' Birse wrote of Pavlov. 'Even Stalin's occasional sharp reprimands, in my opinion undeserved ... left him outwardly unperturbed.' Working together over the course of several years, the interpreters developed a good collaborative relationship: when one struggled with a term the other would suggest something, and they occasionally raised doubts about each other's choices. 'His presence gave me confidence,' Birse recalled, 'and I hope I inspired the same feeling.' On one memorable occasion in Tehran, during one of Stalin's speeches at a banquet, a waiter serving 'Persian lantern' upset the ice-cream dessert over Pavlov's uniform. 'Without hesitation, seemingly undisturbed, he continued to interpret, and completed a long and difficult speech.'

As is common in diplomatic practice, the interpreters worked from their first into their second languages, which was easier as they were more used to the voice and style of their regular clients. While Birse and Bohlen both appreciated Stalin's 'fluency and lack of hesitation in choosing his words', his Russian 'perfectly correct, simple and with no flourishes', they perceived his Georgian accent differently. Not particularly noticeable to Bohlen's ear, it initially bothered Birse: 'It was as if a native of the remote Highlands of Scotland were speaking English.' The bilingual Brit (his father, a Scotsman settled in Russia, never lost his Dundee accent in English) was sensitive to speakers' regional quirks.

Once he had to interpret for Cordell Hull, the US secretary of state, 'who spoke in a low voice with a southern American accent with which I was unfamiliar'. Struggling to understand him, Birse had to keep guessing or ask Hull to repeat his words. 'I had to rely on literal translation of such phrases as I could catch,' he writes. While he thought he was doing badly, no one seemed to mind, 'so I took heart and stumbled on'.

Another historic meeting described by both Bohlen and Birse is the Yalta Conference, hosted by Stalin in February 1945. Again, both mention clarity and logic as the main criteria by which they judged the speeches they had to interpret. Churchill, for instance, would sometimes get carried away. 'He would start a sentence and then repeat it, sometimes two or three times, before the picture would come to his mind,' Bohlen writes. 'Then he would take off on his grand oratory.' Even Birse, well used to his employer's 'words travelling from the depths of his being to burst into life', wrote that at Stalin's dinner party 'both he and Churchill rose to such heights of oratory that Pavlov and I had the greatest difficulty in finding adequate expressions in our respective languages'. A proponent of 'speed, smoothness, and above all accuracy', Birse found it especially hard to deal with rhetorical questions – 'Will the toiler see his home?' – and with such waffle as 'I propose a toast to the broad sunlight of victorious peace.'

As the Big Three continued to dazzle each other with their eloquence over lavish meals, their assistants were too busy to take refreshments. Nearly all diplomatic interpreters I've interviewed mentioned hunger as a professional hazard, but none of them put it as aphoristically as Dollmann does

in his book: 'a wise interpreter either eats a little beforehand or a lot afterwards'. However, the plight of those who
can't afford to have their mouth full is occasionally noticed
by those who can. At the same dinner party, Stalin raised
his glass: 'Tonight, and on other occasions, we three leaders
have got together. We talk, we eat and drink, and we enjoy
ourselves. But meanwhile our interpreters have to work, and
their work is not easy. They have no time to eat or drink. We
rely on them to transmit our ideas to each other. I propose
a toast to our interpreters.' After Stalin clinked glasses with
each of them, Churchill reciprocated, raising his own: 'Interpreters of the world, unite! You have nothing to lose but your
audience!' That, at least, is Birse's version; Bohlen claims it
was he who came up with the witty response, 'having forti-
fied myself with a number of glasses of vodka'. Regardless
of the authorship, the best thing about both speeches was
that they were easy to interpret, even after a few drinks. As
for the rest, the translators must have relied on the Russian
proverb, 'Skill is something you can't drink away.'

Another professional hazard – or a job perk, depending
on the circumstances – for those at summits is the presence
of photographers. While many interpreters pose proudly
in pictures next to the principals, the protagonists of this
chapter seemed to have different attitudes towards it. Dollmann's memoir has quite a few photos of himself at work,
uniform and all, while Schmidt hardly features in any of
the pictures included in the 2016 edition of his book, and
when he does, the caption specifies that he is 'interpreting
as usual'. Neither Birse nor Bohlen had any reason to shun
photo opportunities. As for the self-effacing Pavlov, his tendency to step aside whenever there was a camera around

probably had nothing to do with any aversion to totalitarianism. After retiring from high-stakes politics, he worked in publishing and, by some accounts, remained a loyal Stalinist until his death. The man whose regime cost the USSR more lives than the war did may have been a good speaker to interpret for, but no one (perhaps not even Pavlov) was deluded by his manners. 'I could never rid myself of the thought that I was in a presence of the Absolute Dictator,' Birse concludes in his book, 'and I was thankful that he was not my master.'

Translating for a dictator is similar to translating for anyone, in that your personal view of them shouldn't affect your work. Political disagreements can be easier to come to terms with than linguistic ones, and as any interpreter will confirm, an unpleasant personality doesn't necessarily imply a client from hell. Polite and erudite control freaks, especially those with a smattering of the language they hire a translator for, can be as dangerous as foul-mouthed ignoramuses. To give but one example, they can turn multiple meanings into a real minefield. I once had to fetch a dictionary to reassure a man I was interpreting for that the word 'feckless' does exist and is synonymous with 'irresponsible'. And I no longer frown when someone stops mid-sentence – usually when they are about to say something like 'She literally told me to bugger off' – to warn me, 'Now, I don't know how you're going to translate this,' as if swear words were the hardest to deal with.

When asked about the worst traits in a speaker, many will mention a tendency to interrupt. The jumpy client will hear a familiar phrase and butt in to your interpretation, only to ask you to explain it a moment later. One impatient speaker is described by Hannah Arendt in her account of the 1961 trial of the Nazi criminal Adolf Eichmann, the case that made her reflect on 'the banality of evil'. It wasn't the defendant who created obstacles for the interpreters. 'Judge Landau hardly ever waits to give his answer until the translator has done his work,' Arendt observes, 'and he frequently interrupts the translation to correct and improve it, appearing grateful for this bit of distraction from the grim business at hand.'

Working for a dictator, first-hand accounts suggest, is the same, only worse. Whether our protagonists distanced themselves from or stood by their bosses, there were times when their words were simply ignored, for better or worse. Even Dr Schmidt, despite being good at taking and keeping the floor, sometimes couldn't get a word in edgeways. He recalled a meeting with Horace Wilson, a senior British official who brought Hitler a stern letter from Chamberlain regarding the Sudeten crisis. Schmidt tried to do his job, but everyone talked at once, so that any chance of averting the annexation, however slim, was lost. 'It was one of the rare occasions,' he writes, 'when I failed to assert myself as an interpreter against Hitler.'

There are times when the best way to assert yourself against a dictator is to disregard their words. Ramón Serrano Súñer, the Spanish foreign minister who was present at Hitler and Franco's meeting at Hendaye in 1940, later recalled that the German interpreter, Gross, had not been able 'to comprehend more than half of what we meant to say'. At the end of the somewhat strained negotiations – Hitler was annoyed with Spain for its reluctance to enter the war – Franco overdid it with 'the Spanish custom of repeating formulaic or conventional phrases' when saying goodbye. 'If the day comes that Germany ever truly needs me,' he said to Hitler, 'you will have me unconditionally at your side, with no demands in return.' The minister was worried that Hitler might take this expression of 'hollow courtesy' literally, but Gross either didn't catch Franco's utterance or simply ignored it as verbiage. And so he said nothing. Years later, when Serrano Súñer mentioned the incident to a German diplomat, the latter said, 'We should have erected a monument to Gross, the interpreter, to commemorate what he did.' When no words – not even in the best of translations – are likely to improve things, silence can be truly golden.

9

Little Nothing

In July 1945, Richard Sonnenfeldt, a US private who had ended the war in Austria, was tinkering with a car when he was summoned to General William 'Wild Bill' Donovan, the head of the Office of Strategic Services. Donovan needed a German-speaker to help him interrogate a prisoner. Sonnenfeldt looked like he might fit the bill. A German Jew who fled the Nazis in 1938 aged fifteen, he went first to Britain. Interned because his passport had a swastika stamp, he was deported to Australia and later managed to get entry to America, where he was reunited with his parents. By the time he was called up in 1943, he had not only mastered English vocabulary and grammar but had also shaken off his German accent, or at least managed to sound less foreign than most of his fellow refugees.

The session with Donovan went so well that Sonnenfeldt's commanders flew him to Paris, where preparations for the first Nuremberg trial were underway. Soon he was made, to quote his meticulously detailed memoirs, 'Chief of the Interpretation Section of the Interrogation Division of the Office of the U.S. Chief of Counsel'. 'I received this title for having been first on the scene,' he writes, 'but I kept it because interrogations interpreted by me were never held up by language disputes.'

Once in Nuremberg, Sonnenfeldt was assigned to work with Nazis awaiting trial, among them Hermann Göring. 'I felt the Jewish refugee I had once been tugging at my sleeve,' he recalls. Göring behaved like a celebrity when he surrendered to the Allies. With enough English to understand the questions put to him, he constantly tried to use this to his advantage. At their first meeting, on hearing Sonnenfeldt translate the interrogator's preamble – 'I ask the questions here and you answer them' – Göring corrected the interpreter. Sonnenfeldt was having none of it. Given permission to have a word with the prisoner, he addressed him as 'Herr Gering' – a deliberate mispronunciation to make the name sound like 'little nothing' in German – and told him not to interrupt while the stenographer was recording, to raise any issues afterwards or to ask to be interrogated without an interpreter. (I've made this last suggestion myself when confronted with manipulative speakers, and always found it helpful.) From then on, Göring would always ask for Sonnenfeldt, and as a result the Holocaust escapee spent more than a hundred hours with the mastermind of the final solution.

'The mediocrity ... of virtually all defendants was appalling,' Sonnenfeldt says before mentioning two exceptions: Hjalmar Schacht, 'that financial magician, an arrogant mustachioed Houdini in striped trousers', and Albert Speer, 'that brainy and clear-minded careerist architect'. Reading his memoirs, it's interesting to see how, working on high-profile cases, the interpreter begins to feel rather important himself, sometimes going further than he is supposed to. 'As slippery as he was,' he writes of Göring, 'occasionally I could catch him.' He seems to enjoy these deviations from his brief. When Rudolf Hess, trying to fake amnesia, was examined by specialists, Sonnenfeldt had his reservations, which grew stronger when the Nazi used the word *Kladde*, school slang for 'notebook cover', which suggested a reasonably good memory. The interpreter wanted to challenge Hess but failed to convince 'the learned men who did not speak German' that the teenage term would hardly be used by an amnesiac. This raises a question often faced by translators: how do you restrict yourself to merely translating what's been said or written when you are bursting with comments?

After weeks of work, Sonnenfeldt read out the indictments to all the twenty-one inmates of the Nuremberg jail: 'You are charged with Crimes against Peace, War Crimes, Conspiracy to Commit Aggression, Crimes against Humanity, Genocide.' On 20 November 1945, the first day of the trial, he was asked to interpret during the opening session. What was required of him in the courtroom was a special kind of art. During the pretrial interrogations, the interpreter would wait for the speakers to pause before translating each question and answer. This consecutive mode is still used today where practicable – for instance, when a witness gives evidence in court. When interpreting for a defendant, you usually sit next to them in the dock and employ a technique called *chuchotage*, translating everything live, whispering into their ear as you follow the proceedings, a mode that only works for small groups of listeners. A major hearing such as the Nuremberg trial required a more efficient method than either of the above, one that allowed words to be poured simultaneously into many ears.

A UN-style meeting with interpreters in booths wearing

headsets and pressing buttons might have been an exotic sight in 1945, but equipment comprising several transmission channels and selector switches had existed for a while. Patented nearly twenty years earlier, the Filene–Finlay system, as it was initially called after its inventors, was first tested in June 1927 at the International Labour Conference in Geneva. Colonel Léon Dostert, head of the translation division at Nuremberg, who had been General Dwight D. Eisenhower's interpreter during the war, thought this system should do the job, although many were sceptical about it. Dostert suggested some improvements that would allow it to be used to its full potential (at first, interpreters took notes and relied on pre-translated speeches). The equipment, provided by IBM free of charge, arrived just five days before the trial.

Preparations on the translation side had, of course, started much earlier. Back in those postwar months, finding and recruiting interpreters was a serious matter. The Americans interviewed more than 400 candidates, selecting only 5 per cent of them; Britain, Russia and France provided their own personnel. Before being appointed administrative head of the translation division, Alfred Steer, a scholar of German literature, took a test at the Pentagon, where he had to translate a news clip into German. His examiner, Dostert, didn't speak the language, which annoyed Steer but didn't result in a fail. George Klebnikov, a young Russian émigré, took a test in Paris after a random encounter, and passed; the next day, he caught a train to Nuremberg, where he passed another exam, despite having never heard of simultaneous interpreting. Some of the old guard working for the League of Nations were also approached, but many of them, accustomed to the consecutive mode, couldn't cope with the new arrangements. 'The Paris international telephone exchange was a superb place to pick people up,' Steer remembered. When the proceedings opened, one reporter, seeing a room full of people wearing earphones, thought it actually looked like a telephone exchange.

The successful candidates were a motley crew: refugees and ghetto survivors, journalists and academics in their previous lives. Some of their testimonies are collected in *Eyewitnesses at Nuremberg*, edited by Hilary Gaskin. As all of them agree, the new technology was relatively easy to deal with compared to the other pressures of the job. Once selected, they were put through a training programme; it included mock trials in which some of them played prosecutors and judges, reading sample speeches for others to interpret, gradually increasing the speed. These efforts, combined with miles of cable, hundreds of headsets and dozens of switch boxes, allowed the trial to be effectively conducted in four languages – German, English, French and Russian – with the help of thirty-six interpreters.

Sonnenfeldt wasn't one of them. The proceedings turned out to be drastically different from the sessions he was used to: here the interpreters were physically separated from the speakers and could only request them to pause or slow down by pressing a button. After the first day – during which Göring noticed his interpreter in the glass booth and gave him a familiar wink – Sonnenfeldt declined the offer to join the team; instead, he was tasked with sitting in the courtroom to verify that everyone gave the same evidence as during the earlier interrogations. Well aware of the challenges faced by the interpreters, he praised them for their 'magnificent work'.

Not everyone was equally impressed with them. Perhaps it's the very fact that translation is known to be prone to error that makes people want to control the translator or make a scapegoat of them, or both. Sometimes this is done with good intentions; sometimes for personal advantage. Göring clearly had the latter in mind as he continued to play the system. His tricks are described in Francesca Gaiba's study *The Origins of Simultaneous Interpretation*. He would ask the judges to repeat or reword their questions, claiming that the interpreter had made a mistake or hadn't made themselves clear; he would say that, although the German version was incomprehensible, he'd still be able to answer the question. One of his favourite complaints was that the interpreters were biased against him: for instance, when translating *erfassen* as 'seize' rather than 'register' in the phrase 'the Jewish population was seized'. Siegfried Ramler, accused by Göring's defence of using too strong a verb, later recalled, 'Here I found myself in the odd situation of having to interpret an objection to the accuracy of my interpretation!'

Göring was not alone in his aversion to the interpreters. One of the British judges, Norman Birkett, called them 'a race apart – touchy, vain, unaccountable, full of vagaries, puffed up with self-importance of the most explosive kind, inexpressibly egotistical, and, as a rule, violent opponents of soap and sunlight'.

Double translations unsurprisingly gave Göring ample opportunities to play his games. When he had a German original before him, while the interpreter was translating back the same document read by a judge in English, this inevitably led to discrepancies. If a genuine mistake occurred

– for instance, when someone confused *Endlösung* (final solution) with *Gesamtlösung* (total solution) – Göring was quick to point it out, distracting the court's attention from the fact that both were Nazi euphemisms for 'the elimination of Jews'. All this was done not so much in an attempt to save his skin – he had no doubts about the outcome – as to express his contempt for the Allies and their show trial.

The equipment used by simultaneous interpreters today is based on the same principle as the system rolled out at Nuremberg, and its quality sometimes still leaves much to be desired. Providers like to economise on everything, from booths to headsets, making the interpreter struggle to hear the speaker over other sounds, including their own voice. Meanwhile, some translation agencies also have a very vague idea of what the process actually involves. One of them, shopping around for conference interpreters, surprised me by asking me to quote a fee for ten foreign delegates, as if expecting me to feed them dinner rather than words. But once you are in the booth and your headset is working, the business of listening and talking simultaneously leaves no room for anything else.

Even so, the interpreters at Nuremberg couldn't completely distance themselves from the horrors recounted in the courtroom. 'You didn't have time to think about the content,' the chief interpreter Peter Uiberall, another Jewish refugee who'd made it to America, remembered, 'but it came back to you in your sleep, in nightmares.' That their work was extremely challenging in the technical sense goes without saying; what's harder to comprehend is that one type of stress, resulting from having to fully concentrate

on the task at hand, could often displace the other. Speaking from within the shelter of their professional carapace,
perhaps not wishing to fixate on the greatest trauma they
had experienced, in their reminiscences the interpreters
were more prepared to talk about an everyday nightmare:
the German verb. It comes at the end of the sentence, trying
the patience of English-speakers. Here is Uiberall explaining how a reply to the simple question 'Did you know Mr
Schmidt?' can become an endurance test.

The witness starts, 'Ja, den Schmidt, den habe ich im
Jahre Fünfunddreissig oder nein im Jahre Sechsunddreis-
sig, da habe ich den Schmidt ...' You still don't know.
Has he seen him, has he known him, has he spoken to
him, has he heard of him? All this can follow in the verb
at the end. So the poor interpreter cannot start, unless
he does what they used to call in German 'eine Esel-
brücke bauen', which is a German term, very difficult
to translate, meaning something like 'building a donkey
bridge'. It doesn't exist in English. That is to say, 'Yes,
er, no, er, Schmidt, well, with regard to Schmidt, was it
in thirty-five or thirty-six, was it in Leipzig or was it in
Dresden, I'm not quite sure, it was then that ...'

Another difficulty was the German habit of starting
sentences with *ja*, often used as a filler. Discourse markers
– 'well', 'now', 'you see' – are a special topic in court
interpreting because their omission or alteration puts a
different slant on speech, especially on questions, making
them potentially more or less coercive. To avoid unintended
admissions of guilt, Uiberall told his colleagues to wait and

be absolutely sure the reply was affirmative before translating *ja* as 'yes'. 'There is no such thing,' he later noted, 'as an exact translation of any word.'

In addition to these linguistic hitches, there were episodes when the lawyers made themselves look ridiculous, often through their ignorance of Germany. The focus of Göring's attention was Robert H. Jackson, the chief US prosecutor, whom he corrected at every opportunity: for instance, when the American mangled German proper nouns, so that the interpreter mistook his 'Reichsbank' for 'Reichstag' and 'Wörmann' for 'Bormann'. Their confrontation reached its apogee during Jackson's cross-examination of Göring, which proved a disaster for the prosecutor. Jackson neglected a statement from an earlier interrogation, got into an argument over a botched translation and generally let the defendant have the upper hand, failing to get him to admit that he had ordered 'the final solution to the Jewish question'. Afterwards, Jackson had his excuse handy: 'Göring could always get time to get his speech ready ... He knew English, could understand the question, and while they were interpreting for him he already had the question from me.'

While many of the lawyers, used to rapid-fire questioning, complained about the inevitable delays caused by interpretation (the term 'simultaneous' is used figuratively, of course, as an interpreter always lags a few seconds behind the speaker), the best of them adjusted their style to it. David Maxwell Fyfe, the chief British prosecutor, suggested to Göring at one point, 'Well, witness, you understand English quite well, don't you? Suppose you answer right away?' Unlike his American counterpart, Maxwell Fyfe succeeded in his cross-examination; unlike the majority of his learned friends, he found the interpreting system satisfactory, remarking that 'this was not a high price to pay for what was called a justice in four voices'. Despite having to keep up with his rapid speech, the interpreters admired him for his professionalism.

However monstrous the defendants' deeds, confessed or denied, the interpreters couldn't help establishing a rapport with them. As Uiberall said of this analogue of the Stockholm syndrome, 'We became sort of acquainted with them from daily observation.' Two of the defendants, Speer and Schacht, spoke fluent English and were willing to help the interpreters – after all, it was in their common interests to achieve a good quality of translation. Seeing someone struggle with a difficult word, they would write the relevant term on a piece of paper and pass it along to the booth. 'So we were grateful to them,' Uiberall recalled. 'In the case of Schacht it was a very "innocent" friendship, because he was acquitted; in the case of Speer it was less so.'

It is not unusual for interpreters to develop an 'innocent' relationship with their charges, if only at a linguistic level. Working towards a single goal – to get a message across in another language – can be conducive to bonding, and the longer you spend in the courtroom as an interpreter the easier it is to believe that the most horrible crimes are in fact those committed against language. One of the defendants at Nuremberg, Otto Ohlendorf, sentenced to death for killing thousands in the Holocaust, got a brief reprieve so that he could testify in other trials. While waiting, he wrote a letter thanking the interpreters for giving him the opportunity to have a fair trial. Uiberall called it 'one of the most amazing, though somewhat gruesome, experiences' of his career.

'And that,' he added, 'was the best that was ever said about interpreters.'

Pressure of work notwithstanding, the Nuremberg interpreters continued to practise their preferred style: some acted it out, others remained unemphatic; some repeated everything word for word, others improvised or rephrased. Together they represented a wide range of registers, which sometimes caused irritation. Some listeners found the interpreters' delivery too distracting: for instance, when a woman had to voice the words of a German commander or when a German aristocrat's speech acquired a thick Brooklyn accent. One young woman, interpreting an account of 'humane' conditions in a concentration camp (there had apparently been a library and a swimming pool), baulked at the next word, so that a male colleague had to finish the sentence for her: 'A brothel, Your Honour!' Whenever an interpreter's words were perceived as incongruous, it led to further attempts to control their work, prompting new demands, which they did their best to accommodate. One of them was reprimanded for being, or at least sounding, too laconic. The judge told him to translate everything exactly as it was uttered, then turned back to the speaker: 'Yes, Mr Pine?' The interpreter proceeded: 'Ja, Herr Tannenbaum?'

10

The Last Two Dragomans

In the seventeenth century translators in the Ottoman empire, regardless of their religion, had a number of privileges ordinarily not granted to non-Muslims. They had, for instance, the right to be tried by the grand vizier's court and to travel under armed escort. If they were foreigners, they also had certain rights guaranteed under bilateral agreements between the empire and Christian states. The British Capitulations of 1675 had a provision for the protection of interpreters, which in the English version stipulated that 'in case they shall commit any offence, our Judges and Governors shall not reprove, beat, or put any of the said Interpreters in prison, without the knowledge of the Ambassador or Consul'. The right to protection was their main remuneration; an arrangement that had its consequences, as noted, for instance, by the British consul in Smyrna, Francis Werry, who wrote in 1826, 'The salaries of the dragomen generally are too low to keep them honest.'

As relations between the empire and Europe developed, the number of dragomans grew. Following the Venetian practice of instructing *giovani di lingua*, begun in the sixteenth century, the French founded their own training system for *jeunes de langues* in 1669. In 1821, when the Constantinople

Greeks, suspected of political disloyalty, lost their dominance in the profession, the Turks established their own *Tercüme Odası* (translation office) to counter Christian influence with the help of homegrown Muslim translators. And in 1877, Britain set up the Levant Consular Service to fill diplomatic posts in Turkey, Persia, Greece and Morocco with British-born linguists.

Andrew Ryan's decision to apply for a 'Student Interpretership' in the Levant was a safe career option. 'My inclination would have been for the Bar,' he writes in his memoirs, 'but it seemed too chancy a profession.' Born in Cork in 1876, Ryan chose the civil service, 'which then attracted many lads in Ireland', and although he 'had little real taste for the languages of the East, except perhaps Arabic, the quasi-mathematical precision of which appealed to me', he graduated from Cambridge with 'a fair knowledge of Turkish, a little Arabic, hardly any Persian, the soon-forgotten rudiments of Russian and a tincture of law'. That was the baggage he brought with him to Constantinople in 1899.

As a junior dragoman at the embassy, Ryan attended court hearings that concerned British subjects, essentially acting as an interpreter-cum-solicitor. Much of that work was mundane, but it gave him the opportunity to learn some 'elementary diplomacy' and improve his Turkish. When judges questioned defendants, the interpreter had to 'reduce their answers to the decorous language suited to an official record'. Sometimes the language of his fellow Brits proved irreducible: for instance, when 'a most disreputable old woman' shouted 'Darling!' to the blushing young man over the judges' heads, or when he did his best 'to mitigate the treatment of a very ordinary drunk and disorderly, who in his cups had not only assaulted the police, but had impartially vilified the Prophet, the Sultan and Queen Victoria'. There was nothing Ryan could do about the prophet, for such abuse was too serious to be dealt with on the spot. 'I suggested that I might be left to look after Queen Victoria, but the man got nine months.'

The court interpreter's status was relatively solid, although not cast in stone. 'As it turned a good deal on the interpretation of two words in a seventeenth-century Turkish text,' Ryan writes, referring to the Capitulations, 'it can easily be imagined how difficult it was to agree on the question whether he was a judge, indeed a judge with a veto, as we maintained, or merely an official looker-on, as the Turks contended.' His responsibilities also included dealing with customs declarations (imported goods ranged from toy rifles to lion cubs to New Testaments, which prompted an official to ask, 'Who is this writing to the people of Galata?'), tax matters, detentions in custody, conversions to Islam, slaves taking refuge in the embassy, and so on. When a production of *The Merchant of Venice* was banned in Constantinople, Ryan's protest that 'the play was a work of a British subject named Shakespeare, whom we had never regarded as undesirable, but on the contrary as a credit to the country' didn't work: the authorities replied that 'the treatment of Shylock was calculated to create discord among the Sultan's subjects'.

This was no idle fear. In July 1908, the Young Turks, a nationalist party aiming to establish a constitutional government, came to power after a bloodless revolution. The following year the sultan attempted a counter-coup, and the ensuing turmoil led to the massacre of Christians in Adana, a city in southern Turkey. In April 1909, the British vice consul in nearby Mersina, Major Charles Doughty-Wylie, received a letter from his dragoman in Adana, informing him about unrest. Doughty-Wylie immediately went there and did what he could to restore order. The dragoman and his family, nearly killed by a raging mob, fled to the safety of their house, where they sheltered 500 refugees. Describing it all in his report, the vice consul omits the dragoman's full name (he calls him Mr C. Trypani, while other sources mention Athanasios Trypanis) and refers to other interpreters begging the authorities for help as 'foreign dragomen'. It is estimated that up to 30,000 people were killed in Adana in a precursor to the 1915 Armenian genocide.

By the end of the month, the counter-revolution suppressed, the Turkish parliament was ready to dethrone the sultan. First, however, an Islamic authority had to issue a request for a fatwa, in which the question as to whether or not the sultan should be deposed had to take a form that allowed the answer 'It is' or 'It is not.' Ryan, by then the embassy's second dragoman, provided a close translation of the question that took up nearly a page, in line with 'the old Turkish practice of couching long official documents in one breathless sentence'. The answer was in the affirmative.

With the approach of the Great War, Anglo-Turkish relations deteriorated. British diplomats tried to ensure Turkey's neutrality, not knowing that it had already pledged its support to Germany in the event of war with Russia. The position of foreign residents in the country grew more precarious, their loyalties shifting to whichever side was more likely to protect them. Ryan, never too sympathetic to the

Turks, no longer tried to conceal his feelings, warning that whatever their role in the war, 'they may give a lot of trouble in the future'. As the situation came to a head, he and his colleagues were busy preparing 'reproachful notes on all sorts of subjects to the Porte'.

It all exploded in October 1914, when Turkey bombarded a number of Russia's Black Sea ports. The Russians, French and British left on the same ship, and on 5 November, still at sea, they commemorated Guy Fawkes' day by burning an effigy of the kaiser. In one of his last dispatches, Ryan quoted a Turkish minister's outburst against the Entente Cordiale, slightly tempering his French in translation, omitting the epithet 'pig' but keeping 'devil'. Initially cut by the ambassador, the passage was picked up by *The Times* as 'brilliantly written', even though Ryan didn't bother to abbreviate the d-word to the family-friendly 'd—l'. That commendation aside, the British press mostly blamed the embassy for its failure to keep things under control. The *Daily Mail* described the state of consular affairs as 'worthy of *Alice in Wonderland*, with no one who knew Turkish, no one who had been long in Constantinople, no one who understood Turkish methods and habits'. Once accusations, justified or not, are made against someone's language skills by someone who has none, respect is hard to regain.

After the war, Ryan returned to Constantinople. An experienced player of word games, he continued to deal in verbal formulae, approaching translation as an exact art. In March 1924, when the young Republic of Turkey abolished the caliphate, he translated the first article of the new constitution into English with his usual pedantry:

In translating, as literally as possible, the legal text, I use the word 'Caliphship' to mark the distinction between two uses of the Turkish word *Khilafat*. As there is no definite article in that language, it may and commonly does mean the Caliphate, but it can also be used in an abstract sense to describe the functions of a Caliph.

His translation reads, 'The Caliph is deposed. As Caliphship is fundamentally comprised in the sense and significance of government and republic, the office of Caliph is abolished.' He thought the wording 'sufficiently subtle to suggest perhaps to wishful thinkers that the old Caliphate was in some sense preserved in the personality of the Republic', though the ruling party had rejected such suggestions.

As Ryan went about his various duties, another contender for the title of the last of the dragomans arrived in Turkey. Johannes Kolmodin, a Swedish orientalist, had studied languages in Uppsala and Berlin before coming to Istanbul in 1917 to conduct scholarly research. His scholarship money soon proved insufficient, and to support himself he joined the Swedish legation as an attaché, becoming a dragoman within a few years. Unlike Ryan, who remained at loggerheads with the nationalist government, particularly over its treatment of the non-Muslim population of Turkey, Kolmodin was a loyal friend of the new republic and an avid supporter of its founder, Mustafa Kemal Atatürk. In 1922, when the Kemalists massacred Armenians and Greeks in Smyrna, he called the reports of these events 'mendacious', 'malevolent and coloured', and when the atrocities could no longer be denied, he blamed anyone but the Turks.

While Ryan tried to be, or at least appear, neutral between the republicans and their opponents, Kolmodin took sides unreservedly, an attitude which manifested itself in his work. Translating the Turkish constitution, he didn't pussyfoot around with any ambiguous terms. His Swedish version reads, 'The Caliph is deposed. The Caliphate, as a part of the very concept of the state of republic, has been abolished.' Two years earlier, he had written in a private letter, 'It is very important to call the system "republic" because the Caliphate, which is to remain, is on no account a papistry, but a secular general representation of Islam for which the Turkish people's state will be the foundation.' He also noted that 'Sweden's relationship with the new establishment shapes up well,' patting himself on the back: 'I personally drove in the peace delegation.'

Kolmodin's feelings towards Gustaf Wallenberg, the head of the Swedish legation, were more complicated than the foreign policy they implemented. If Ryan remarked that a dragoman is doomed to be the ambassador's alter ego, Kolmodin had no doubts about his own importance. The legation's main job was reporting, and it was he who did most of it. *The Last Dragoman*, a collection of research papers edited by Elizabeth Ozdalga, comments on Kolmodin's academic language: heavy on parentheses, dashes, double negatives and subordinate clauses. In the reports over his own signature, however, he 'expressed himself rather more simply and freely ... without risking objections from Wallenberg'. The envoy didn't deny his dragoman credit, acknowledging that 'the account of the decisive events ... was entirely due to Dr Kolmodin, whose eminent knowledge and great proficiency in the Turkish language were essential for describing these interesting war movements'.

Kolmodin, for his part, complained about his boss: 'Unfortunately he is quite dull in his head, but does not want to admit it and let me assist in the talks he conducts. When things become messy afterwards, I have to try and set them right.' Was he being oversensitive, as some translators tend to be when stuck in a chicken-and-egg cycle of feeling unfulfilled and undervalued? In December 1919, he wrote, 'I may be so bold as to claim that, at the moment, I am the most respected foreigner in Constantinople.' Ryan, on the other hand, had few illusions about his own notability. When stopped by two French gendarmes in the occupied city in March 1918, he failed to explain himself, so they had to consult a native interpreter, 'who cautiously replied that he did not know, but that, to judge by the gentleman's language, he might well be British'.

'Here you have to try to interpret even the very worst for the best, especially when you pretend to be a diplomat,' Kolmodin wrote. If he (or his English translator) sounds somewhat vague on his allegiances in government service, his views emerge very clearly from his personal correspondence. He translated a speech Atatürk gave in 1922 – 'Both among Muslims and Christians there have unfortunately been some traitors, against whom the Government has acted, as was its right and duty, regardless of their religion' – and tried to get it into the Swedish press to suppress 'alarmist reports' about the Turks persecuting Christians. 'There will hardly be room for a separate non-Turkish-speaking community,' he predicted. 'The Ottoman Christians will have to bring themselves to learn Turkish.' Today, when many governments want all immigrants to learn the language of their adopted countries, professional translators tend to fret about these policies. Either we are more liberal than our predecessors, or less keen on a future in which everyone is fluent in our working language.

The paths of the two dragomans were to cross again at the Conference of Lausanne, called in 1922 to settle matters between Turkey and the Western powers. French was the main language at the conference, and although the British foreign secretary, Lord Curzon, knew it quite well, 'all his speeches were delivered in English', to quote Ryan, 'and had to be interpreted in the presence of their author, who was perfectly capable of catching out the interpreter'. When he finally accepted a document he had ordered to be redrafted, Curzon would cry, 'Admirable!' – 'though we realised that what he admired was his own reflection in our mirror', Ryan recalls. Their collaboration captures the balance of power within the speaker–interpreter–audience triad, where the translator acts as the indispensable, and ideally impartial, middleman but often remains unnoticed. Kolmodin, who came to Lausanne as an expert assistant to Sweden's representative, remarked that Curzon's main concern was 'not the minorities but ... the petroleum wells'. In his letters he continued to insist on the innocence of the Turks, referring to 'the so-called "atrocities"' as a story concocted by Near East Relief, a humanitarian organisation founded in 1915, to raise more funds.

Kolmodin left Turkey for Ethiopia in 1931 and died two years later in Addis Ababa, shortly after being visited in hospital by his latest employer, Emperor Haile Selassie. He is remembered in Sweden as 'our last, most illustrious dragoman'. Ryan went on to have a long, successful diplomatic career, occupying high posts in Morocco, Saudi Arabia and Albania. Among their differences, perhaps the one most worthy of reflection was their translation styles. What's interesting is that Kolmodin, for all his love of Turkey, comes across as more casual than Ryan, who took great pains with a language he didn't care for much. Yet the fact remains that Kolmodin's work was informed by his loyalty to all things Turkish, while Ryan tended to stick to his own cultural and political guns. Although these two modes are sometimes viewed as mutually exclusive, translators can, and should be able to, employ both, sometimes within a single paragraph. Debates around the two approaches, so-called foreignisation and domestication, tend to be restricted to literary translation, but those working in other fields constantly face similar choices.

A century on, interpreters continue to choose between taking sides and remaining above the fray. These positions become polarised when the future begins to look uncertain. A list of 'dying professions' recently circulated in the media includes lawyers but not interpreters. This is because people either consider us to be as good as dead already, or are unfamiliar with the name of the profession (I've heard colleagues introduce themselves as 'spoken translators', and once barely managed to keep a straight face at being called an 'interpretator'). Back in 1909, when being a dragoman felt more secure than choosing the 'chancy' bar, Ryan already had reservations about the prospects for his trade: 'If all goes well with the Constitution, and Turkey really regenerates herself on European lines, we are bound to disappear sooner or later, as no civilized European Government would tolerate a class of foreign officials whose business it was to meddle directly in all their public offices.' Indeed, the Treaty of Lausanne, signed on 24 July 1923, put an end to the Capitulations and, consequently, to the title. Dragomans had to go – to give way to progress.

11

As Oriental as Possible

'It is an amusement to me to take what Liberties I like with these Persians,' Edward Fitzgerald wrote to his friend Edward Cowell in 1857. It was Cowell, a British orientalist, who had introduced Fitzgerald, a wealthy Suffolk gentleman and a lover of literature, music and plants, to Persian poetry, drawing his attention to an eleventh-century manuscript kept in the Bodleian Library. Attributed to one Omar Khayyam, it contained a set of *rubaiyat*, or quatrains, ordered alphabetically by the last letter of the rhyme word. The poems captured Fitzgerald's imagination and he set out to translate them. In 1859, he privately printed his work under the title *Rubaiyat of Omar Khayyam, the Astronomer-Poet of Persia*, without mentioning his own name. The book didn't sell, but two years later Dante Gabriel Rossetti spotted a remaindered copy, loved it and told other Pre-Raphaelites about it. By the turn of the twentieth century, it had become one of the most widely read and quoted poems in English.

'There was no original to which Fitzgerald ... owed a debt of faithfulness,' J. M. Cohen writes in *English Translators and Translations*. 'It was merely a Victorian poem in the oriental convention.' Scholars have compared the translation with the manuscript line by line, concluding that nearly half of Fitzgerald's quatrains have direct correspondences in the original, a few can't be traced back to anything in it, and the rest are composites. Fitzgerald selected his material from this 'strange succession of Grave and Gay' and arranged it so as to create a narrative: his protagonist, driven by a desire to catch the day, begins his quest in a garden and, after taking much delight in wine, love and nature, returns to the same place, convinced that hedonism is the only philosophy worth pursuing in a world where all things are transient. The selected stanzas, Fitzgerald writes in his foreword to a later edition, are 'strung into something of an Eclogue, with perhaps a less than equal proportion of the "Drink and make-merry," which (genuine or not) recurs over-frequently in the Original'.

The foreword talks of the author's genius, presenting him as a 'Philosopher, of scientific Insight and Ability far beyond that of the Age and Country he lived in'. Referring to him as 'Omar', Fitzgerald apologises, as if anticipating rebukes: 'I cannot help calling him by his – no, not Christian – familiar name.' Indeed, decades later his remarks alerted the translation police, who, guided by the motto 'All cultures are equal but some are more equal than others,' accused Fitzgerald of patronising 'these Persians'. How dare he call Khayyam 'this remarkable little Fellow' and 'my property'? This last phrase appears in another exchange with Cowell: 'I take old Omar rather more as my property than yours: he and I are more akin, are we not?' Quick to detect ignoble motives in Fitzgerald's words, his critics overlook the fact that he is talking about an affinity he feels with his hero. Any translator who has ever fallen in love with their source text must have felt a similar impulse to call it their own.

'It should be kept as Oriental as possible,' Fitzgerald says about his version of Khayyam, 'only using the most idiomatic Saxon words to convey the Eastern metaphor.' To do this, and following the principle 'It is better to be orientally obscure than Europeanly clear,' he adorns his translation with Persian landmarks absent in the original. His gravitation towards the East, however, doesn't clash with the Saxon drift he permits himself now and again:

> Into this Universe, and *Why* not knowing,
> Nor *Whence*, like Water willy-nilly flowing;
> And out of it, as Wind along the Waste,
> I know not *Whither*, willy-nilly blowing.

'Willy-nilly' – which at the time connoted comedy among other things – might have been chosen by Fitzgerald in the belief that 'at all Cost, a Thing must live: with a transfusion of one's own worse Life if one can't retain the Original's better'. The only word this quatrain has in common with the original is 'know'. Does that imply a tendency to take too many liberties or a natural desire to lend your soulmate your own voice?

'There is a cliché in the U.S. that the purpose of a poetry translation is to create an excellent new poem in English,' the poet and translator Eliot Weinberger said in his lecture 'Anonymous Sources'. 'I have always maintained ... that the purpose of a poetry translation into English is to create an excellent translation in English.' Which of these schools did Fitzgerald belong to? Many commentators, starting from his early biographers Thomas Wright and A. C. Benson, insist on calling his work an adaptation, although Wright concedes that 'beyond a few extravagances, we get a faithful representation of Omar'. New or not, the *Rubaiyat* was widely, and deservedly, praised. The omission of the translator's name in the first edition led some to mistake it for an original work, the mystery only contributing to its popularity. Khayyam clubs opened in Britain and the poem travelled across the Atlantic, where its fame spread high and low. In a short story by the American humorist O. Henry, the narrator muses:

> This Homer K. M. seemed to me to be a kind of a dog who looked at life like it was a tin can tied to his tail. After running himself half to death, he sits down, hangs his tongue out, and looks at the can and says: 'Oh, well, since we can't shake the growler, let's get it filled at the corner, and all have a drink on me.'

'The greatest pessimism about the feasibility of translation has been concentrated on poetry,' the Mexican poet Octavio Paz writes in an essay, 'a remarkable posture since many of the best poems in every Western language are translations, and many of those translations were written by great poets.' To counter the French writer Georges Mounin, to whom 'poetry is a fabric of connotations and, consequently, untranslatable', Paz emphasises the universal nature of poetry as well as that of translation. He argues that no text is completely original as it's already a translation (from mentalese, one could say) and that every text, including the closest of translations, is unique. Weinberger, in his turn, asserts: 'There is no text that cannot be translated; there are only texts that have not yet found their translators.' The relationship he developed with Paz allowed many texts to find the translator they deserved. Working with Paz, Weinberger recalls, was a collaborative process, whereby the author would make suggestions, always leaving the last word to the translator. Moreover, certain nuances highlighted in translation would occasionally prompt Paz to change something in the original. 'I have many doubts about myself in Spanish,' he once said, 'but I love myself in English.'

As theoreticians insist, there are two approaches in literary translation: domestication and foreignisation. According to the textbook definition, when Fitzgerald describes a certain establishment in Khayyam's text as 'this batter'd Caravanserai', it's an example of foreignisation, while 'the Tavern Door agape', used in another stanza, is an attempt to domesticate the same establishment. Leaving theory aside, these are clearly relative notions, each meaning different things to the author and the reader, whereas to the translator they look like two sides of the same coin. It always takes me a moment to remember that domestication stands for cultural adaptation, while to foreignise means to preserve exoticism. The logic of this dichotomy is as vague as why it should be a dichotomy in the first place. After all, what any act of translation inevitably domesticates is the source, whereas what sometimes undergoes foreignisation in the process is the target language. Since these techniques apply to different things, contrasting them with each other is like comparing apples with oranges. Isn't the task of the translator to create a hybrid of the two?

Hailing translation as a prerequisite for a truly international culture, Weinberger doesn't see these principles as irreconcilable either. Both authors and translators, he suggests, should try to combine the domestic and the foreign in their work, so as to avoid unnecessary explanations and at the same time not alienate the reader. His dialectical reasoning extends to multiculturalism and its (not always positive) effects on translation, bringing to light 'the reigning cliché of Orientalism – namely that scholarship follows imperialism'. The example he gives is the flourishing of translation, particularly from Sanskrit and Persian, in nineteenth-century Germany, despite its having no stake in either India or Persia. Weinberger's view of perceived controversies around cultural ownership is captured in a maxim the translation police would do well to remember: 'Translation is not appropriation, as is sometimes claimed; it is a form of listening that then changes how you speak.' And if you think of it as a dialogue, it's only natural that the act of conversing should also change how your interlocutor speaks in more ways than simply replacing their words by your own one at a time.

The notions of foreignisation and domestication were formulated long before translation studies emerged as a subject. In a lecture given in 1813, the German scholar Friedrich Schleiermacher said, 'Either the translator leaves the author in peace ... and moves the reader towards him; or he leaves the reader in peace ... and moves the author towards him.' Schleiermacher favoured the former approach, the one that had led to the German translation boom, whose agents were unwilling to let the reader and the author meet halfway, worried that they might miss each other altogether. Writing in the mid-eighteenth century, the philosopher Johann Gottfried Herder expressed the same view: 'Homer must enter France a captive, clad in the French fashion, lest he offend their eye ... We poor Germans, on the other hand ... just want to see him as he is.' One of the targets of his sarcasm must have been the renowned seventeenth-century translator Nicholas D'Ablancourt, who preferred his classics to look inconspicuously French, for 'ambassadors usually dress in the fashion of the country to which they are sent'.

The oft-used sartorial metaphor applies to any outsider adopting local cultural codes in order to be more readily understood in a foreign tongue. One nineteenth-century figure famous for such assimilation was the British explorer, author and translator Richard Burton. The most impressive episode in his travels across Asia and Africa was his 1853 trip to Mecca, where foreigners were banned under the threat of death. Burton, who claimed to speak thirty-five languages and dream in seventeen, made it there disguised in Muslim dress and, to be on the safe side, circumcised. When it came to translating the East for his compatriots, however, he didn't pass it off as a Victorian fantasy. His version of *The Arabian Nights* shocked the public familiar with earlier translations, in which Scheherazade's characters were fully dressed in respectable English clothes.

Burton printed *The Book of the Thousand Nights and One Night* and *Supplemental Nights* – sixteen volumes in all – between 1885 and 1887, using a press he had set up with the purpose of publishing erotic oriental texts. An admirer of the *Rubaiyat*, he dabbled in poetry too, while channelling his adventures into engaging prose. Was he a good translator? In a biography published in 1906, after Burton's death, Thomas Wright calls his subject a great linguist and anthropologist, before comparing his version of the *Nights* with an earlier one, by John Payne, and concluding that Burton had borrowed at least three quarters of his translation from it. Some called Wright's charge absurd, insisting that Burton had collected his material long before Payne began his work. Payne had provided Wright with all the papers, telling him, 'Wherever there is any doubt, give Burton the benefit of it.'

It wasn't Burton's alleged plagiarism, however, that outraged British literary circles. Their reaction was caused by sexually explicit – along the lines of 'she sported with him while he toyed with her awhile' – scenes, previously excluded from translations, and especially by Burton's extensive footnotes (their authorship was never challenged). These offer a wealth of information about Islam, local traditions, mythology, architecture, geography and much else, including anthropological observations on Arab sexual practices. The book was by turns censored, bowdlerised and pilloried in Britain for over a decade; an 1885 review recognised it as a 'monument of labour and scholarship and of research'; more than a century later, Robert Irwin in his *The Arabian Nights: A Companion* exposed Burton's racism, calling his notes 'obtrusive, kinky and highly personal', 'extraordinary specimens of rostered bigotry' and a 'parade of barmy erudition'.

'Burton's translation was estranging to the English reader who was used to chastened tales of tender English orientalism,' Colette Colligan writes in an academic study of a public debate about pornography in literature provoked by the publication of the *Nights*. In his foreword, Burton talks of the 'long-sought opportunity of noticing practices and customs which interest all mankind' and tells the English that they mustn't denounce it in the name of 'Respectability' and 'Propriety'. He wishes to educate them in these matters, to free them from 'that most immodest modern modesty which sees covert implication where nothing is implied and "improper" allusion when propriety is not outraged'.

Another reason to learn about the intimate life of the Arabs, Burton suggests, is that doing so would facilitate the imperial cause. He believes that Britain's recent failures in Afghanistan resulted from its 'crass ignorance concerning the Oriental peoples', and that the only way to avoid 'the contempt of Europe as well as of the eastern world' is to learn more about a 'race more powerful than any pagans – the Moslems'. Quite how knowledge of their sexual customs would advance British imperial interests, he doesn't say. His observations are frequently as patronising towards 'the Oriental peoples' as you'd expect from a stalwart of colonial rule and, to quote Irwin, 'a man of many prejudices'.

Burton's Victorian detractors were no great cosmopolitans either. One of them, upon reading that not only did Arabs enjoy vanilla sex, often extramarital, but they also engaged in sodomy, bestiality and racial interbreeding, wrote, 'Is there any reason why we should laboriously import the gigantic muck heaps of other races ... and charge a high price for the privilege of wallowing in them?' The price (a guinea a volume) caused more indignation at the time than Burton's bigotry. With all the commentary available now, it's still hard to see where his interest in the countries he explored ends and racism begins.

Before Burton embarked on his translation (in 1872, while on consular service in Trieste), *The Arabian Nights* had already been noticed by British critics, one of whom found the first European edition – Antoine Galland's *Les Mille et une nuits*, published in France in the early eighteenth century – improper, for it presented 'an Oriental

... in the fashionable French hat, gloves, and boots of the last century'. No matter what costume translators picked to cover the bare foreignness of the exotic original, there was always a risk that the result would be perceived as inappropriately dressed. 'Galland's version is the most poorly written of them all,' Jorge Luis Borges writes in 'The Translators of *The Thousand and One Nights*', 'the least faithful, and the weakest, but it was the most widely read'. Since then, numerous versions of the tales have been produced the world over, the translators often going for a homogeneously smooth or an elaborately archaic style. Recently, Yasmine Seale has tried to turn the tables, aiming in her edition of *Aladdin* 'to bring out the modernity that is already in the text'. Her translation of the rest of the *Nights* – a handful from Galland's French and the rest from Arabic – will be released over the next few years. Judging by the first volume, in which the narrator's wit and charm reveal humour previously wrapped up in layers of tradition, she has found a new, elegant outfit for her Shahrazad.

In *Lectures on Russian Literature*, Vladimir Nabokov categorises translation errors as those arising from genuine ignorance, deliberate obfuscation and – the worst crime of all – attempts to embellish the original. Mistakes of the first kind are standard-issue howlers, mostly false friends and calques, such as 'public house', which, translated into Russian literally, means 'brothel'. Illustrating the second point, Nabokov cites 'the most charming example of Victorian modesty' he has ever come across, from an early English translation of *Anna Karenina*. Asked what's wrong with her, Anna replies, 'I am *beremenna*', 'making the foreign reader wonder what strange and awful Oriental disease that was; all because the translator thought that "I am pregnant" might shock some pure soul'. And then he goes on to the most serious offender: 'the slick translator who arranges Scheherazade's boudoir according to his own taste and with professional elegance tries to improve the looks of his victims'.

Back in Victorian England, it was Burton's risqué manner that scandalised his contemporaries, many of whom believed he should have tidied up the boudoir to make it look more like a drawing room. Nabokov, whose commentary to his word-for-word translation of *Eugene Onegin* runs to 1,200 pages (the text itself takes up about 220), might have approved of Burton's decision to provide detailed notes, but he would have certainly condemned him for not being sufficiently accurate as a translator. Like many literalists (as well as their opponents in the creative corner), Nabokov didn't believe in compromise. Yet when it comes to taking the author to the reader or the reader to the author, these choices needn't rule each other out. What's interesting about Burton's text is its versatility: he wants the reader to see the East in its exotic splendour, but also to be entertained, not inundated with unfamiliar paraphernalia. Thus, his characters wear *turbands* and *bag-breeches*, but also *mantillas*, *gaberdines* and *bonnets*; drink *sherbet* and eat *scones*; beat their *tabrets* and enjoy *belle-lettres*; frequent *bazars* and *saloons*; lie on *divans* and hide in *closets*; variously *salute* and *salam* each other. Among them are *eunuchs* and *castratos*, *fellahs* and *courtiers*, *wazirs* and *chamberlains*. Once ceremoniously introduced, 'Lord Sulayman son of David (Allah accept the twain!)' becomes 'Solomon Davidson' in an erudite note that only benefits from this jocular abbreviation.

Burton's version of the *Nights* was the first Borges ever read, and he was still enchanted by it when he came to write his comparative analysis. Commenting on another edition, *Le Livre des mille nuits et une nuit*, published in France between 1926 and 1932, he praises its translator, J. C. Mardrus, for his 'happy and creative infidelity'. It's possible to be eclectic, Borges insists, to respect the primacy of the original without becoming its slave. Giving the reader the chance to experience a work as its author intended (provided their intention is known or can be guessed), not just in a different language but also in another era, culture, climate, is fidelity in its most dynamic sense.

Imagine translating an old text for a liberal-minded twenty-first-century audience: *The Bacchae*, say, a classical play in which a macho ruler wants his women to stop indulging in Dionysiac rituals and return to their looms. What's truer to Euripides: portraying his character as a bigoted tyrant or as a product of his time, no more or less conservative than your average ancient Greek king? And wouldn't leaving Lady Chatterley and her lover the way they were back in the day when their behaviour defied conventional morals render them too prudish by today's standards? Wouldn't a truly faithful translator have to produce something worthy of obscenity charges?

The translator's licence to change is a useful tool of their trade in every genre, but most of all in poetry. Before performing his dance on ropes, in the preface to Ovid's *Epistles*, John Dryden talks of three principal moves: metaphrase, or word-for-word translation; paraphrase, or 'translation with latitude'; and imitation. This last one is 'an endeavour of a later poet to write like one, who has written before him, on the same subject: that is, not to translate his words, or to be confined to his sense, but only to set him as a pattern, and to write, as he supposes that author would have done, had he lived in our age, and in our country'. Implementing the same idea in *Imitations*, Robert Lowell said of his selection from the European canon, 'I have been reckless with literal meaning, and labored hard to get the tone ... I have tried to write alive English and to do what my authors might have done if they were writing their poems now and in America.' Some accused him, predictably enough, of appropriation; some noted that the poems sounded a lot like Lowell; some said they could now hear Homer, Rimbaud, Baudelaire, Rilke, Montale and others speak in natural American idiom.

Poets dabbling in translation, or translators who also happen to write poetry, are criticised left, right and centre. Vain to the point of self-obsession, the argument goes, they hunt for ideas to steal wherever they can, passing their raids off as a quest for inspiration; often they can't be bothered to learn the language of those they imitate, working from a crib; and even when translating from the original, they believe that their status, sealed with the cliché 'Poetry is what gets lost in translation,' gives them the right to be freer than any diligent translator can ever afford to be. What their accusers tend to ignore is that the works they allegedly appropriate don't end up in their private collections, but are shared with the world. As for where their loyalty should lie, Emily Wilson, whose translation of *Odyssey* came out in 2018, puts it well:

We need to remember that translations are always partial, always interpretative, always products of the manifold choices and long, hard labours of their creators, each of us trying, in our very different ways, to be as responsible and truthful as we can be, with respect both to the original poem and to the readers of our own place and time.

Why turn translation into a one-way street if we can move in both directions, looking for a place where the author and the reader can happily meet, both enriched by their respective journeys? Our search for a golden mean would be more fruitful if, instead of arguing who owns the words on the page, we treated them as our collective property, agreeing that the entirety of world literature belongs to us all: its writers, translators and readers alike. Does this plan sound too utopian? Where does it leave the notion of authorship? Can authors and translators ever collaborate on an equal footing? What's known about their relationships mainly comes from stories told by the translator alone (which in itself is somewhat telling), and it's only rarely that we have both parties' accounts, however subjective, to compare. Rarely, but not never.

12

Fifty Per Cent of Borges

'For nearly the past three years, I have been lucky to have my own translator by my side,' Jorge Luis Borges wrote in 1970, 'and together we are bringing out some ten or twelve volumes of my work in English, a language I am unworthy to handle, a language I often wish had been my birthright.' Borges met Norman Thomas di Giovanni, a young and energetic American, while visiting Harvard in 1967. In his memoir *The Lesson of the Master* di Giovanni recalls attending one of Borges' lectures and being 'struck by the gentle quality and humanity' of his words. He wrote to the master, mentioning a Spanish poetry collection he had recently translated and suggesting they collaborate to produce a volume of Borges' poems in English. Borges, who had been blind for fifteen years, dictated a reply inviting di Giovanni to call him. It was the beginning of a relationship that would bring about unexpected developments – literary, financial and personal – in the lives of both men.

Their collaboration got off to a good start during Borges' stay in the US. On their very first afternoon together, as they talked about one of Borges' recent poems, a bond was formed of 'poetry and the music of words'. 'Within a month,' di Giovanni continues, 'Borges and I had planned the whole book.' Before returning to Argentina in 1968, the poet asked the translator to join him there so they could carry on working together. Six months later, di Giovanni was in Buenos Aires, ready to resume. He didn't come empty-handed, having managed to secure a lucrative right-of-first-refusal contract with the *New Yorker*, whereby both of them would be paid equal sums for translations of Borges' new work. Signing it was 'like reaching nirvana in this world', di Giovanni told me in 2010, adding, 'Mind you, 50 per cent of Borges is not exactly an oil well.' While famous enough to be invited to lecture abroad, Borges wasn't a household name outside Argentina, and English translations of his work never made it onto bestseller lists. The opportunity to introduce him to the *New Yorker* readership was unique. At first, however, the dream project seemed destined to fall through: Borges, who was approaching seventy and had not had a book out in eight years, was only composing poetry at the time. He refused to publish anything new for fear that it would be judged inferior to his earlier work. As di Giovanni puts it in *The Lesson*, 'He felt he would never write again.'

Despite Borges' writerly insecurity, di Giovanni persevered: if no new work was forthcoming, there were still old pieces to be translated. Every afternoon at four sharp, he would pick Borges up from his flat and they would walk to the Argentine National Library, where Borges was the director. There they would work together. Borges' English was excellent – he adored English literature – and the method they devised proved fruitful. Di Giovanni would make a rough draft in advance; sitting with Borges in his office, he would read half a line to him, first in Spanish and then in English, and they would discuss possible improvements.

Back home, he would type up his notes and prepare another batch for the next day. As their work progressed, Borges put more and more trust in his collaborator. The translator's suggestions would sometimes persuade him to go back to the original and make changes to it or, when it came to new poems, to switch from his beloved sonnet to other forms.

Soon the pair grew close: they would chat, go to parties, take walks together. On one of their excursions, Borges sketched out the plot of a story he had in mind, but when di Giovanni asked about setting it down, the master demurred. As time went on, he mentioned other stories he had been composing in his head, and the translator 'began a subtle campaign of egging him on, shoring up his confidence, and proving to him that his writing days were far from over'. To cajole Borges out of his decision never to publish again, di Giovanni alternated between praise and teasing: 'Tommyrot ... Eight pages. You can do it.' At one point he lied that he needed money. Borges immediately reached for his wallet, but di Giovanni said that while he couldn't accept a loan, if they submitted something to the *New Yorker* that would be enough to get him out of trouble. A few days later, Borges gave him a typescript he had dictated, a draft of what was to become 'The Meeting', a short story about a duel fought with knives and the secret lives of the weapons. Over the next couple of weeks, they translated it into English, amending the original in the process. The story appeared in the *New Yorker* and in the Argentine daily *La Prensa*. 'After that, it all became a whirlwind. There was no stopping him now.'

Meanwhile, the poetry collection they had been working on, *Elogio de la sombra*, came out in Spanish in 1969, on

Borges' seventieth birthday, and he gave di Giovanni a copy signed 'Al colaborador, al amigo, al promesso sposo' (it was the eve of di Giovanni's wedding, which Borges and his wife Elsa attended as witnesses). Two of the poems in the book were translated back from their English drafts, and there were other changes resulting from their collaboration on what eventually became *In Praise of Darkness*. Di Giovanni's plan was to stay in Argentina for a few months; he ended up spending almost three years there. Among other books he and Borges produced together were *The Aleph and Other Stories* (based on the first edition of 1949, it included a short autobiography of the author written with the translator's help); a new collection of short stories, *Doctor Brodie's Report*; and *The Book of Imaginary Beings*, a series of earlier miniatures 'revised, enlarged and translated' jointly by them. These publications, as well as new stories that continued to appear in the *New Yorker*, did a lot for Borges' popularity in the anglophone world, which seems to have worked wonders for his confidence: he published six more volumes of poetry and seventeen more stories before his death in 1986.

'Translation, in my workaday life, amounts to saying it in English,' di Giovanni writes in *The Lesson*. 'Is it English? is the question I put to myself a hundred times a week.' He and Borges, himself a translator, both saw translation as a creative practice with plenty of opportunities for self-expression; they also believed that 'words immediately suggested by the Spanish should be avoided in English', showing a tendency towards, some would argue, overtranslation. In the poem 'Everything and Nothing', for instance, where Borges describes Shakespeare's words as 'copiosas, fantásticas y agitadas', they rejected 'copious, fantastic and agitated' (a version that appears in another translation; yet another uses 'multitudinous, and of a fantastical and agitated turn'), rendering the phrase instead as 'swarming, fanciful, and excited'. Dismissing 'word-for-word slavishness', di Giovanni states their idea of a good translation: 'Aspiring to inconspicuousness, invisibility, [it] should bear no telltale trace of the original.'

Their motto echoes the words of another American translator, Norman Shapiro, quoted by Lawrence Venuti in *The Translator's Invisibility*: 'A good translation is like a pane of glass. You only notice that it's there when there are little imperfections – scratches, bubbles. Ideally, there shouldn't be any. It should never call attention to itself.' Traditionally popular among translators working into English, this approach is the opposite of that promoted by Vladimir Nabokov, who wanted a translation to read like a translation. However, he didn't always hold this view: at the beginning of his literary career, he translated *Alice's Adventures in Wonderland*, renaming the heroine Anya and adding plenty of his own cultural heritage to her adventures. He cleverly reworked Carroll's wordplay (in one of his puns, invented to replace 'We called him Tortoise because he taught us,' he has an octopus going around with a rod, introduced purely for the sake of homophony) and substituted the original's verses with parodies of well-known Russian poems – in other words, he thoroughly Russified the text. Reading this scintillating translation, you wish he hadn't grown into such a pedant.

There were literalists among the ranks of Latin American

academics too, and their reaction to the work of team di Giovanni–Borges was predictably intolerant. Years later, talking to me, di Giovanni was still fuming as he remembered his skirmishes with them.

> They constantly picked on this word or that. In one story, we've got 'he looked up to the sky'. The original says *cielo*, which in Spanish means both 'sky' and 'heaven'. When we were working on it, Borges told me he meant the sky, so that's what I wrote. And this academic got all het up: why did I say 'sky'? The translation is signed by the author, but does it matter? No, they always know best.
>
> I used to know another Argentine academic: she taught translation studies. If anyone wants to talk to you about translation studies, run for your life. So she says to me, 'Di Giovanni, I've got a question for you. Borges' story "Pedro Salvadores" has 703 words, while your translation has 753.' That's right, I say. She wants to know why. So I explain to her that such is the peculiar nature of the English language. She says, 'OK, but here's another thing I've noticed. Borges' original is broken into four paragraphs, whereas you've got seven.' A crime has been committed!

What did he make of Borges' famous story 'Pierre Menard, Author of *Don Quixote*', I asked, and of its protagonist, whose 'ambition, an admirable one, was to produce a handful of pages that matched word for word and line for line those of Miguel de Cervantes'? Quite how one can complete this impossible task is unclear, which makes it even more worth trying. A parable of translation, surely? 'They often wanted me to do just that,' di Giovanni replied, 'to turn into him and translate him word for word.'

The master, by contrast, was 'unfailingly co-operative' and treated his collaborator with the utmost respect. When they first thought of a joint venture, Borges worried that adding his name as a co-translator would diminish di Giovanni's status. Told that it would only raise the work's standing, he said that in his country 'a translator would be far too jealous to share credit with the author'. Later, discussing the terms of their contract with the *New Yorker*, di Giovanni was touched by Borges' reaction to the fifty-fifty arrangement: 'Is that enough for you? Perhaps you should take more.' Talking about their work in public, Borges was no less generous: 'When we attempt a translation, or re-creation, of my poems or prose in English, we don't think of ourselves as being two men. We think we are really one mind at work.'

That harmonious state – two men, one mind – was often interrupted by a third presence. Elsa, whom Borges had married shortly before travelling to the US in 1967, wasn't prepared to share her husband with anyone. 'With me along,' di Giovanni's version goes, 'Borges had an ally, and she was not in sole control of him.' In his book *Georgie and Elsa* he spares no ink in telling 'the untold story' of the marriage that floundered before his eyes, describing in tedious detail Elsa's unreasonable demands, petty insults, bossiness, vanity, avariciousness and lack of interest in Borges' intellectual life. According to di Giovanni, Elsa oscillated between crying on his shoulder, telling him how 'Georgie had failed her as a man', and mounting smear campaigns against him, once going as far as accusing him of theft. Reading this account, full of bile and gossip, often smacking of sour grapes, it's hard to tell who was more jealous of whom; the only person you feel really sorry for is Borges.

Di Giovanni remembers Borges confiding stories of 'conjugal torture' to him, beginning from the early days of their acquaintance. Eventually the ultimate confession came. 'I've committed what seems to me now an unaccountable mistake,' he said of his marriage, 'a huge mistake – a quite unexplainable and mysterious mistake.' But if Borges did tend to overshare the minutiae of his private life, di Giovanni went on to tell urbi et orbi all of it and then some. In 1970, when the idea of a divorce was floated, he took it upon himself to secure his friend's escape from Elsa's 'stranglehold'. He dealt with the lawyers and helped Borges compile a list of his grievances, which was needed to start proceedings. Reproduced in *Georgie and Elsa*, it consists of twenty-seven points, including: 'She wants me to replace my friends, who share my literary tastes, with others of a more commercial persuasion.'

When matters came to a head, the men conspired to flee Buenos Aires until things settled. One day Borges left the flat he shared with Elsa, ostensibly to go to work as usual. Instead di Giovanni took him to the airport and they made their getaway, returning a few days later to the house of Borges' mother, where he had lived before getting married. The story reads like a bad comedy, full of unfunny gags and barely concealed bitterness on the narrator's part. Despite all that, I remember di Giovanni, who died in 2017, as a talented translator who loved his métier and a man with a wry sense of humour. Telling me about their complicated relationship, at one point he said, 'I'm not going to lie to you now and say, you know, we were so close Borges cried every time he saw me.'

There is a photograph of Borges and di Giovanni walking down a Buenos Aires street, the old man leaning on his young companion's arm. When it appeared in an Argentine weekly, di Giovanni thought of it as his moment in the limelight. A young American coming to Argentina, a country under a military dictatorship, unpopular among democracies, to secure international recognition for its most famous writer – it was a gesture the nation appreciated. 'Which was why the story was about me,' di Giovanni says in *The Lesson*, 'why the pictures were of me with the National Treasure on my arm and not of Borges with me on his.' So much for the translator's invisibility, it's tempting to say; pity the author couldn't see any of that. But then again, visibility is a relative notion, defined by where you stand. To make yourself 'invisible' in a translation, you have to put a considerable amount of effort into it, which in itself can hardly go unnoticed. If the reader doesn't know that the book they have before them is a translation, it may appear to them merely as a text written in their language; otherwise, it's only natural that the translator's fingerprints should show on the transparent surface. Whatever their strategy, it's never hard to detect that the words they use are, ultimately, their own.

To Borges, the translator was, first and foremost, 'a very close reader', and he believed that good readers are 'even blacker and rarer swans than good writers', their activities 'more modest, more unobtrusive, more intellectual'. The epithets 'modest' and 'unobtrusive' do not readily come to mind when you are reading di Giovanni's memoirs, possibly because he wrote them after a divorce that was even more acrimonious than the one he had helped to arrange. After an eventful five years together, Borges and di Giovanni drifted apart. In 1986, the terminally ill Borges married his assistant, María Kodama, and after his death she discarded di Giovanni along with the latest publishing contract he and Borges had signed (also based on equally split royalties), commissioning new English translations to replace their joint works. When we met, di Giovanni had a lot to say about Kodama and his other foes, who 'never knew the real man' and envied their friendship, not to mention the terms of their agreement. As he talked about his role as Borges' translator, amanuensis, agent and confidant, I imagined him forty years younger, even more charismatic (he still had a magnetic presence in his late seventies), able to inspire an author resigned to darkness to write again.

As for the quality of their collaborative works, they do sometimes read as if there is no barrier between the two men. A short piece they called 'Borges and Myself' (others translated it as 'Borges and I') has these lines, originally written about selves co-existing in a single person but open to wider interpretations:

It is not hard for me to admit that he has managed to write a few worthwhile pages, but these pages cannot save me, perhaps because what is good no longer belongs to anyone – not even the other man – but rather to speech or tradition. In any case, I am fated to become lost once and for all, and only some moment of myself will survive in the other man ... And so my life is a running away, and I lose everything and everything is left to oblivion or to the other man.

Which of us is writing this page I don't know.

While not an expert on Borges, I mostly prefer the texts he and di Giovanni created together to other English versions, and I am not alone in that. On reading one of the new translations published by the estate after their falling-out with di Giovanni, Paul Theroux wrote to him, 'It is not Borges. You are Borges.'

'If writing is an art, translation is an art,' di Giovanni says in *The Lesson*; 'if writing is a craft, translation is a craft.' While many of his fellow translators equate the two activities, Eliot Weinberger expounds a different view in 'Anonymous Sources': 'A translation is a translation and not a work of art – unless, over the centuries, it … becomes a work of art.' Rather than insisting on absolute equality, he praises translation as an 'utterly unique genre' that doesn't have to be defined by analogy; and if translators are often perceived as a 'problematic necessity', this fact deserves wry remarks, not angry protestations. Weinberger's tongue-in-cheek suggestion 'to raise the banner of the translator's essential and endearing anonymity' might leave some (not this translator) sceptical, but his stance on the role of translation in literature, expressed in a quietly ironic, self-effacing yet dignified manner, has probably done more for the profession than other people's louder calls for visibility.

While readers of literature in translation rarely judge a book by its translator's relative prominence, they never forfeit their right to know the author's name. There are many theories about the identity of Elena Ferrante, an Italian writer whose anonymity is said to be essential to her work. According to one of them, 'the real Ferrante' is Ann Goldstein, the American translator of Ferrante's books. Even when meant figuratively, the claim has been emphatically denied by Goldstein. She neither sees herself as the author's alter ego nor believes her translations to be reinterpretations of the originals; yet she is the only one Ferrante fans can meet in person.

Incidentally, attempts to unravel this unusual set-up have revealed another translator in the picture. In 2016, a reporter sifted through records of royalties payments and concluded that the person behind the pseudonym must be Anita Raja, an Italian translator working from German. A year later, after analysing a number of texts, experts identified Raja's husband, the writer Domenico Starnone, as the likeliest author of Ferrante's novels. For the story to turn even more intriguing, the next discovery would have to be that the books were originally written in a language other than Italian.

The translator's (in)visibility is perhaps most deeply linked not to their style, which can change from one work to the next, but to the duality inherent in any act of translation, or indeed writing. A vivid example of that is 'Borges and Myself', whose narrator measures himself against his double. Here is a typical juxtaposition: 'I have a taste for hourglasses, maps, eighteenth-century typography, the roots of words, the smell of coffee, and Stevenson's prose; the other man shares these likes, but in a showy way that turns them into stagy mannerisms.' After losing his eyesight, Borges would often ask people to read him something from Stevenson, whose *Fables* he had translated into Spanish. Was he perhaps hoping for some kind of a Jekyll-and-Hyde effect when urging his own translators to 'Simplify me. Make me stark ... Make me macho and gaucho and skinny'? What a pleasure to imagine him walking in Buenos Aires with di Giovanni at his side, composing a story narrated by its own translator, who goes missing, investigates his own disappearance and finally confesses that he and the author are essentially one and the same.

13

Word-worship

In July 2018, someone with time on their hands, or with an IT column to write, entered 'ag' into Google Translate. It was recognised as Irish (at the time of writing it still is, its primary meaning given as 'at'); put in twenty-five times, it produced 'As the name of the Lord was written in the Hebrew language, it was written in the language of the Hebrew Nation.' That and similarly eerie results led to the assumption that Google had been using the Bible to train its algorithms. Google refrained from comment but removed the cryptic phrases, mostly related to rare languages. That only strengthened the suspicion about the role of the Bible in machine translation, since where few sources are available, the code will fall back on one of them and try to 'hallucinate' something out of the nonsense it has been fed.

It was such languages that researchers at the University of Copenhagen had in mind in 2015 when they began training their software on the biblical corpus to map a well-studied language onto a 'low-resource' one, in which there is less material available. Another research group, based at Dartmouth College in the US, also makes no secret of using the Bible, analysing thirty-four different English-language versions, in this case to improve the style of machine translation. The fact that it is a vast data set, with hundreds of parallel texts available, all having a uniform structure and usually arrived at through conservative translation (or so the scientists say), means that linguistic software developers should benefit from its use.

Anyhow, human translators have known this all along. There is nothing more satisfying than coming across a biblical quote in a text you are working on: unlike the majority of quotations, it's easily located, saving you the trouble of translating it yourself. This bonus is available thanks to the efforts of an entire army of translators battling through the eras, the first recorded campaign taking place some 200 years before Christ. According to the legend, seventy-two translators, each in his cell, worked from the Hebrew Old Testament into Greek and after seventy-two days produced as many identical texts. As Philo of Alexandria put it, 'they, like men inspired, prophesied, not one saying one thing and another another, but every one of them employed the self-same nouns and verbs, as if some unseen prompter had suggested all their language to them'. The miracle confirmed the divine nature of the original, and the translation, called the Septuagint after the Latin word for seventy (but one in a long line of apocryphal approximations), was considered the canonical text for several centuries, until the time came for an authorised Latin version.

That task fell to Eusebius Hieronymus, who went down in history as St Jerome, a figure familiar from numerous images depicting him in his study, sometimes wearing an anachronistic cardinal's red robe and even more implausible spectacles, always surrounded by books. These must have included the Septuagint, from which he initially worked, the

Hebrew and Aramaic originals, to which he turned afterwards, and earlier Latin translations. His Vulgate Bible,
translated between 391 and 415 CE, comprised revisions of
the New Testament and a new translation of the Old Testament; it remains the authoritative biblical text of the Roman
Catholic Church to this day.

While Jerome's Latin has been praised as the closest to
the standards of classical Rome, his translatology is envel-
oped in contradictions. In his writings, often irascible and
not always logically watertight, he denounces literalism,
though he makes an exception for the sources he regards as
sacred. In his 'Letter to Pammachius', the earliest surviving
translation manifesto, dated 395 CE, he says, 'Not only do I
admit, but I proclaim at the top of my voice, that in translating from Greek, except from Sacred Scripture, where even
the order of the words is God's doing, I have not translated
word for word, but sense for sense.' The word L. G. Kelly
translates as 'God's doing', *mysterium*, rendered elsewhere
as 'holy sacrament' or 'mystery', is in itself mysterious: we
can only guess what exactly Jerome meant and where he
drew the line when taking liberties with his sources, including the Bible. Be that as it may, the dilemma posed by the
patron saint of translators – fidelity vs freedom – has continued to baffle his successors ever since.

Translation is not an exact science, and Jerome constantly
oscillates between sense and word, returning to the problem
on another occasion: 'If I translate word for word, it sounds
absurd; if from necessity, I change something in the word
order or in the language, I am seen to abdicate the responsibility of a translator.' Whichever strategy he chooses, there
is no shortage of criticism. 'My enemies tell the uneducated

Christian crowd that Jerome falsified the original letter, that Jerome has not translated word for word, that Jerome has written "beloved friend" in place of "honourable Sir", and that – more disgraceful still – Jerome has maliciously condensed by omitting the epithet "most reverend",' he rages in 'Letter to Pammachius'. Sometimes he lurches from linguistic objections to ethical ones: 'I wish to interrogate those men who call cunning and malice prudence. Where did you obtain your copy of my translation? ... What place will be safe when a man cannot keep his secrets even behind his own walls and in his private desk?' Still, he continued to translate, and to waver between fidelity and freedom, professional principles and religious agendas.

In that last respect, Jerome was not unlike those of his twenty-first-century detractors who begin with his personality before going on to suggest that his views affected his work. The novelist Anne Enright, in her essay 'The Genesis of Blame', takes 'fake old Saint Jerome' to task for his misogyny. One charge against him is that his angle on the Fall scene – where, naming the unspecified forbidden fruit, he cleverly plays on the Latin *malum*, meaning 'evil' and 'apple' – is skewed: for instance, he uses 'seduced' rather than 'deceived' and describes Adam and Eve as 'naked' rather than 'vulnerable'. As several specialists have pointed out, Enright is wrong: the word in the first example, *seductus*, in fourth-century Latin did not have the sexual overtones of its modern English equivalent; as for 'naked', this is the standard translation of the Hebrew *erom*, used in reference to adultery elsewhere in the Bible. 'Jerome was an unlovely individual,' one of the commentators concludes, 'but too good a translator to allow his personal opinions to distort a text he considered sacred.'

Some of Enright's objections are justified: where the Hebrew Genesis says 'your desire will be for your husband', the Vulgate has 'you will be under the power of your husband' (elsewhere Jerome gets the Hebrew word for 'desire' right). Jane Barr also quotes this deviation from the original in her thoroughly researched article 'The Vulgate Genesis and St. Jerome's Attitudes to Women'. First, she acknowledges Jerome's stylistic talent and good command of Hebrew, citing his improvements on earlier versions. There follow a number of examples, not all of them exposing the translator as a bigot. In one verse, Jerome translates 'he spoke to the heart of the girl' as 'he soothed her in her sadness with soft words', expressing sympathy; in another, 'she is with child' is changed to the crude 'she has a swollen womb'; in yet another, where Joseph turns down a woman asking him to lie with her, two words are added, *molesta* (bothersome) and *stuprum* (illicit intercourse or unchastity). Barr summarises his interventions as follows: 'Some betray Jerome's antipathy to women, some show a deep sensitivity and awareness … Jerome is a faithful translator of the Hebrew as a rule, and therefore any divergence from it is unusual and assumes importance.'

To all appearances, Jerome was indeed a misogynist; he also had a tendency to shift blame. He mentions inaccuracies introduced into the Bible by its earlier translators and, while he's at it, by the evangelists, simply to justify his own free style – a wise pre-emptive move on his part, since criticising the Septuagint, that miracle of a text, or the Gospels would have been deemed heresy. But for all his human traits, he was a solid professional. His approach can be compared to that of another variety of translator: the missionary, whose vocation informs how they go about rendering religious texts into different tongues.

Eugene A. Nida, a renowned biblical scholar, spent most of his life working to bring the word of God to places far and near. Soon after the Second World War, employed as a linguist by the American Bible Society to oversee translations of the Bible, he began travelling all over the world to advise people working into local languages, often from one of the English versions available. He worked on the project for several decades, bringing together native and non-native speakers to discuss any potential difficulties, from basic Christian concepts to religious subtleties, and from linguistic peculiarities to the cultural traits of the peoples they sought to enlighten.

Nida and his colleagues took especial trouble with the word-or-sense problem because their main concern was maximum accessibility. Believing that everything in the Bible can be fully comprehended in any other language, together they compiled a commentary for translators, explaining how possible meanings could be best expressed, as well as a dictionary of New Testament Greek, in which each word's definitions were listed according to the frequency of their appearance in the corpus (the same idea is used by machine translation algorithms). Nida's thoughts on religious texts are applicable to most translation genres: 'The greatest obstacle ... is the prevalence of "word-worshiping", the feeling that seemingly important words must always be translated in the same way.' Promoting the idea of dynamic equivalence, he urged translators to be culturally sensitive when introducing new terms and notions. He was delighted when a missionary in Panama, struggling with 'sanctification', a concept unknown to the Valiente Indians, saw laundresses by a stream and in a moment of inspiration came up with 'washed by the Spirit of God and kept clean'. Nida's own suggestions included replacing 'white as snow' in countries where it never snows with 'white as egret feathers' or 'white as fungus'. He was, however, unimpressed when certain translators in Latin America discarded *burro* (the Spanish for donkey or ass, including in the non-zoological sense) in the description of Jesus' arrival at Jerusalem and referred instead to an 'animal with long ears', making some readers think it was a 'very large rabbit'.

When religious beliefs need to be transplanted into a new language, glossing is key. The Jesuit Matteo Ricci, upon establishing a Catholic mission in China in 1583, dressed as a Confucian scholar to be taken seriously. He allowed his converts to continue honouring their ancestors in the traditional fashion and introduced into their vocabulary the word *Tianzhu*, or 'Lord of Heaven', a neologism that, consisting of two terms from the Confucian canon, was more acceptable to the Chinese than the Latin *Deus*. The Dominicans, however, disagreed with their Jesuit rivals' culturally sensitive approach, accusing them of mixing idolatry with true religion. The Chinese rites controversy lasted until 1939, when China's Catholics finally had their traditions officially approved.

Back in the sixteenth century, the Jesuits saw the introduction of Christianity to China as a multidisciplinary project, calling alike on the sciences and arts. They developed their own education system, which began with Latin and Greek, continued with natural philosophy, mathematics and astronomy, and deferred theology to the end. In their view, there was a profound connection between Western scientific ideas and true faith, which should prove useful in China, where scholarship and intellect were held in high regard. Between 1583 and 1700, missionaries published about 450 works in Chinese, at least fifty of them translations, usually done collaboratively with native speakers, whose help was crucial. Sometimes a Jesuit would recite a text to his Chinese co-translators, who would then put it in writing; sometimes he would give them a draft to revise.

'I am of little talent,' Ricci wrote of his translation exercises. 'Moreover, the logic of East and West are so supremely different. In searching for synonyms, there are still many missing words. Even if I can explain things orally ... to put it down in writing is extremely difficult.' Yet the historian R. Po-chia Hsia calls him a 'graceful stylist' who 'adopted Chinese syntax and idiom, trying to persuade by means of a Christian discourse decorated by Chinese rhetorical flourishes'. Engaging with the Chinese literati, Ricci treated them as fellow intellectuals, 'colleagues who assisted my progress left and right'. His main achievements, apart from converting a number of prominent figures to Christianity, were the earliest European-style map of the world printed in China and a Portuguese–Chinese dictionary, the first for any European language, which he and a fellow missionary compiled using their own transliteration system.

The Bible didn't appear in China until the late eighteenth century, when ex-Jesuit Louis de Poirot produced a version based on the Vulgate, but it was from Ricci that the Chinese learned their first Gospel stories, some of which he translated from memory. True to the principle of cultural adaption, he sought to make them more appealing to Chinese notions of morality and fate. He also illustrated them with pictures brought from Rome, often tweaking story content according to what images he had handy. His editorial skills were impressive. In one story he had Christ standing on the sea-shore rather than walking on the sea, to match a picture relating to a different episode. Another, given the catchy title 'Two Disciples, After Hearing the Truth, Reject All Vanity', was published alongside the right illustration, but Ricci still had to cut one episode to ensure the words and the image worked together. The story, taken from Luke and full of hidden meanings allowing for various theological interpretations, has Jesus encountering two men on the road to Emmaus, breaking bread with them and being recognised as a result. Ricci's version omits the key scene – not because bread was insufficiently Chinese but because the artist who carved the vignette into a printing block couldn't reproduce this detail. Most translators have made similar compromises, an intricate figure of speech forcing them to reject all vanity and make a cut.

With so many factors – ideological, practical and random – affecting Bible translations, and with so many translators involved, no wonder most versions come with mistakes. Besides the apple invented by Jerome, there are numerous others, some of them by now part of the Christian tradition. A much-quoted example is Isaiah 7:14, where it is predicted that an *almah* (young woman) will give birth to a child who will bear a symbolic name. When *almah* became *parthenos* (virgin) in the Septuagint, it was probably chosen as an analogue of 'childless' rather than to prefigure the virgin birth of Christ, as some commentators believe. When flagging mistranslations, critics often express their own religious and philosophical tastes. Thus, radical Protestants of the early-modern era criticised translations of the New Testament for not being sufficiently literal, insisting that *episkopos* should actually read 'overseer' rather than 'bishop', and *ekklesia*, 'congregation' rather than 'church'. The freethinking Dutch scholar Adriaan Koerbagh stated in the seventeenth century that the correct meaning of the Hebrew word usually translated as 'devil' in the Old Testament was 'accuser' or 'libeller'.

The most illuminating examples in translation, those best able to display the spectrum of its possibilities, arise from multiple meanings, a curse but also a blessing. The King James Bible – produced collaboratively by fifty-four translators, who between 1604 and 1609 worked from Hebrew, Latin, Greek, Spanish, French, Italian, German and English texts – is brimming with them. It is true that 'gave up the ghost' should be 'breathed his last', but whoever chose the former coined a colourful English idiom. Similarly, 'and on earth peace to those on whom his favor rests', as the New International Version has it, doesn't have the same ring as 'and on earth peace, good will toward men'.

Nida and his associates had to deal with mistranslations too, explaining, for instance, that when people ask to have 'their debts forgiven' they mean sins (the word suggested by the Greek text, sometimes translated as 'trespasses') rather than financial obligations, and that a group of disciples 'serving tables' are in fact in charge of finances (some of the English translations of Acts 6:2 refer, somewhat confusingly, to 'the distribution of food'). They highlighted a number of potentially confusing turns of phrase, such as 'Lead us not into temptation', with its implications of God tempting people to sin (later, in 2018, Pope Francis suggested that the phrase should be changed to 'Abandon us not when in temptation'). In Nida's view, certain 'awkwardly literal renderings', such as 'our daily bread' and 'to know God', could also do with some revision.

A more serious obstacle to the goal of maximum outreach is a feature that makes the King James beautiful and incomprehensible at once: its outdated language. An archaic version is often valued more, Nida wrote, as 'the more old-fashioned a text seems to be, the more it appears to be closer to the original events ... Furthermore, many people believe that their ability to understand a strange form of their own language is evidence that they have received from God a special gift for interpreting God's mysterious use of words.' But then Nida realised that many of his mentees, all university and seminary graduates, didn't understand such anachronisms as 'hallowed be' and 'Your kingdom come'. Prepared to sacrifice some of the atmosphere for the sake of clarity, the Bible Society launched a large-scale revision programme. In Latin America it began with a vox pop generating 1,700 pages of proposals. The missionaries set to work implementing them, undeterred by a question put to them by some Japanese translators, 'If the Bible becomes that clear, what will the preachers have to preach about?'

Period language is one of the most fascinating topics raised by the Bible. When King James commissioned his new version, which was to become a single authoritative text, the brief was to produce a conservative translation, and so expressions such as 'verily' and 'it came to pass', already archaic by 1604, were kept. The idea was perhaps similar to that expressed by Nida: an antiquated text, validated by its very quaintness, breathes history. 'We hoped that we had been in the right way,' the King James translators say in their preface, 'that we had the Oracles of God delivered unto us.' The sheer number of idiomatic expressions they coined more than justifies their approach, although their achievement does not preclude other versions. When Atar Hadari, a translator from Hebrew, first told me of his project of retranslating the Bible, I looked at him in disbelief, but then he read some of his verses, and there was light.

> If he'd only give me one kiss from his mouth
> for a touch from you is sweeter than Champagne

is how he renders two lines in 'The Song of Songs', trying to bring a faint motif of 1920s dance music into it, 'because popular songs from back then still have an antique tinkle in my ear while still being living song'.

I enjoyed Hadari's jazzy translation more than I expected, my own preferences gravitating to the other end of the scale. For one thing, once you start modernising a text it's easy to let newspeak get the better of you. Every time an opportunity to update something arises, I can't help recalling a joky (I hope it was only that) proposal to reissue Dostoevsky's *The Adolescent* as *The Teenager*. Of course the risk of overdoing it also exists if you set out to stylise in the other direction, but I've been fortunate in this regard. One of the most enjoyable books I've ever translated is Peter Ackroyd's *Hawksmoor*, a 1985 novel written in two registers, its odd chapters narrated by the eighteenth-century protagonist in period language and the rest written in modern English. I used a pastiche of late-eighteenth-century Russian as the closest analogue to Ackroyd's stylised idiom, compiling a dictionary based on period sources for myself and a grammar manual for the editor, so that they wouldn't take my historical touches for errors. I was uncharacteristically pleased with the result. Some years later, writing a piece about *Hawksmoor*, I was researching online reactions to it. One of the posts caught my eye: 'Really glad that I had picked a translated copy. 17th century English? Haha, no thank you.' I asked what language their copy was in. The reply floored me: 'Russian :)'.

When Jerome interpreted certain passages according to his beliefs, his main principle was that 'it is sacrilegious to conceal or disregard a mystery of God'. When he claimed that 'in dealing with the Bible one must consider the substance and not the literal words', it wasn't just to avoid criticism but also to state that in this case the end justifies the means. His translations, he insisted, were done in the name of a sacred cause, and so despite being proud of his work and knowing his worth, he was prepared to make sacrifices when confronted with that all-important *mysterium*.

Which is better? To foreignise or to domesticate? Many Bible translators understood the importance of cultural glossing and did what they could. Their respect for the languages they worked into is laudable, but the question remains: where do you stop? Imagine spending a long time getting your head around some term with no direct equivalent in the target language when you can solve the problem by introducing a new word. A classic example of a translator lagging behind linguistic developments is Vladimir

Nabokov with his 'blue cowboy trousers', a phrase he used in his Russian translation of *Lolita*, unaware that *dzhinsy* had already become common (the word, that is; the garment itself was still a rarity in the USSR of the 1960s). One of the reasons I've stopped translating into Russian is my inability to keep up with a language where *fastfud*, *skvot*, *feïk* and numerous other loanwords continue to mushroom, recognisable but impossible for me to fit into my active lexicon.

If new tricks are hard to learn, things get easier when you come across a familiar phrase in a book and reach for a ready-made translation, a product of all those old controversies. The Bible remains one of the most useful dictionaries, provided you can identify a quote as such; otherwise you risk turning into the protagonist of 'Translator', a satirical short story by Teffi. In the self-styled wordsmith's rendition, a passage from a theological treatise specifies good prospects awaiting a person 'capable of procuring one ram'. The narrator has to use all her imagination to figure out that the original in fact refers to the parable of the lost sheep. But suppose you do recognise a Bible quote in your source text: assuming you are working into a language steeped in biblical allusions, you'd need a really good reason to translate it from scratch. Indeed, the Bible's near-omnipresence makes it the epitome of translation as a joint venture, a process spanning epochs, languages, tastes and principles. Alexander Pushkin once scribbled next to one of his poems, 'Translators are stage horses of enlightenment.' In the Bible, we have a rare opportunity to look back and see how much ground has already been covered for us since the creation of the word.

14

Journalation

Starting in the early eighteenth century, a wave of new periodicals swept through Europe and beyond. *Zuschauer, Le Spectateur ou le Socrate moderne, Der Patriot, La Spectatrice, El Pensador, Patriotiske Tillskuer, Zritel', O Carapuceiro* and many others were all inspired by the *Spectator*, a paper edited by Joseph Addison and Richard Steele in London. The trend began in 1714 with European publishers translating selected articles from the English periodical for their audiences. The preface to *Le Spectateur*, a French enterprise launched in 'the hope of bringing men back from their deviation and inspiring them with the principles of Honour and Virtue', has the unnamed translator positioning themselves as a mediator between Britain and 'foreign countries', whose readership stood to benefit from the British example. The venture soon gained popularity: in France alone, at least a hundred imitations of the *Spectator* had appeared by the time the French Revolution flared up in 1789; in the Netherlands, there were about seventy, published in Dutch or French; in the German-speaking countries, according to one of the translators, Louise Gottsched, there were too many of them to list.

Most of these papers alternated between free translation

and imitation. Thus, in an essay reflecting on the immortality of the soul, St Paul's Cathedral turned into the Kremlin in Russian, while another piece acquired slaves and tropical fruit juices in Brazilian Portuguese. Imitations of the *Spectator* soon developed into a special genre, becoming more popular than straight translations. The most prolific of the imitators was Jacques-Vincent Delacroix, who produced no fewer than fifteen publications with *spectateur* in the title. Referring to *Le Spectateur anglois* in a 1791 issue of his *Le Spectateur français*, he said that 'there are original books which are inimitable' and that 'it would be against the artistic rules to employ the same colour to paint two different nations'. Delacroix was praised by Voltaire, who promoted him to the position of Addison and Steele's true heir; his detractors, in their turn, denounced his pretentiousness and lack of modesty. Unlike his English colleagues, Delacroix had to please not only the public but also the censors. He had high hopes for the revolution, but after a few cautious attempts to criticise the new regime, he was arrested and labelled a public enemy.

News had begun to be treated as an international commodity even earlier. The first English newspapers, or *corantos*, were mainly translations from Latin, German and French. Around 1618, when news fever caused by the Thirty Years War spread through Europe, it led to the emergence of the weekly *Corante, or News from Italy, Germany, Hungary, Spain and France*. Later in the seventeenth century, the *London Gazette* followed suit, relying in particular on French sources to report on continental wars, and the *Daily Courant*, first published in 1702, consisted of highly interpretative translations of French and Dutch papers. Nowadays major media outlets carry stories from all over the world, using foreign correspondents (if they can be afforded) and news wires: Reuters, Associated Press and others. Whichever model is used, journalists translating news are not translators in the usual sense of the word. Some argue that their task is closer to interpretation since they constantly have to rephrase, summarise, adapt, gloss and contextualise foreign sources, framing stories for their audiences. They are sometimes called journalators, their job known as transediting. These composite neologisms may sound awkward, but they serve as a fairly accurate code for a process that requires translators to localise, simplify and stereotype: to put things in context.

Localisation is, of course, not unique to journalism. For any consumer good – such as an ad, a computer game, a website, a film or a newspaper article – to be safely transplanted from one country to another, translation in the conventional sense is not enough. These products all have to be packaged differently if they are to win hearts and purses. Cultural reframing, that old translation device, is indispensable in the age of globalisation, when the success of any venture is defined by how easily it can travel across borders. The adjustment of global content for particular audiences, with their linguistic, cultural and political characteristics taken into account, assumes especially interesting forms in the news media.

On the one hand, events unfolding in some distant corner of the world are inevitably perceived as foreign; on the other hand, the very fact that they are worth reporting so far away from where they are happening implies that the intended audience should be able to relate to them. Reading a novel, we may or may not care if it's a translation, but we usually realise that it's a work of fiction, whereas a news item is something we turn to for facts, rather than to enjoy the style of the original. Besides, we often think of it as the original, only remembering that it's a translation when there appears to be something wrong with it.

Any text that needs translating has room both for deliberate distortions, often made in the name of ideology, and for genuine mistakes. Journalism is always done in a hurry, bringing a high risk of common translation pitfalls, such as false friends. Spelled or pronounced similarly in two given languages, these words often smuggle themselves into news. That's what happened in 1966 when France announced its withdrawal from the NATO Integrated Military Command Structure and requested all foreign troops to leave the country, taking America and its allies by surprise. Asked if the decision was irreversible, President De Gaulle made a statement that was taken as a promise that France would 'eventually rejoin' the NATO structure, whereas he merely said that it might happen *éventuellement*, meaning 'potentially'. It did happen, eventually, in 2009.

The usual mistakes and misunderstandings aside, journalistic translation errors can result either from treating the original too liberally or too literally; in other words, overlocalising a story can be as unhelpful as preserving too much of its foreign colour. To give but one example: in 2006, Ayman al-Zawahiri, al-Qaeda's second in command, said that the Egyptian militant group al-Jamaa al-Islamiya had joined his organisation. However, the group 'categorically denied' the claim in a statement on its website, which was in turn translated by a number of international news outlets.

One of them, the Russian broadsheet *Izvestiya*, used the verb *otkrestit'sya* in its headline; a perfectly ordinary, slightly colloquial word meaning 'to deny vehemently', it literally translates as 'to cross one's heart (to swear one's noninvolvement)'. This prompted an avalanche of jokes hinging on the Islamists' apparent religious conversion. It is a small mercy that Russian has no direct analogue of the idiom 'to cross one's heart and hope to die'.

It was another journalator's blunder that generated the Hungarian word for 'mistranslation', *leiterjakab*. In 1863, when the French photographer Nadar first flew in his balloon, a Hungarian reporter used a piece in a Viennese newspaper as the basis for his article. The German original read, 'Empor, empor, wir wollen so hoch hinauffliegen wie Jakobs Leiter,' or 'Up, up, we want to fly up as high as Jacob's ladder,' but the journalist missed the biblical reference and wrote 'as high as Jakob Leiter'. (Reading about it for the first time, I was confused myself, mistaking the balloon, named *Le Géant*, for Nadar's companion.)

Every news journalist has a few similar stories to tell. Gaffes can result from rushing to the most frequently used definition of a polysemic word, so that 'the US lifted sanctions' becomes 'the US raised sanctions'; or from a tendency to simplify and generalise, so that *éradicateurs*, a government faction in Algeria, is replaced by 'hardliners'. The BBC World Service, sometimes described as 'the translation factory' to the annoyance of its employees, is an especially rich source of such anecdotes. The writer Hamid Ismailov remembers an occasion in the early 1990s when the staff of the Central Asian Service had to translate the news from

English for their listeners. They got a script from the newsroom that announced in its opening line, 'A member of the Kyrgyz parliament, Jokorgu Kenesh, died today.' One of Ismailov's colleagues proceeded to translate this as 'A member of the Kyrgyz parliament, Mr Jokorgu Kenesh, died today.' They didn't realise until after the broadcast that 'Jokorgu Kenesh' meant 'Supreme Council'. 'So that day,' Ismailov says, 'we buried the entire Kyrgyz parliament.'

Linguistic challenges arise daily in newsrooms the world over. One morning in 2010, BBC Radio 4's *Today* programme broadcast a news item that began, 'Some translations suggest that the Iranian president, Mahmoud Ahmadinejad, dismissed the latest UN sanction package as a "used handkerchief", others as a "used tissue". Either way, they are fit for the waste bin, President Ahmadinejad said.' A few minutes later, presumably following an editorial decision, the newsreader stuck to 'used handkerchief', and the BBC Tehran correspondent commented, 'It was a predictable response from Iran, with a characteristically colourful metaphor.' The broadcast, analysed by Robert Holland in a research paper, provides some insight into the present-day global media. The unusual reference to two translations brought up a number of questions: which was the more accurate? Why was the difference between them important? Why did the editors draw the audience's attention to them before choosing one over the other? Holland suggests a number of possibilities: the producers might have wanted to avoid an international scandal, to show off their 'interlingual awareness' or simply to make a joke, evoking past problems caused by inaccurate translations from Farsi. These included a scandal in 2006 when CNN was temporarily banned from working in Iran after it modified Ahmadinejad's statement that the country had the 'right to use nuclear technology', replacing the last word with 'weapons'.

One source of such ambiguities is the growing tendency of non-English-speaking countries to use their own translations into English, for instance, when covering their leaders' speeches. In 2009, a sentence in Ahmadinejad's controversial UN address, in which he questioned the Security Council's power of veto, was translated by Iran as follows: 'How can such a logic comply with humanitarian or spiritual values?' The BBC's version was worded less categorically: 'With which human and divine value is this logic compatible?' That Ahmadinejad's words required extra care had been clear since 2005, when linguistic disagreement reached a peak. Speaking at a conference entitled The World Without Zionism, he quoted Ayatollah Khomeini. The Western media first translated the Farsi phrase in question as 'Israel must be wiped off the map'; however, after much indignation, this was corrected to 'this regime occupying Jerusalem must vanish from the page of time'.

Another moot point is, as always, impartiality. Journalists may aspire to it, but translation, with its necessary trade-offs, is not particularly conducive to fairness. It's especially hard to remain unbiased when selecting an extract from a source text, which has to be done all the time and involves judgements that can't be fully offset by putting things in context. 'In the spirit of promoting informed, democratic choice', in the same paper Holland proposes to introduce on-air warnings, similar to those concerning 'strong language' or 'scenes of sexual nature', to let audiences know that an upcoming story involves translation and 'has a rather different import for English-speaking listeners than the original speech would have had'. Localisation, however cleverly done, can't change that, but without it news won't travel very far.

The winter of 2011–12 saw a surge of anti-government protests in Russia, held in response to parliamentary elections won by the country's ruling party. Accusing the Kremlin of ballot-rigging, the protesters demanded a rerun. The rallies were attended by people of different political persuasions and ages, all of them feeling disenfranchised in a country trying to present itself as democratic. One of their slogans read, 'Vy nas dazhe ne predstavlyaete.' A pun on the Russian verb *predstavlyat'*, meaning 'to imagine' and 'to represent', it can be translated as 'You can't even imagine us' or as 'You don't even represent us.' Understood in the former sense, the remark 'You can't even imagine' often crops up in everyday speech; the other interpretation is less likely as the clash of the formal 'represent' and the emotional 'even' makes it somewhat forced. When it came to activism, it was an ingenious way to highlight the chasm between the people and their so-called representatives, desperate to remain in power at all costs.

The slogan went viral, becoming the main meme of the protests (which petered out after a few months, bringing no tangible results). Like any pun, it was bound to get mangled in translation, but I tried to make up for that by extending the context in two directions. In the years leading up to the protests, the Kremlin prided itself on its modernisation programme, promising to transform the country and to catch up with the West, both economically and politically. However, widespread corruption and the lack of democracy meant that whatever changes they attempted to introduce, most of the population were left no better off. Contemplating the slogan, I remembered another one, 'No taxation without representation,' a precursor of the American Revolution. First used by eighteenth-century colonists to protest against being taxed by Britain while having no representation in Parliament, it has since been employed by various other activists. With that in mind, I went for 'No modernisation without representation.' The original pun is inevitably gone, but the demand for representative democracy, set against a relevant background, is rephrased via an anglophone slogan, and a rhyming one at that.

In the world of fast news, even a transeditor of genius usually has to sacrifice the best gems – 'Foot Heads Arms Body' (the *Times* headline of 1986 referring to Michael Foot being put in charge of a nuclear disarmament committee); 'Trump Slips on Ban Appeal' (thought up by the *Huffington Post* for a 2017 piece about US courts rejecting the president's proposal to ban visitors from certain countries); 'May Ends in June' (the *Daily Mirror*'s announcement of Theresa May's resignation in 2019) – for something less catchy. Most headlines, and not just those based on wordplay, get rewritten; a similar strategy is applied to book titles. Although you are not supposed to judge a book by its cover, the importance of a title – intended to grab attention, to summarise the plot, to intrigue – cannot be overestimated. Faced with a double entendre, a local reference, a quote or a neologism on a book's cover, the translator should, ideally, try to match the author's inventiveness, and if an equivalent can't be found, they can always play the original up or, to be on the safe side, down.

One example of title-making raised to the level of high art is Peter Handke's novella *Wunschloses Unglück*. Handke reversed a German idiom that means 'happier than one could ever dream', turning it into 'extreme unhappiness', and then Ralph Manheim translated the result as *A Sorrow Beyond Dreams*. In another example, the title of Tom McCarthy's novel *Remainder* was jazzed up by its French translator Thierry Decottignies to sound like a line of verse: *Et ce sont les chats qui tombèrent*. Translated back, it reads 'The cats it was that fell,' a reference to a recurring episode in the book. And Paul Hammond, translating Michel Houellebecq's debut novel *Extension du domaine de la lutte*, went for the brilliantly concise *Whatever*.

A long title trail accompanies Victor Pelevin's cult novel *Generation 'П'*. Originally published in Russian in 1999 under this interlingual title, featuring *П* for *P*, which in turn is for 'Pepsi', it is a tale of one adman's journey to greatness in the heady days of early post-Soviet capitalism. Andrew Bromfield's translation came out in the UK as *Babylon*, a nod to the protagonist, Vavilen, affectionately called Babe in this version. The book's US title, *Homo Zapiens*, is Pelevin's own invention: a term for the model consumer, it appears in the text in its abbreviated Cyrillic form, *ХЗ*, a popular euphemistic acronym that stands for the Russian equivalent of 'Fuck knows.' However, Pelevin's titles were far from the only thing Bromfield had to localise.

The Russian original is bursting at the seams with copywriting puns, some of them judiciously dropped in translation. When 'half an hour of the most intensive intellectual exertion' produces yet another moronic slogan, cutting it provides a welcome respite from the wordplay overload. In other passages, Bromfield more than makes up for the omitted puns, coining new ones: 'Ariel. Temptingly tempestuous' (washing powder); 'Three More White Lines' (Adidas trainers); 'A first-class lord for you happy lot!' (the Almighty). The God ad concept is rewritten in the English version to match the slogan, but the ending is translated verbatim. Having finished the job, the copywriter looks at the result and asks, fighting tears, 'Dost Thou like it, Lord?'

Some of the slogans devised by Pelevin and Bromfield are quite good, while others deserve – as the author intended – to be included among history's worst copywriting disasters. Here are a few classics from this ever-expanding collection. When the slogan 'Come alive! You're in the Pepsi generation' was translated into Chinese, it came out, according to some sources, as 'Pepsi brings your ancestors back from the dead,' or words to that effect (like translation tales, ad anecdotes often have an apocryphal tinge, what with so many working versions to choose from).

Similarly unsuccessful was a campaign the French mobile network operator Orange launched in Northern Ireland in the late 1990s. To the local Catholic population, 'The future's bright, the future's Orange' connoted Protestant loyalism. Amid headlines of the 'Orange Gets Red Light' variety, the campaign produced little revenue, and though it may not have been the resulting associations with the Orange Order alone that got the company into trouble, it's hard not to conclude that their creatives could have applied a bit more local colour, so to speak.

Then again, even when a message is suitable for its audience, it might not sound quite right. Another much-quoted story concerns the slogan 'Nothing sucks like an Electrolux,' invented by a British agency in the 1970s to advertise a Swedish vacuum cleaner. Despite many Americans laughing at what they saw as a brand blunder, UK consumers were happy because the slang usage of 'suck' hadn't yet reached these shores. Words, it appears, travel faster than their contexts, a phenomenon dating back to at least three centuries ago, when it produced a whole stack of *spectateurs*.

15

Dealing with the Natives

On 11 April 1870, an excursion party of seven Britons and two Italians set off from Athens to visit the historic battle-field of Marathon. They were accompanied by a Greek guide named Alexander Anemoyannis, who, to quote the historian Romilly Jenkins, had 'a wide, if somewhat dubious, reputation among foreign travellers'. At the time the Greek kingdom was overrun by brigands, its countryside notoriously unsafe. On the way back, the tourists met a detachment sent out to escort them, but pressed ahead without the guards. A band of brigands captured them; the women were released, the men held. Anemoyannis tried to slip away but the abductors caught him, shouting, 'The dragoman too!'

Negotiations ensued, conducted partly through Anemoyannis. The robbers demanded a ransom – an exorbitant £32,000, later raised to £50,000 – plus amnesty for themselves and their imprisoned associates. One of the captives, Lord Muncaster (his name somehow led the brigands to believe he was a cousin of Queen Victoria), was released to arrange for the ransom to be paid. The British, suspecting the Greek government of being in cahoots with the *klephts*, were prepared to pay the requested sum, but instead a rescue expedition was organised.

Dealing with the Natives

It didn't go to plan. The leader of the gang told the prisoners many times that unless his terms were met immediately, he would cut their throats. Anemoyannis interpreted the demands but left the threat out. Pursued by soldiers, the bandits sent the guide to deliver another message to their commander. As reported by Ioannes Gennadius in *Notes on the Recent Murders by Brigands in Greece*, the colonel told the messenger 'to hasten back and inform the brigands that they might remain tranquilly and without fear at Sykamenos, for the soldiers had orders not to fire upon them; and that there they could receive the money and go out of the state on the conditions of safety which the Government had promised them'. Anemoyannis failed to convey this reply to the brigands, perhaps because he couldn't catch up with them as they fled towards the village of Dilessi. The remaining four captives – secretaries of the Italian and the British legations, a lawyer and a young aristocrat – couldn't keep up with the gang and were killed.

'The part played in the abduction by the dragoman Alexander is one of the most puzzling features of the whole episode,' Jenkins writes in *The Dilessi Murders*, calling him 'a most untrustworthy agent and witness'. He was charged with general complicity with the gang, including wilful negligence throughout the negotiations. During the inquiry, one of the guards testified that he had warned the tourists several times, urging them not to proceed on their own, but they paid no heed. Anemoyannis' statement that he had translated the warning was contested. He was also alleged to have revealed to the brigands the details of a conversation between the captives and an emissary of the rescue party, held in Italian.

In defence of the Greek nation, Gennadius stresses that

even if 'the treachery of the Cicerone' played its part in the tragedy, this doesn't mean that the government should be held responsible for the conduct of a privately hired guide. He also challenges some of the accusations against Anemoyannis: 'It is far more probable for Lord Muncaster to be mistaken than for two men ... who understood the language better than his Lordship.' But regardless of Muncaster's knowledge of Greek, the interpreter was, of course, not supposed to omit anything in his English version. It is common for people to make wrong assumptions about mediated speech: for instance, that the intermediary should only translate what they think the listeners don't understand, and stay silent otherwise, to minimise their interference or simply to save time. Such an approach can turn any interpreting session into a metalingual minefield.

Despite the evidence against him, Anemoyannis was cleared of all blame and, according to Jenkins, managed to return to his trade, accompanying foreign tourists on country trips for many years afterwards. Word must have spread of his questionable track record, but in those days, as indeed much later, many travellers expected their guides to be cheats, projecting their worst suspicions about the local population onto the profession. Baedeker books contained some patronising advice on 'Dealing with the Natives', including guides, as well as on the best places to hire them and the costs involved. 'There are about ninety dragomans in Cairo, all more or less intelligent and able,' a 1892 Baedeker claims, 'but scarcely a half of the number are trustworthy.'

Late-nineteenth-century travelogues usually portray the guide as part and parcel of the oriental scene; the more exotic and picturesque the better. Yet it's difficult to please tourists: they want both colourful wildness and solid professionalism, even though – that most basic of predicaments – they have no way of evaluating the accuracy of the alien-sounding words uttered by their interpreters. 'The Eastern dragoman is not averse to talking,' Charles Dudley Warner recalls in *Winter on the Nile*, 'but he always interprets in a sort of short-hand that is fatal to conversation. I think the dragomans at such interviews usually translate you into what they think you ought to say, and give you such a reply as they think will be good for you.'

Self-employed linguists of that era – as always in the history of the trade – were expected to do much more than translate: they had to negotiate and spy, to wait on and protect their clients, to run errands, mediate, procure goods and services, and so on. If something was not to the clients' liking, they blamed the guide, while giving him little credit for his work, no matter how diligent, and often abusing him. One happier story is told in Rachel Mairs and Maya Muratov's book *Archaeologists, Tourists, Interpreters*. Solomon Negima would have been forgotten along with the majority of his fellow translators had it not been for his book of testimonials, which contained letters from his clients, photographs and other proof of his employment history. Take this, dated 18 April 1891: 'Lord Dalrymple begs to state that he travelled in the spring of 1891 through Palestine and Syria with Suleiman Negima as his dragoman, and has much pleasure in stating that he found him most intelligent, obliging, and useful in every way, and can most strongly recommend him to all parties wishing to travel through the above mentioned districts.'

A Syrian Roman Catholic, Negima went to a German
mission school and spoke excellent English and German.
He started as an interpreter with the British army in 1885,
serving in Egypt and Sudan, and after the campaign began
working with tourists. Praised for his calm temperament as
much as for his language skills, Negima – like many interpreters then and now – had to deal with some difficult clients.
An Englishwoman named Miss Ellen E. Miller (the title of
her travelogue, *Alone Through Syria*, refers to the fact that
she had no European companions) found him too timid. She
was cross when he didn't encourage her bold attempts to
peer into the tents of locals; on falling ill, she expected him
to nurse her. Negima was more fortunate with the Reverend Joseph Llewellyn Thomas, an Anglican minister from
Oxford, who also treated him as a servant, of course, but
was less hungry for exotic adventures. He too left a glowing
review in Negima's equivalent of a LinkedIn profile.

It is not known whether Alexander Anemoyannis had a
similar book, or how he persuaded tourists to employ him
after his acquittal. The fact that there were still tourists in
those parts was, in a way, down to sheer luck. A European
cause célèbre, the Dilessi murders jeopardised Greece's relations with Britain, which had supported it in its fight against
Ottoman rule during the 1821–28 War of Independence and
had been one of its protectors since the 1830s. At the same
time, many in Britain believed that Greece deserved to be
treated like a colony, perceiving the whole Greek nation as a
race of *klephts* unworthy of their great Hellenic past.

Charles Tuckerman, the American minister in Athens,
whose 1871 pamphlet, *Brigandage in Greece*, was widely
discussed, considered *klephtouria* to be the basis of a

political system rife with corruption, crime and blackmail. Years later, his Greek translator, a bureaucrat at the Ministry of Foreign Affairs, deployed a subtle linguistic argument to exonerate his country. As Rodanthi Tzanelli relates in her paper 'Unclaimed Colonies', he omitted the word 'blackmail' in his translation of Tuckerman's article, explaining in a footnote, 'This is part of the English and Scottish tradition because ... the proper word for the description of the process can be found in the vocabulary of those languages; on the contrary, in our language the term does not exist, and there is no fear or reason for it to be invented.' The translator's argument was clever but not watertight. Greek does have a word for blackmail: *ekviasmos*. While not an exact equivalent of its English counterpart – a cognate of *via*, 'violence', it is, as contemporary native speakers tend to think, less suggestive of tangible benefits – it would never the less have done the job.

Seen through the prism of language, the Anglo-Greek relations of that period appear especially complex and reflect more general policies. Some early-nineteenth-century British sources, according to the 1933 edition of *The Oxford English Dictionary*, linked Ireland and Greece. The 'unruly districts' of Ireland were often called 'Grecian'; the *Telegraph* called brigands 'Fenians after the continental fashion'; the *Standard* suggested that 'Greek' was colonial slang for 'Irish'. Following the Dilessi murders, politicians often referred to brigands as *banditti*, a word that was also applied to the Ribbonmen, members of a secret society that operated in rural Ireland. British imperial attitudes crossed borders with ease, even if that meant travelling in the company of unreliable guides.

*

There are numerous ways for any translator to discredit themselves: silence and talk, initiative and passivity, sometimes a single word, omitted or used, are all fraught with pitfalls. The translator's fidelity to their source, at times ignored altogether, can also be constantly questioned. And so it should be. I say this as someone who has betrayed in my capacity as an interpreter. That I acted in good faith and was, in most cases, prompt to correct myself may be mitigating factors, but they don't absolve me completely. Yet even if I were completely innocent of any errors (difficult though it is to imagine, given the nature of the job and its constraints), I'd still be amazed at the trust many of my clients place in me. Meeting me for the first time – in a police custody cell, for instance, or a court witness room – they assume that, as someone who speaks their language and is there to assist them, I am in their corner, so they can share anything with me. I tell them not to mistake me for their solicitor, to think of me as a machine, to say only what they want the English-speakers to hear. I remind them that once the tape is rolling, I'll have to interpret everything they say, including 'You reckon I'd better not mention I threw the first punch?' Explaining all that is sometimes the hardest part.

And then work begins for real, with many opportunities for mistakes and little time to correct them. Remembered afterwards, they sometimes make me distrust myself. Once, during a domestic abuse trial, I interpreted the victim's words as 'he was drunk' (she used a very popular and versatile Russian word, *vypivshi*, which doesn't typically amount to 'completely drunk'), having momentarily considered and rejected 'he was tipsy' as too quaint, 'he was in a state of inebriation that can be described as low to medium, possibly slightly above that, but definitely not high' as too formal and lengthy, and having for some reason not thought of the perfectly suitable 'he had been drinking'.

Sometimes my mind registers an error mid-sentence and I catch myself just in time to say, 'The interpreter would like to make a correction ...' A post-mortem usually sends me back to my glossaries, notes and reference materials. Occasionally, though, I manage to get both the content and the form right. One such instance was an interview with an alleged rapist. Speaking in Russian, with me interpreting, he told the police that the intercourse was consensual and, clearly desperate to make a good impression, described his encounter with the victim (which took place in a local park, under some bushes, in the middle of a rowdy drinking session) in the language of a nineteenth-century romantic novel. My rendition of his account went something like this:

> As I looked out yonder, my gaze fell upon a comely young lady leaning against a tree in a most seductive position. My spirits suddenly inflamed, I rose from the bench, leaving my good fellows to carry on with their badinage, and, approaching the lady in her solitary reverie, found her well disposed towards my attentions. Having accommodated ourselves under the said tree, we soon found ourselves engaged in a carnal embrace ...

I improvised away, trying to reproduce both the vocabulary and the style as faithfully as possible, even though we all understood that the monologue was probably not the whole truth.

Translation is not cricket. It involves three main players – the source, the target and the intermediary – with at least one of them unable to grasp what's going on, so they assume, not unreasonably, that the game is skewed and not in their favour. When they start losing, or think they do, their gut instinct is to blame the one who understands everything – the intermediary. If a written text looks unconvincing or an utterance sounds false, communication breaks down. Conversely, the less solid the source, the more difficult it is to translate. This circle of mutual mistrust is hard to break. Many translators and users of their services will find familiar motifs in a postcard from Egypt dated circa 1917. It features a picture of a brown-skinned man – dressed in native costume, a tarboosh on his head, his open gaze intended to symbolise honesty – captioned 'A Trusty Dragoman'. The message reads, 'This is a guide and interpreter, it says a <u>trusty</u> dragoman don't believe it.'

16

Rectify the Names

'I do not know,' A. Henry Savage Landor writes in *China and the Allies*, 'who invented the name "Boxers" as a translation of the words Ih-hwo-Ch'uan, by which the antiforeign societies in China call themselves, but whoever did so was wrong.' The English author, anthropologist and adventurer was in China in 1900, when the Boxer Rebellion, an uprising against all things and beings foreign, swept through the country. An experienced explorer who travelled through Tibet in the 1890s and knew several local dialects, Savage Landor considers different names given to these secret (and often secretly supported by the Qing government) societies. His translation of one of them, *Yihequan*, reads 'Volunteer United Fists'; another, *Yihetuan*, is rendered as 'Volunteer United Trained Bands'.

The journalist Dmitry Yanchevetsky, Savage Landor's Russian colleague, also reported from China during the uprising. His account, *By Never-Changing Cathay's Walls*, covers the same events as *China and the Allies*, but the two books are quite different in style. Yanchevetsky's title, taken from a patriotic poem by Pushkin, sets the tone for his reports, which occasionally border on jingoistic and are full of flourishes. The reserved Savage Landor is usually careful with his facts, while the poetically inclined Yanch-evetsky sometimes lets his imagination lead him astray. If there is one thing the graduate of the Oriental Faculty of St Petersburg University is pedantic about, it is the Chinese language, both its numerous regional varieties and the official written version used throughout the empire. The latter alone presented enough challenges for its students. Where Savage Landor skirts around two Chinese characters in the society's name – one meaning 'harmony', the other usually translated as 'righteousness' – ending up with 'united', Yanchevetsky combines both with some improvisation, rendering *Yihequan* and *Yihetuan* in Russian as, literally, 'Truthful and Harmonious Fist' and 'Truthful and Harmonious Militia'.

Translating Yanchevetsky's book, I went for 'Righteous and Harmonious Fists' and 'Righteous and Harmonious Militia', names widely used in English-language literature on the subject, along with 'Boxers United in Righteousness' or simply 'Boxers'. I also had to compile a spreadsheet of proper nouns for the copy editor to choose from numerous variants, historical and contemporary, spelled according to different transliteration systems. Turning for reference to Savage Landor, who in the first few pages alone spells one Chinese word in several different ways, was no use; luckily, Yanchevetsky proved more consistent. What both agree on is that 'Boxers' is misleading: the rebels were not fighting with their bare hands. Although martial arts were an important part of their practices, which included physical exercises and magic rituals designed to make them invincible, their main goal was to put up a united front against the technologically advanced foreigners who had come to their land uninvited and were threatening to destroy their traditional way of life.

The actions of the insurgents were anything but harmonious, and the imperial court was equally unpredictable in its attitude to them, issuing an order to 'annihilate' them one day before returning to its policy of encouraging them the next. According to Savage Landor, Empress-Dowager Cixi 'in one of her messages approving of the so-called Boxers, gave severe instructions never to mention the word ... *Harmony*, in the presence of strangers', so the corresponding character was changed to an officially endorsed one, meaning 'united'. The word was incorporated into some translations, while others stuck to 'harmonious'. Neither version, however, reflects the brutality the rebels showed towards the foreigners and their Chinese associates alike.

Our correspondents were reporting from the city of Tientsin (known as Tianjin today) before going to Pekin (now Beijing). In June 1900, as storm clouds gathered over both cities, the situation became especially dire in the capital: the rebels were setting things on fire, and foreign residents dared not venture outside the legation quarter. An international rescue force was slowly making its way from Tientsin to Pekin. The troops' progress was hindered by the Boxers, to whom the telegraph was as evil as the railway, so the Europeans often got their wires cut – or crossed. Perhaps it was the scarcity of non-fake news that prompted Yanchevetsky, stranded in Tientsin, to add an especially lurid piece to his reports.

His description of a Boxer gathering at the Temple of the Spirit of Fire, done from imagination, is a study in red. Hidden in the depths of the native city, the temple is lit by red lanterns, full of half-naked men wearing red headbands, belts and scarves embroidered with mysterious hieroglyphs. Their red-clad leader makes a dramatic entrance and addresses the crowd with an inflammatory speech, inciting them to go and kill all the foreigners. 'We executed a Japanese interpreter from the Japanese Legation in Pekin,' he says. 'When he tried to pass through the city gates, despite the prohibition, the leopard soldiers of Tung Fu Hsiang caught him, cut off his nose, ears, lips and fingers, stabbed his body, cut his back into belts for themselves and ripped the heart out of his chest.' More gory details follow, culminating in the ultimate propaganda message: 'We dissected the heart of the enemy and ate it. Now, having a piece of an enemy heart in my chest, I fear no enemy.'

Savage Landor gives a shorter account of the incident: 'Mr. Sogiyama, Chancellor of the Japanese Legation, had been barbarously murdered by the soldiers of General Tung's cavalry when on his way to the station.' Akira Sugiyama (as most English-language sources spell his name) was indeed the chancellor of the legation. On his way to the railway station to meet some Japanese troops, the soldiers seized him at the city gate and killed him while a crowd of Chinese watched. This was the first casualty Pekin's international community had suffered in the conflict, and when the mutilated body was found the next day, it was said that the victim's heart had been cut out and sent to General Tung as a trophy. Savage Landor doesn't mention these rumours, while Yanchevetsky spares no red paint in his vignette. Did he throw in the interpreter bit to embellish someone else's report, or did he simply misunderstand it? A translator mistranslated into existence, only to be brutally killed: what a metaphor for a war fought in many languages.

As for real interpreters caught up in the hostilities, those recruited from the locals often paid a high price for their involvement with the 'foreign devils' (as early-twentieth-century sources often rendered the Chinese expression). After a group of European railway engineers working some hundred miles from Pekin had to flee from a threatening mob, Savage Landor reports, 'three Chinese who were interpreters to the engineers came weeping into the Belgian Consulate, saying the Boxers had attacked their masters, and that if immediate relief were not sent they feared all would be massacred'. A party of volunteers was promptly sent to their rescue, with one of the interpreters joining them. Later, the survivors told of another Chinese interpreter trying to shield the Europeans from enemy fire as they cowered in the cabin of their junk. Most of the refugees managed to reach the safety of Pekin; the chief engineer, his sister and two associates perished; the fate of the loyal interpreter is unknown.

Despite the danger of reprisals, some locals continued to consort with foreigners. Yanchevetsky speaks fondly of 'a Chinese gentleman named Liu but more widely known as Leonid Ivanovich', a schoolteacher in Tientsin and an interpreter to the viceroy of the province. An intelligent man, he knew Russian very well and sought the company of Russians. At one of their outings, over 'Chinese sweets, a European meal and French champagne of a Shanghai variety', he filled his companions in on the history of the Boxer movement, mocking it for its backward ideas and comparing it to other rebel movements that had existed in China since the late eighteenth century. Boxers United in Righteousness had evolved from Big Fist, its predecessors including Big Knife, Big Swords, Clay Pot, Protection of the State, Destruction of the Devils, Red Lantern Shining and Armour of the Golden Bell. As for Liu's own full name, it is lost to history, and so are those of most of his colleagues. Elsewhere, Yanchevetsky mentions an engineer who travelled around the country accompanied by his helpful interpreter, 'a Chinaman by the name of Petr Ivanovich'. Whatever Chinese gentlemen made of being christened in such a fashion, they probably thought it best to be friendly with their big neighbour.

As I ploughed my way through the Chinese names in Yanchevetsky's book, stumbling over obscure titles, places, institutions, I thought of *The Analects of Confucius*, in which the ancient sage, asked what he would do if put in charge of a country, says (in Simon Leys' translation) that he would 'rectify the names' first of all: 'If the names are not correct, language is without an object. When language is without an object no affair can be effected ... rites and music wither, punishment and penalties miss their target [so that] people do not know where they stand.' The importance of names is something translators feel strongly about, as do authors, especially when expecting to be translated. Perhaps the Boxers should have given more thought to the naming of their society, if only to ensure that no one confused it with a sports club.

During the rebellion, Yanchevetsky sometimes acted as an interpreter too, interrogating prisoners. On one such occasion, after getting a few noncommittal words out of a wounded, barely conscious man, he remarks sympathetically, 'I do not know what they eventually did to the prisoner. I doubt that the Allied soldiers spared his life. It was not worth a straw.' The nationalist in him retreated when basic human values were at stake. As for his linguistic duties, despite his concerns about being insufficiently versed in local dialects, the Sinologist managed fairly well. Still, he felt humbled in the presence of experts like the erudite Liu, doubly so on his visit to Li Hungchang, the chancellor of the Chinese empire, for whom Liu now worked as an interpreter full time, having fled Tientsin after the Boxers burned his school. 'What could I possibly say to this great man?' Yanchevetsky muses. Fortunately, Liu came to the rescue, telling the chancellor that 'the Russian journalist would be extremely flattered and grateful if he could impart his valuable opinion of this year's events in China'.

Visiting the Russian consulate in Tientsin, Yanchevetsky listens in amazement as the ladies chat to a Chinese servant: 'How marvellously they spoke the language of Confucius!' Their fluency, in his view, is to do with the fact that, compared to written Chinese, with its thousands of characters representing morphemes rather than phonemes, the spoken language is not too grammatically involved and therefore relatively easy to learn (the emphasis surely being on 'relatively'). His examples range from Cossacks being able to get by after a short time in the Far East to an officer who, after studying Chinese for only two years, makes an impressive diplomatic career.

Diplomacy and translation were, as usual, inextricably linked. The Boxer Rebellion occurred forty years after the end of the Second Opium War, when China was forced to allow foreign legations into Pekin and open several ports for international trade. In *Changing China*, William Gascoyne-Cecil relates what happened in 1860 when the British and the French made treaties with the empire, which was by then too weak to oppose their demands. One of these documents had several unexpected clauses in it. According to Gascoyne-Cecil, the French minister, unable to read Chinese, relied on his interpreter, 'a very able Jesuit', to go over the Chinese version. While doing so, Père Delamarre added two provisions to the text: one permitted Christians to practise their religion in China; the other gave French missionaries important property rights. 'When this pious fraud was discovered,' Gascoyne-Cecil writes, 'the French Minister thought it would do no good to denounce his interpreter, and therefore the treaty was treated by the French as binding and never questioned by the Chinese.'

Paul A. Cohen gives more details in *China and Christianity*, writing that 'the allied armies forced the Chinese authorities to consent to additional agreements which buttressed still further the privileges of the Christian missionary and convert'. While the French text of the treaty merely affirmed an earlier imperial edict, promising to compensate the Catholics for their losses during the war, the Chinese version was indeed more far-reaching. Under its terms, French missionaries were allowed to rent and buy land throughout the country and to build on it; Catholicism was permitted everywhere in China; and arresting Christians with no legal justification became punishable. 'The Chinese ... accepted the Chinese text as authoritative,' Cohen writes, noting that while the differences were 'apparently due to the duplicity of one of the interpreters on the French side ... just who was responsible for this interpolation remains a matter of speculation'. Some historians attribute it to Delamarre, while others blame another French interpreter, Baron de Mèritens, 'on the basis of his own admission'. One study implicates Baron Gros, the French commander during the war, suggesting that he connived in the doctoring of the text to secure special rights for his compatriots. Perhaps the trick was achieved by a collective effort and not, as one might think, by a single stroke of a translator's pen.

Translating Yanchevetsky, I felt tempted to change not just the more impenetrable names but also his jingoistic outbursts. In the end I didn't, simply because most of my energy was spent on looking up proper nouns. The Romanisation and Russification of Chinese have both undergone a number of revisions over the past century, and historical documents, including Savage Landor's and Yanchevetsky's reports, can differ wildly in their spelling of certain names. Sometimes the easiest way to identify a particular person or place in both books was to look at the illustrations: with only a handful of cameras around, the correspondents on the scene all shared the same photographs. Besides, Russian and English translations of official Chinese documents were often close enough to each other, so that, sifting through them, I managed to find some relevant English excerpts to paste into my text. Translating them from scratch would have been quicker, but I took the trouble in the name of authenticity.

When the allies marched into Pekin to liberate the legations after the eight-week siege, documents were the least of their worries. Savage Landor recalls going inside the *Yamen* (the 'War Office', to use his own term) shortly after it was taken. He found the place a complete mess: scattered everywhere were drill manuals used by the Chinese army, scientific books on explosives, navigation and chemistry, photographs, maps and charts, as well as original manuscripts of the treaties between China and other countries (possibly including the one fudged by the French four decades earlier). As he wandered around, 'a number of coolies entered and began to sweep all these valuable papers into the canal'. He also mentions a missionary who, upon discovering some important documents in one of the viceroy's buildings, offered them to the British authorities, along with their translations. 'He was in return treated far from civilly.'

Missionaries were generally enthusiastic about the written word, an instrument of both enlightenment and soft power. Savage Landor praises Timothy Richard, a Welsh Baptist missionary 'beloved and revered in all China', who translated a great many literary, scientific and religious works into Chinese. The books proved popular, especially with the younger generation, eager 'to know all that "foreign devils" know'. A prominent public figure, an agent of modernisation in China, Richard tried to protect his fellow missionaries as the rebellion took over the country. That summer, 239 of them were killed, along with more than 32,000 Chinese converts. As Joseph Esterick says in *The Origins of the Boxer Uprising*, 'to the ordinary villager of north China, the unequal treaties, the gunboat diplomacy, the concessions along the coast were of little significance. If such folk ever saw a foreigner it was certainly a missionary – and the foreign presence meant "foreign religion".' In other words, even if the Boxers didn't see Christianity as yet another manifestation of Western imperialism in China, they hated its encroachment on their traditional life as much as they did foreign technology. Whoever tweaked the Sino-French Convention in 1860 had a hand in forming that attitude too.

As the uprising raged across China, both missionaries and

translators got more than they bargained for, often having no option but to take an active part in the events. One of the better-known interpreters, Mr Munthe, admired by Savage Landor and Yanchevetsky, was a retired Norwegian officer, a polyglot who had been employed as a Chinese army instructor. When the hostilities flared up, Munthe resigned and, as Savage Landor writes, 'offered his services to the Allies, refusing all remuneration, and making the sole condition that he must be at all times in the front'. He served under the British before joining the Russian army, 'while other Generals preferred in many cases to employ men who, although very worthy in themselves, could be of no great assistance to the troops'. In the storming of Pekin, he showed himself not only a capable interpreter but also a brave soldier. When a general was mortally wounded, Munthe and Yanchevetsky carried him away under fire. Both interpreters were justly praised – unlike many of their Chinese colleagues, for whom the risks were even greater.

Language skills also came in handy for some in the aftermath of the rebellion. On taking Tientsin, the allied authorities initially allowed free looting of the city. However, the next day, when many foreigners carted their booty to the gates of the legations, they ran into officials instructed to seize any valuables. To avoid this 'looting of the looters', as Savage Landor puts it, some used a simple ruse. When rickshaws carrying plundered goods were stopped by, say, a British officer, he 'would be met by a jabber of French' from the plunderer. Since it had been agreed that each representative should confiscate only what had been stolen by his fellow countrymen, the officer would 'bow courteously and acknowledge that subjects of the much-respected

French Republic were not under his jurisdiction', letting them through. 'So folks – not military – who were fortunate enough to speak various foreign tongues,' Savage Landor concludes his account, 'brought home quite a nice collection of things.'

Yanchevetsky also mentions the looting, always insisting that the Russians never took part in it (I had to translate these passages through gritted teeth). Estherick describes the plundering as perpetrated by 'troops of all nationalities (though the Europeans were the worst, and the Japanese the best behaved), and missionaries, who would later justify their activities in articles with such delightful titles as "The Ethics of Loot"'. It's not clear, however, what proficiency level in a foreign language was required for one to get away with the speaking-in-tongues trick. Any strange-sounding mumble would have probably been enough to deceive a monolingual officer, the success of the deception relying not so much on the chancers' linguistic abilities as on everyone else's lack thereof.

During the Boxer Rebellion, as in most conflict situations, collaborators found themselves between the foreign devil and the deep blue sea. Native interpreters always have to live with the threat of revenge from their own people, and once official hostilities are over, they are often left behind. For a more recent example of the same dynamic at work, consider the military interpreters employed by the British army in Afghanistan in the past two decades.

They were initially told they would be allowed to move to the UK, but then things didn't go as agreed. First, the so-called Intimidation Scheme (let's hope no one ever has to translate that) was introduced to protect those whose safety was compromised because of their collaboration with the Taliban's enemy. Four hundred and one interpreters applied and were eventually relocated to Britain. In 2018, with their temporary visas due to expire, 150 ex-terps, some of whom had served on the front line in Helmand, realised they would have to reapply to remain in the country, to pay £2,400 for new documents, and in some cases would not be allowed to bring their families over. The alternative was deportation to Afghanistan, where the risk of being killed by the Taliban was significant. The interpreters petitioned the Home Office to reconsider its policy and were supported by the defence secretary as well as by their former colleagues. One of them, Captain Ed Aitken, said, 'The value our interpreters gave us in such an alien environment is difficult to overstate and the trust we put in them to work with us in often horrific conditions was extraordinary.'

In May 2018, the fee was finally waived and fifty former personnel were granted UK visas. At the same time, a number of other Afghan interpreters were denied entry to Britain despite being hunted by the Taliban. In April 2019, the families of those who had settled in the UK were allowed to join them, but a year later some are still waiting for their visas. Considered traitors in their own country, these 'unsung heroes of the military campaign in Afghanistan' (as the media called them on the few occasions they did make it into the news) were initially abandoned by the state they had served, and when it eventually accepted them it wasn't exactly with open arms. Their stories were underreported; the only people who remember them now, it seems, are their comrades-in-arms. While the places where the war was fought – Helmand, Lashkar Gah, Marjah – still ring a faint bell, the names of those who can't return there are buried under the dead weight of their asylum papers.

The interpreters who worked for the US army have been treated similarly, if not worse. 'Any combat veteran from Iraq and Afghanistan will tell you that his best asset is a great terp,' the *Armed Forces Journal* reported in 2011. The best of them didn't just translate but were also 'culturally attuned and adept at recognizing nonverbal clues or shifts'. They enlisted on the understanding that they would be allowed to resettle, but only a tenth of them have managed to move to America; the rest don't qualify, however dangerous their situation in their home country. One of the interpreters I spoke to, Raz Mohammad Popal, spent more than three years with American and Canadian forces in Kandahar. His father asked him not to return to their village for fear of retribution. Popal applied for a US visa under the special immigrant scheme in 2015, but after four years' anxious waiting, it was rejected. Living in Kabul now, he calls the process 'a lottery' and does his best to look after his family.

The case of one Iraqi interpreter, Imad Abbas Jasim, is equally disheartening. He got the job in 2003 after a chance encounter at the gate of an American military base in Baghdad (he was selling cans of Pepsi outside) and worked with US forces for three years. In 2006, he was wounded in an explosion; his brother, who also worked for the Americans, was kidnapped and never found. Fearing for himself and his family, Jasim applied for resettlement to the US. More than ten years and several reapplications later, still in Iraq, he got a final rejection on security grounds. He sees the American army motto 'No man left behind' as 'the biggest lie ever'.

Rectify the Names

Translators in armed conflicts often draw the short straw. They can never rely on the warring sides to trust them fully, nor can they expect much help from peacekeepers. The threat of retaliation is always there. Attempts are being made to change this state of affairs. Red T, a not-for-profit organisation supporting translators and interpreters worldwide, is petitioning for a UN resolution to protect linguistic contractors in high-risk settings. If the stories recounted here make the reader reflect on the plight of the front-line translator, we might be one step closer to the day when the only battles they have to fight are over their choice of words, such as the tug of war between 'united' and 'harmonious'.

17

The Obligation of the Competent Authorities

'I can't speak a word of English,' the Chinese author Yan Lianke recently said in an interview, 'so I don't care whether my work is translated well or not.' It's all very well for a man of letters to say that. If literature, like all art, is useless, then there's no point imposing any criteria on a literary translation besides purely artistic ones. Things are different in the pragmatic worlds of business and public affairs. When it comes to translating commercial or legal documents, interpreting at a business meeting or a court hearing, the end users of these services have the right to expect certain standards from the providers. Yet even here, the fact that translation is so little understood by those on the receiving end – and not just because they are unfamiliar with languages per se – makes it hard to evaluate. 'A job well done,' an experienced UN interpreter once told me, 'is when no one complains.' Whatever quality in translation means, it's easier to define it by negatives. Standards may be a hard notion to nail down, but it's usually evident when they start slipping.

Iqbal Begum was tried in an English court in 1981 for killing her abusive husband. She pleaded guilty to murder and was automatically sentenced to life in jail. It didn't transpire until later that her interpreter, a Punjabi-speaking solicitor, failed to convey the difference between murder and manslaughter to her, possibly because they spoke different dialects of the language. 'It is beyond the understanding of this court,' reads the record of her appeal hearing, 'that it did not occur to someone from the time she was taken into custody until she stood arraigned that the reason for her silence … was simply because she was not being spoken to in a language which she understood.' It was concluded that 'the reason for the apparent lack of communication lay in the inadequacy of interpretation'. Begum was released on appeal in 1985 and, disowned by her family, committed suicide a few years later. Her case, as well as a number of other miscarriages of justice, led to calls for an independent body regulating interpreters in Britain.

As the need to move from community-based interpreting to a regulated system became apparent, the National Register of Public Service Interpreters was established in 1994. To join it, one had to pass an exam that involved several modules, oral and written, and covered specialised medical, legal or administrative terminology, depending on one's choice of course. The admission criteria have since been lowered to include candidates with a diploma based on a distance course with no exam. The register is still freely available to anyone looking for a qualified interpreter to attend a court hearing, a medical appointment, a meeting with a social worker or a job centre interview, but fewer and fewer public services go down this route.

The move towards the private sector began with criminal courts and tribunals, where the right to have the free assistance of an interpreter is guaranteed under Article 6 of the European Convention on Human Rights. In 2011, when I began working as a court interpreter, we were employed directly by the courts and paid £85 for the first three hours, with a lower rate afterwards, plus travel costs. The arrangement was thought too costly in the post-2008 austerity climate, and in 2012 the Ministry of Justice (MoJ) outsourced its court interpreting services. A £90 million contract was awarded to a small agency, which was promptly bought by the outsourcing giant Capita.

Chaos ensued as Capita began using unqualified interpreters, paying them £16 per hour, with no minimum time and lower travel remuneration. Many professionals boycotted the agreement for financial or ethical reasons; there were protests outside Parliament, letters to MPs and 'dossiers of shame' detailing instances of unprofessionalism. Numerous no-shows, delays and double-bookings aside, they mentioned such blunders as a man charged with perverting the course of justice being called a pervert. Yet the new system, despite being called 'nothing short of shambolic' in a 2013 report, remained in place. When Capita's contract expired in 2016, another agency, thebigword, took over as the MoJ's service provider, still paying its subcontractors peanuts, still not fussed about quality. On day one of the new agreement, a slave gang trial was adjourned because the interpreter who had worked on the case could no longer afford to attend; eight weeks on, a man who tried to steal £600 worth of groceries was held in custody for forty-eight hours before an interpreter could be found.

The MoJ claims to have made multi-million-pound savings on court interpreting since the outsourcing began, but the figures don't include the cost of delays. Numerous cases have been adjourned because there was no interpreter available. For instance, the case against Colonel Kumar Lama, a Nepalese army officer accused of torture, temporarily abandoned in 2015 because an interpreter couldn't be found, finally collapsed a year later, having cost the taxpayer £1 million. Other damaging consequences, moral and physical, are harder to quantify – if one can talk about them in quantitative terms at all. Tragedies caused by inadequate translation happen not only in the justice system but across the board. In 2015, a Romanian construction worker lost the use of his legs after an incident at a building site. The investigation revealed that he had had to rely on unofficial interpreters for health and safety instructions.

As more and more professional interpreters stop working for the public sector, standards keep slipping – yet more evidence, if it were needed, that outsourcing doesn't improve services. Mistakes in translation, from linguistic inaccuracies to cultural subtleties, can never be entirely avoided, but some of the errors reported from the courts are egregious: 'bitten' confused with 'beaten', 'charge' translated as 'fine' rather than 'accusation', 'Home Office' mistaken for a study, and so on. Given how easily translation lends itself to improvisation, I was prepared to take some of these stories with a pinch of salt until I witnessed several such incidents myself. The MoJ, clearly aware of them too, appointed another contractor to provide 'independent quality assurance', using assessors to conduct random checks ('mystery shopping' in the agency's jargon) in courtrooms, at fees only slightly above the pittance offered to interpreters.

As for the clients, when provided with an interpreter,

some people are grateful for any help they can get, some are past caring, and some trust no one but themselves. A defendant once asked me just to sit there quietly, as all his previous experience of interpretation had been negative. Interpreters, meanwhile, are struggling to make their case: some call for the outsourcing agreements to be scrapped; others brandish their diplomas and blame novices for undercutting their fees. There are ongoing discussions about unionising and forming professional collectives. Little recognition and low pay mean that even those going into public service interpreting with the best of intentions can't afford to invest in training or put in the hours to prepare for an assignment. What the free market has created is not healthy competition but a vicious circle of poor wages and poor workmanship.

Worrying trends in translation are a worldwide phenomenon in the age of late capitalism. The global language services market is dominated by large companies – US-based LanguageLine Solutions leads with a revenue of more than $450 million; thebigword is ranked fourth – the majority of them relying on public-sector contracts, most heavily in the US, Scandinavia, the UK and the Netherlands. Many of these contracts, valued between $10 million and $80 million, are in the healthcare market, which is estimated to be growing, especially in America. Does that make providers more aware of the standards they should set? In 2014, a young woman in Oregon died because of a mistake made by a call centre interpreter, who sent the ambulance to the wrong address, causing a fatal delay. Can tragedies like this be overlooked in favour of performance metrics?

In the fight between quality and costs – or between sense

and nonsense – some countries fare better than others. Germany, for example, takes public service translation seriously, whereas Spain suffers from the same problems as Britain. Italian court interpreters complain about facing threats from the Mafia, while in Denmark they threatened to go on strike when in 2018 a contract to provide nationwide translation services to the justice system and law enforcement bodies was awarded to a single agency. Strikes among translators are not unusual, and sometimes they do bring results. In 2016, the Home Office reversed its decision to reduce pay for its pool of interpreters after they announced plans to strike over the proposed cuts; in 2018, simultaneous interpreters disrupted European Parliament proceedings over working conditions.

Alarming reports of institutionalised unprofessionalism can be heard on both sides of the Atlantic. A recent case in Canada led to an Iranian woman's asylum application being rejected because of a disputed translation. A trained midwife, she told the immigration hearing that she had performed 'virginity restoration surgery' in her home country. After the family of one of her patients discovered what she had done, they threatened to kill her and reported her to the authorities, leaving her no choice but to leave Iran. When the immigration adjudicator asked the applicant to describe the procedure, she did so in Farsi, and the interpreter used the terms 'virginity curtain' and 'virginity tissue' instead of 'hymen'. That was taken as evidence that the applicant's story was fabricated, and she and her daughter were refused asylum. Fortunately, the decision was overturned on appeal after it was pointed out that 'translating medical terms from Farsi to English was an imprecise exercise'.

The US has strict language access regulations – people with limited English proficiency must be provided with an interpreter in medical and public service settings – but the legislation is changing. In 2019, the Trump administration announced its decision to get rid of interpreters at initial immigration hearings. To learn their rights, migrants will now have to watch an 'orientation video' with subtitles in their language (only Spanish at the time of writing, although there are plans to add twenty more). Lawyers have warned that this is likely to create problems, as in their view the video is confusing, and migrants will no longer be able to ask the judge for clarification unless their lawyer happens to speak their language. Judges have the option of looking for an interpreter inside the courthouse, or of requesting telephone interpreting services, but, as one of them told the *San Francisco Chronicle*, these are often 'woefully inaccurate and substantially delayed'.

The cost cutting will inevitably affect migrants' ability to make their case in court or even to understand their fate – provided they get to this stage in the first place. To give one example, of 250,000 Guatemalan refugees stopped at the US border in 2019, at least half were Mayan, and many spoke little or no Spanish, but that was the only language on offer, which led to deportations. Meanwhile, the US immigration authorities have been using online translation tools to study refugees' social media profiles before making decisions about their future. When it was pointed out in 2019 that such services come with disclaimers, the government replied that it 'understands the limitations of online translation tools'.

*

The Obligation of the Competent Authorities

'The obligation of the competent authorities is not limited to the appointment of an interpreter,' a guide to the European Convention on Human Rights says, 'but ... may also extend to a degree of subsequent control over the adequacy of the interpretation provided.' The lowest bidders contracted by 'the competent authorities' are under no such obligation, their main criterion being costs (they wouldn't have won the tender otherwise). When asked about their selection principles for interpreters, agencies go as far as to insist that their contractors are 'reliable and responsible', with linguistic competence sometimes coming second. It is of course easier to verify attendance than competence.

What do professionals make of all this? Jonathan Downie, a conference interpreter and the author of a book on the subject, talked to me about the notion of value in the industry, stressing the difference between absolute value, or the actual costs to the end user, and perceived value, or the impression they are left with. 'If it's just numbers on a spreadsheet,' he said, 'they'll try to get it cheaper; if they know they can't do without you, price becomes a far less important factor.' While quality is a more elusive concept than quantity, one way to assess it is to ask whether the interpreter performed in a way that met the client's expectations. In one of his articles, Downie argues that people tend to 'commission translations to fulfil a certain purpose', which 'could trump strict linguistic accuracy in some cases'. Do people still need quality, I asked, thinking of the decline in public services. 'The argument made to defend the expense on interpreting in the public sector,' Downie said, 'is very much a human rights argument.' If translation is needed only because the law says so, people will try to get it as

cheaply as possible. The alternative is to show that getting
it right will help you achieve your goal and make savings at
the same time: having patients spend less time in hospital,
for instance, or prisoners in custody.

Another interpreter, Hiromi Sakai, also has a fairly opti-
mistic attitude towards her job, despite knowing how badly
things are going in some areas. She told me about an occasion when, having been double-booked for a conference, she
stayed and listened in. What she heard was so awful that she
wrote to the agency that had hired the interpreters. 'They
cut me off,' she remembered. 'I never got another offer from
them.' Having realised that whistleblowing doesn't work,
Sakai concentrated on what is in her power: to be as accurate as possible, but also to create an atmosphere of mutual
understanding and, ultimately, to make clients happy. Edu-
cating the end user about what they often see as irrelevant
details – from the quality of equipment to the pace of
speeches – is another thing professionals can do. Last but
not least, if you want to be valued, you shouldn't be selling
yourself cheap. 'I raised my fees, even if it meant losing some
of my clients,' Sakai said, 'and I'm not going to give in.'

The question of multilingual communication became especially poignant when Britain voted to leave Europe. The
2018 Brexit white paper, published in twenty-two EU languages, was in parts translated spectacularly badly – or
appeared 'very mythical', as one German-speaker politely
put it. Another asked, 'What does *Fischergemeinden* even
mean? People praying for fish?' (The made-up compound is
slapped together from 'fisherman' and a word whose meanings include 'community' and 'parish'.) The document

misspelled 'Estonia' in Estonian, 'Finland' in Finnish, 'German' in German and 'UK' in Croatian. In French, 'principled Brexit' acquired moral overtones: a Brexit with, rather than based on, certain principles. In Welsh, the word *cenhadaeth* was used to mean 'mission' in a corporate sense, despite its religious connotations. The German text, apparently the worst, judging by native speakers' reactions, also had 'letter (of the law)' translated as 'letter (of the alphabet)'. A Dutch-speaking Twitter user wrote, 'Dear UK government. We appreciate the effort and you probably have no clue, but please stick to English if you want us to understand you. This is horrible. Kind regards, The Netherlands.'

Many Europeans believed that the fiasco illustrated how badly the UK government was prepared for Brexit and how little it cared about Europe. However, the explanation might be more prosaic: language skills in Britain have long been in decline. In 2018, Britain paid the European Commission £1.5 million for translation services, expenditure condemned by some politicians as 'an embarrassing waste of both time and taxpayers' money'. The bill included fees paid to EU interpreters used during Brexit negotiations, one of whom translated a speech Jean-Claude Juncker gave in December that year. Talking about the UK's position on leaving Europe, the EC president used the French word *nébuleux*; rendered as 'nebulous', it provoked an angry reaction from Theresa May, who took it personally. Explaining himself later, Juncker said (in English), 'I didn't, by the way, know that this word exists in English.' What he meant was that he couldn't see where the British parliament was heading, and in any case, he wasn't referring to May but to 'the overall state of the debate in Britain'.

With plenty of examples showing that it pays to have quality translation, some positive signs are appearing in the UK: for instance, the word 'insourcing'. British analysts reported in 2019 that '78 per cent of local authorities believe it gives them more flexibility, two-thirds say it also saves money, and more than half say it has improved the quality of the service while simplifying how it is managed'. 'The days of large-scale outsourcing,' to quote Downie again, 'are coming to an end.' There are indications that the tide might be turning, and depending on what happens with the economy, the state of things might improve. 'Give it five to ten years,' Downie says, 'and I think we won't recognise the pessimism about interpreting in the public sector.'

'Current trends in several countries go in the direction of de-professionalism due to shortage of financial means, absence of specialized training and lack of awareness of the risks of using non-professional legal interpreters,' reads a standard on legal interpreting issued by the International Organization for Standardization in April 2019. It contains a number of requirements, from general to technical, but, unsurprisingly, no hard-and-fast rules. Translation is as impossible to evaluate as it is to perform absolutely right. That doesn't mean we should stop trying. Whether quality is needed or not, translators carry on, sometimes doing better and sometimes worse.

'I tend to equate what I do to the work of a gas fitter, providing a basic service which I have studied to master,' Robert Walkden wrote in a letter to the *London Review of Books* in 2018, responding to another correspondent's claim that translation of any kind can amount to art. 'There is more to non-literary translation than mechanical activity, but that doesn't make the people who do it artists.' To prove his point, he mentions the popularity of computer-assisted translation tools: essentially memory databanks that allow one to look up entire fragments previously used by translators in relevant contexts. Having employed such tools for decades, some professionals are now moving towards fully automated translation, with mixed results.

Translation aids were invented to improve the output of translators' efforts, but do they always work as expected? One typical story, related by a colleague, concerns a court ruling he translated using a software tool built from a database of existing translations. His client ran a checking program on the text and detected four passages for which 'the translation delivered was 100 per cent machine translation (verbatim) with no effort to transform this into human legal translation'. However, all the segments flagged were articles of law always cited in rulings of that kind in their standard form. The version suggested by the machine was 'perfect, exact, and any modification I would have made would have actually decreased the quality of the translation', according to the translator. And yet the client refused to pay. Whether translation tools are designed to make things generally better or just to speed them up and cut costs, the question of how to define quality still stands.

18

Alogical Elements

> What I refer to is this: he says my Jumping Frog is a
> funny story, but still he can't see why it should ever really
> convulse any one with laughter – and straightway pro-
> ceeds to translate it into French in order to prove to his
> nation that there is nothing so very extravagantly funny
> about it. Just there is where my complaint originates. He
> has not translated it at all.

This is from Mark Twain's introduction to a book he pub-
lished in 1903 under the title *The Jumping Frog: In English,
Then in French, Then Clawed Back into a Civilized Language
Once More by Patient, Unremunerated Toil*. It contains three
short stories: 'The Notorious Jumping Frog of Calaveras
County', 'La Grenouille sauteuse du comte de Calaveras'
[*sic*] and 'The Frog Jumping of the County of Calaveras'.
The first was one of Twain's earliest works, originally published in 1865, a humorous piece set in California during the
Gold Rush era; the second appeared in 1872 in the *Revue des
deux mondes*; the last was the author's revenge against the
French translator (much criticised, never named): his own,
deliberately literal translation of the unfunny version back
into English.

Whether or not Twain's French readers found the story funny, the original certainly is, though not as hilarious as the double-translated piece. 'There was a feller here once by the name of Jim Smiley,' the former begins; the latter reads, 'It there was one time here an individual known under the name of Jim Smiley.' The character is described as a compulsive bettor – 'Any way that suited the other man would suit him – any way just so's he got a bet, he was satisfied' – and the same can be concluded from the other text: 'All that which convenienced to the other, to him convenienced also; seeing that he had a bet, Smiley was satisfied.' The next sentence is transformed more substantially: 'But still he was lucky, uncommon lucky; he most always come out winner' becomes 'And he had a chance! a chance even worthless; nearly always he gained.' It goes on for twenty pages, 'no more like the Jumping Frog', to quote Twain's introduction again, 'than I am like a meridian of longitude'.

Back-translation, the trick that allowed Twain to doubly defend his reputation as a humorist, is an often-amusing multilingual analogue of Chinese whispers. In the early 1990s, it was used for a practical purpose: to evaluate the quality of machine translation. It worked as follows: first humans translated newspaper articles from English into different languages, then machines translated them back, and then other humans answered questions about their content. Known as comprehension evaluation, the method was soon abandoned as inconclusive since the texts provided by human translators, although originating from the same source, were so different that it was hard to tell if comprehension gaps were caused by these discrepancies or by errors made in the course of machine processing. This and other evaluation methods all have two things in common: they involve some human input (at least at the time of writing) and remain, to a greater or lesser extent, subjective.

In 2018, when 352 experts were asked to estimate the probability of AI outperforming humans in various tasks in the near future, their combined predictions suggested that this would happen in translation by 2024. The report, published by Oxford and Yale researchers, defines equal performance in this area as machines being 'about as good as a human who is fluent in both languages but unskilled at translation'. Among 'specific AI capabilities' listed, 'language translation' is mentioned next to 'folding laundry'.

The practice of translation is prone to misconceptions. Perhaps it was to be expected that a lack of understanding would accompany the development of translation algorithms, which to many seem as impenetrable as the process itself. And yet the basic principles behind them can be explained in layman's terms, since they are not that different from those underpinning any human act of translation. The field of natural language processing emerged in the postwar years, when the Cold War generated a need for more texts to be translated. Americans led the way, with Warren Weaver introducing a new approach to translation in a 1949 paper that proved influential. Behind it was a mathematical model of communication developed by another American scientist, Claude Shannon. Weaver helped to popularise Shannon's ideas and applied them to translation, arguing that – aside from 'alogical elements in language' such as 'intuitive sense of style, emotional content, etc.' – it could be reduced to a logical problem.

The first to tackle this problem were rule-based algorithms. Developed in the 1950s and 1960s, they used bilingual dictionaries as well as complex systems of rules that allowed a computer to determine the word order in the target language. Having thousands of sophisticated, language-specific rules meant that the systems were difficult to maintain, yet their early promise was encouraging enough for funding bodies, particularly in the US, to invest in further research. And then, after the initial burst of enthusiasm, the tables turned. In 1959, Yehoshua Bar-Hillel, who had led the research in the early 1950s, published a highly negative report on machine translation, pointing out some limitations of the existing systems. They were, he claimed, not sophisticated enough to analyse sentence structure in a satisfactory way, especially when translating between grammatically distant languages. If computers were to generate anything better than 'The Frog Jumping', more complex rules were required.

Bar-Hillel's criticism contributed to work in the field slowing down, although his influence alone wasn't enough to bring it to a standstill. In 1964, funding organisations behind machine translation research in the USA commissioned a report on the field. Produced in 1966 by the Automatic Language Processing Advisory Committee, the report analysed the needs for machine translation and associated costs. One of its conclusions was that 'the majority of requested translations are of negligible interest, and ultimately are either partially read or not read at all' (indeed, this must be true for most texts ever produced). 'There is no emergency in the field of translation,' was the verdict. 'The problem is not to meet some nonexistent need through nonexistent machine translation.'

With the main players thus convinced that their trouble and investment had been unjustified, the first wave of natural language processing subsided. The trough was followed by another peak, which came in the 1980s with the dawn of the internet age. It was the availability of electronic texts that allowed researchers to come up with the idea of statistical machine translation. The key element of any statistical model is a parallel corpus: a set of pairs of texts that are translations of each other, preferably of good quality, however that is judged. These texts have to be aligned, or matched, unit by unit: at word, phrase, sentence or paragraph level. Sentence-level alignment, for instance, can be done by length, a relatively simple and robust method that takes into account the fact that the number of words in a sentence usually changes in translation. Another way to do it is lexically, whereby similar strings of characters – acronyms, proper names or numbers – serve as correspondence points whose presence allows the program to map texts onto one another, sentence by sentence.

Given a large corpus of texts aligned at sentence level, a statistical model is implemented as follows: first, a word alignment algorithm is applied, building a dictionary of sorts, in which each translation of a given word is associated with the probability of this particular meaning. The probabilities are determined by the relative frequency of each pair appearing in the corpus. Next, the model uses the newly compiled dictionary to translate each sentence, choosing the most likely translations – not just of individual words, but also of phrases and sentences – suggested by the corpus. It also compares the obtained draft with a monolingual corpus to ensure the result makes sense and reads smoothly in the target language.

As this (very rough) outline shows, the machine follows its human counterparts in the main stages of translation: both look things up in a dictionary; both avoid the notoriously unreliable word-for-word approach; both try to use common sense, albeit differently. Faced with a range of contexts to choose from, humans act intuitively, while algorithms have no option but to pick the most probable meaning of a given word or phrase. The possibility of translation is grounded in the fact that most things people say have already been said before and can be found in a vast data set stored on a computer server, in a human brain or elsewhere in the coffers of civilisation.

As statistical models kept improving, another approach was conceived, conceptually based on the same idea – that there is no need to reinvent the wheel, trying to express a thought or concept anew when it's already available in a multitude of languages – but radically different in its implementation. Neural networks have made their way into translation in the past decade, gradually replacing the earlier methods. A neural algorithm also analyses a large data set, but the outcome of this stage is so-called word embeddings. The code considers a given word together with a few surrounding ones, treating this group as one context in which the word can be used, in line with the words of the linguist John Rupert Firth, 'You shall know a word by the company it keeps.' At an AI exhibition in 2019, I tried experimenting with a word embedding generator developed by Google. When I typed in 'translation', it returned 'colonisation', 'misinterpreted' and 'literary', demonstrating once again that machines only replicate what they have learned from their creators.

Each word typically belongs in many different contexts, so the algorithm limits these to a manageable number by discarding the less common ones. Then the word is represented as a set of features, or certain characteristics expressed in numbers, each measuring how likely it is to belong to one of the identified contexts. This structure of word embeddings is built for both the source and the target language, either separately, when the algorithm is trained on each monolingual corpus independently, or jointly, with the use of bilingual corpora of aligned texts. If the former method is chosen, the two structures are mapped onto one another afterwards, which again results in an alignment between them. This process, known as deep learning, generates a kind of superdictionary that stores a colossal amount of information about the usage of words and other units.

The models described here may still look like black boxes (to understand them fully would require a degree in computer linguistics, and by the time you get there they will have been replaced by another generation of algorithms), but one thing is clear: it's all about data. The earliest corpora used by translation software developers were legislative texts, widely available and easy to align sentence by sentence. Examples include Canadian parliamentary debates, transcribed in English and French; EU documents, provided in more than twenty languages; and UN proceedings, published in six. As the internet conquered the world, multilingual sites became useful sources, the largest of them being Wikipedia. Although not all of its articles on a given topic are translations of each other, taking a single, often quite narrow subject and comparing the texts can work better than consulting a traditional dictionary with its direct equivalents.

Biblical corpora are a treasure trove of data; TED talks are routinely translated into a variety of languages; the list goes on. The ubiquity of multilingual information allows search engines to harvest more data online, building new training corpora that may be lower in quality but still helpful due to their sheer volume. Quantity, it seems, is more important than quality here; furthermore, the discipline is much more about computers than it is about linguistics.

It hasn't always been like this. At the dawn of machine translation, computer scientists and linguists worked closely together, beginning with the rule-based systems in the 1950s, but the emergence of the statistical approach in the 1980s caused them to drift apart. As the work gained pace, it became unfashionable to involve linguists in the process. Frederick Jelinek, a renowned figure in the field of information theory who headed IBM's speech recognition research group from the mid-1970s for two decades, supposedly said, 'Every time I fire a linguist, the performance of our system goes up.' An apocryphal story perhaps, and even if true, the remark was no doubt made for effect. The main reason for getting rid of linguists was cost efficiency, since things produced by humans are notoriously difficult to integrate into a complex system. To train an algorithm autonomously is a lot quicker and cheaper than to employ specialists for the task, and as new data becomes available, systems have to be constantly retrained, leaving even less time and money for human intervention, however expert, in this highly competitive industry.

Thierry Poibeau, a researcher specialising in digital humanities – his book *Machine Translation* makes a welcome contrast with numerous other works on the subject, which read as if they've been written in some rare language before being put through a shoddy translation app – tells me that over the last twenty-five years, there have been suggestions to bring linguists back on board on equal terms with developers, but now that deep learning is expected to work automatically, their return looks less likely. Instead, they have become, in Poibeau's words, 'the lumpenproletariat of machine learning'. In 2016, as Google moved from statistical methods to neural networks, trumpeting the move from supervised to unsupervised learning as the next step forward, *Wired* magazine reported that the company employed a 'massive team of PhD linguists' called Pygmalion to manually annotate heaps of data for algorithms to be trained on, a task described by a former project manager as 'very click, click, click'. By 2019, according to the *Guardian*, 'the appetite for Pygmalion's hand-labelled data, and the size of the team, has only increased'. Google's claims about the self-sufficient nature of its networks go against the experience of its employees. 'Artificial intelligence is not that artificial,' one of them told the *Guardian*. 'It's human beings that are doing the work.'

With or without linguists, automatic translation tools have been improving fast. Their applications today include cross-language information retrieval (when multilingual online sources are queried in search of keywords), automatic subtitling and captioning, text-based messaging, direct speech translation for voice messaging systems, and much else. The technology is also making inroads into the publishing industry, with more and more books being translated by machines and then post-edited (usually there is also a pre-editing stage, designed to make the text easier for the algorithm to process). One example of this is *Deep Learning* by Ian Goodfellow, Yoshua Bengio and Aaron Courville, which came out in English in 2016 and two years later appeared in French, translated by DeepL, one of Google Translate's competitors. This involved some preliminary work whereby a dictionary of technical terms was compiled for the computer to use, and afterwards the text was 'validated' by unnamed editors. The French edition did well, although it's hard to tell how much of its success was due to human input. Poibeau's experience was different: working on a French edition of his own book, he updated the conclusion and put it through a translation tool. 'It was French,' he says, 'but it was too literal, too close to the English original, so it was easier to rewrite it from scratch.' Another relatively recent addition to the list of jobs about to be taken over by machines is the translation of EU documents. Curiously, it is texts produced by the EU, translated by professionals, that form the large data set known as Europarl, one of the most useful multilingual sources for training algorithms. The corpus has taught the machines all they need to replace its creators.

Despite the revolutionary developments of the machine age, most of the challenges that human translators have faced since the early days are still there, a reminder that machines are man-made products. Take pivot languages, for instance, used as an intermediate stage to translate between rare languages. Where the amount of data available is still insufficient for sophisticated neural networks to be trained properly, it makes sense to use English, with its breadth of texts available, as an intermediary language. Yet the dangers

of introducing an extra obstacle remain. The digital humanities scholar Frédéric Kaplan, the inventor of the term
'linguistic capitalism', mentions an example dating back to
2014, when Google Translate, confronted with the French
idiom 'Il pleut des cordes' (literally 'It rains ropes'), translated it into Italian as 'Piove cani e gatti' (literally 'It rains
cats and dogs'), which makes no sense. The metaphor had
been extended too far, clearly through the pivot of English.

Then again, there are languages more universal than
English. 'Thus may it be true that the way to translate from
Chinese to Arabic, or from Russian to Portuguese, is not
to attempt the direct route, shouting from tower to tower,'
Weaver wrote in 1955. 'Perhaps the way is to descend, from
each language, down to the common base of human communication – the real but as yet undiscovered universal
language.' By this he might have meant mentalese, the language of thought. Analogies with the way the human brain
works don't end at the theoretical level either. To mimic the
natural procedure, software engineers devised a combination
of an encoder – which translates the source into so-called
interlingua, a formal language specially developed to make
it easier for computers to process – and a decoder. The inter-
lingua-based approach, the most ambitious of all, has never
been applied on a large scale. Still, it's telling that the search
for a universal representation of meaning has moved from
an innate language to a machine equivalent of mentalese.
The latter, in its turn, is intended to fully automate translation, allowing us to stay monolingual if we wish.

Among other problems faced by machines and humans
alike are polysemy and, more generally, anything that
requires semantic or syntactic disambiguation. In his

scathing report Bar-Hillel used the example 'The box was in the pen' to demonstrate the infeasibility of high-quality automated translation. The sentence is logical in certain contexts as the word 'pen' can refer to a writing instrument or to an enclosure, but the latter meaning, Bar-Hillel argued, would be impossible for a computer to arrive at probabilistically. While he was right, other, more predictable contexts are not beyond present-day algorithms. Poibeau cites another example, 'The motion fails,' to show that, although the most likely French equivalent for 'motion' is *mouvement*, any decent model will dismiss 'La mouvement est rejetée' as nonsensical and choose instead 'La motion est rejetée.' More ambiguous utterances, such as 'There was not a single man at the party,' are indeed impossible to translate outside the context (or even within it), but that's hardly specific to machines; any human would usually find this statement confusing.

Turning from abstract examples to practical matters, it's clear that machines need all the help they can get from humans. In August 2019, Facebook was investigated by the UN for failing to stop incendiary Burmese-language posts about Myanmar's Rohingya Muslims, tens of thousands of whom had fled Myanmar as a result of ethnically motivated violence. Found to be 'a useful instrument for those seeking to spread hate' against the minority group, Facebook was also criticised for providing misleading translations. One post in Burmese, for example, read, 'Kill all the *kalars* that you see in Myanmar; none of them should be left alive,' the pejorative *kalar* referring to the Rohingya. Facebook's translation of it read, 'I shouldn't have a rainbow in Myanmar.' The company admitted being 'too slow to prevent misinformation and hate' and removed the Burmese translation feature. It's still unclear whether the errors were generated by the software alone or with the help of human translators.

Translation challenges are too many to test comprehensively here, but let's look at a few to see if machines are any better than humans at coping with them. Discussing the issue in his blog, the linguist Mark Liberman mentions three things computers can't get right: pronouns, idioms and common sense. He opens a book at random, takes the French phrase 'qu'on me pose un lapin', meaning 'that somebody stands me up', feeds it into Google Translate and gets a literal version; doing the same now, I still get 'I'm asked a rabbit.' The algorithm deals more sensitively with the title of the famous Hungarian translation of *Winnie the Pooh* – *Micimackó* ('Mici the bear'), recognising it as 'Winnie the Pooh'. Moving on to swear words, Google is fairly inventive: 'fuck', for instance, generates a decent range of expletives. Puns, predictably, fall through the cracks, just as they always do unless rescued by luck or genius. Finally, to test them to the extreme, can machines distinguish between registers? The sentence Twain had much fun with, 'But still he was lucky, uncommon lucky; he most always come out winner,' translated into French and back, reads, 'But he was still lucky, a rare chance; he comes out most often winner.' Were the reader to conduct the same experiment now, the results would likely be different (the algorithms are constantly changing as more data is being fed into them), perhaps so much as to suggest that computers have already outperformed humans in translation, though that might be a matter of definition.

*

'The chief drawback hitherto of most of such machines is, that they require the continual intervention of a human agent to regulate their movements.' Luigi Menabrea, the scientist whose notes Ada Lovelace translated and expanded, wrote this of Charles Babbage's Analytical Engine in 1840. In a sense, our relationship with technology hasn't changed all that much since then. The most debated AI question today is whether machines can be truly artificially intelligent and do things that humans haven't taught them. Judging by the difficulties experienced by translation algorithms, so far they have been following in their inventors' footsteps, and when it comes to evaluating the quality of their translations, the benchmark is also decidedly human. There are a number of assessment methods based on different scores, designed to quantify such qualitative characteristics as adequacy and fluency, and their proponents talk of 'fully automatic' evaluation, but the fact remains: each of these procedures involves comparison between a translation produced by a computer and one done by a human professional, the latter considered optimal. As for the automated part, Poibeau mentions 'the poverty of the information used for evaluation, which completely eliminates notions such as style, fluency, or even the grammaticality of sentences'. My own experience – I once spent a long time salvaging a text mangled by some software package – also makes me want to side with the Luddites, at least for now.

Another popular evaluation method consists in getting a translator, preferably a novice, to post-edit a text generated by a software tool, noting the time it takes them to complete the task. This way of measuring quality, linked to the human ability to process language, is also highly subjective: whatever their level of experience, there is no telling how long it might take a given individual to polish a given text. The same applies not only to fully automated solutions but to all translation aids. Some translators shun technology, preferring traditional work methods as ultimately more efficient, others rely on available resources, using computer-assisted tools to query stored and tagged texts; some say automatic translation should be avoided like the plague, others believe machine-produced texts are often easier to proofread and post-edit than those translated by humans. One useful aspect of machine translation is that the errors it generates are easier to spot than human mistakes: more often than not they result in gibberish, with neither rhyme nor reason to it. Machines are certainly much broader in their knowledge than humans, but until they achieve a comparable depth, it's too early to concede defeat.

When it comes to computer-assisted interpreting technology – tools combining speech recognition with machine translation to provide real-time assistance, for instance, to suggest terminology, make corrections, note down numbers – it's currently at an even less advanced stage. No wonder many interpreters see these tools as a hindrance. The most frequently heard concern (apart from the fear that robots are coming to take our jobs) is that developers have no idea what interpreters really do. And with a process as deeply wired as live translation, every little tweak takes some getting used to. As often with technology, those who don't have to use it are a lot more enthusiastic about it than those who do. Law practitioners predicted in 2018 that human court interpreters would be obsolete within 'a few years'. When sceptics ran the sentence 'Replacing interpreters with technology will lead to miscarriages of justice' through Google Translate out and back into English, they got ample proof that their scepticism was justified. Bulgarian, for instance, initially produced 'Replacing translators with technology will lead to a spontaneous assassination', although it now has a more plausible ending, 'disputes over justice'. Long-term prospects aside, we can be sure of one thing: the principal aim of using computers in translation of any kind, written or oral, is to provide professionals with some help and to allow end users to decide how much human input is needed for a particular task.

'Translation is not about data-crunching, smooth information flows, circuit topology or input-output,' Derek Schilling, a learned enthusiast of multilingual Oulipian experiments, writes in 'Translation as Total Social Fact and Scholarly Pursuit' (lipogrammatically, the better to defy rules, algorithms and all things programmable). 'It's not just typing a word, chain of words or full paragraph in a backlit dialog box and obtaining instant satisfaction with a touch of a button (voilà!). Such popular notions notwithstanding, translation is a philosophical notion of broad historical import; a practical activity or vocation; and a socio-cultural act.' Indeed, the advent of the machine age has only brought the human nature of translation to the fore. Computers do their job – which includes sifting through terabytes of data to remind us of what we've already said many times over – while we keep doing ours. Until language is reduced to putting more or less right words into a more or less right order; as long as people continue joking and swearing, praising and ironising, uttering and writing things they mean or not; while human communication still involves all of the above and much else, we can safely say, paraphrasing Twain, that the reports of the translator's death have been greatly exaggerated.

Notes on Sources

Since this is a popular book, I thought it unnecessary to provide an academic-style bibliography. The key sources I have consulted in my research are listed below instead.

Introduction

The events leading up to the Hiroshima bombing are summarised in Edward Wiley's report 'The Uncertain Summer of 1945' (https://www.nsa.gov/news-features/declassified-documents/cryptologic-quarterly/assets/files/The_Uncertain_Summer_of_1945.pdf, declassified in 2011) and, in greater detail, in John Toland's *The Rising Sun: The Decline and Fall of the Japanese Empire, 1936–1945* (New York, Random House, 1970).

José Ortega y Gasset's essay 'The Misery and Splendour of Translation', translated by Elizabeth Gamble Miller, appears in *The Translation Studies Reader*, edited by Lawrence Venuti (London and New York, Routledge, 2000, pp. 49–63). Eliot Weinberger's lecture 'Anonymous Sources', printed in Esther Allen and Susan Bernofsky (eds), *In Translation: Translators on Their Work and What It Means* (New York, Columbia University Press, 2013, pp. 17–30), is a rich font of thoughts on translation.

John Dryden's preface to his translation of Ovid's *Epistles* can be found at https://www.gutenberg.org/files/54361/54361-h/54361-h.htm.

1 Shaking the World

William Taubman's Pulitzer-Prize-winning biography, *Khrushchev: The Man and His Era* (New York, W. W. Norton, 2003), is a mine of stories about the Soviet leader's ambiguous relationship with the West. The speeches he delivered during his 1960 trip, collected in *Khrushchev in America* (New York, Crosscurrents Press, 1960), were reported in numerous magazine and newspaper articles; a comprehensive survey of these can be found in Peter Carlson's *K Blows Top* (New York, Public Affairs, 2009). The interpreters' memoirs are available in their Russian editions: Oleg Troyanovsky's *Through the Years and Distances (Cherez gody i rasstoyaniya*, Moscow, Vagrius, 1997) and Viktor Sukhodrev's *My Tongue Is My Friend (Yazyk moĭ – drug moĭ*, Moscow, AST, 1999). The latter title is a play on yet another Russian proverb, 'My tongue is my enemy.'

2 Comic Effects

A video of Presidents Yeltsin and Clinton laughing can be watched online at https://www.youtube.com/watch?v=mv7Moxmq6io. David Bellos' *Is That a Fish in Your Ear? Translation and the Meaning of Everything* (London, Penguin, 2011) is an engaging, informative book written by a translator with several decades of experience. Its chapter on humour and puns is especially delightful. Umberto Eco's reflections on the theory and practice of translation can be found in *Experiences in Translation*, a series of lectures translated by Alastair McEwen (Toronto, University of Toronto Press, 2001), which is full of entertaining examples. Some of the Oulipian exercises can be found in *Translating Constrained Literature*, a special issue of *Modern Language Notes* edited by Camille Bloomfield and Derek Schilling (*MLN*, vol. 131, 4, 2016).

3 The Arts of Flattery

The adventures of Joseph Wolff are recounted in his *Narrative of a Mission to Bokhara in the Years 1843–1845, to Ascertain the Fate of Colonel Stoddart and Captain Conolly* (London, John W. Parker, 1846). Charles Stoddart's correspondence and eyewitness accounts of his imprisonment appear in 'Papers Respecting the Detention of Lieutenant-Colonel Stoddart and Captain A. Conolly at Bokhara' (British government publication, 1839–44). Arthur Conolly talks about his travels in *Journey to the North of India, Overland from England, through Russia, Persia and Affghaunistaun* (London, Richard Bentley, 1838). Alexander Burnes' experiences are described in his bestselling travelogue *Travels into Bokhara* (London, John Murray, 1834).

The last year of Alexander Griboedov's life is the subject of Yury Tynyanov's historical novel *Smert' Vazir-Mukhtara*, first published in 1927–28 and translated from the Russian by Anna Kurkina Rush and Christopher Rush as *The Death of Vazir-Mukhtar* (New York, Columbia University Press, 2021). A fictionalised account of the Great Game is woven into *The Devils' Dance*, a novel by Hamid Ismailov translated from the Uzbek by Donald Rayfield (Sheffield, Tilted Axis, 2018). Detailed studies of the historical events this chapter draws on can be found in Peter Hopkirk's *The Great Game: On Secret Service in High Asia* (London, John Murray, 1990) and in *Tournament of Shadows: The Great Game and the Race for Empire in Asia* by Karl E. Meyer and Shareen Blair Brysac (London, Little, Brown, 2001).

4 Observation and Analysis

The original works of Giovanni Virginio Schiaparelli, *Le opere di G. V. Schiaparelli* (Milano, U. Hoepli, 1930), and his correspondence, *Corrispondenza su Marte di Giovanni Virginio Schiaparelli* (Pisa, Domus Galilaeana, 1963), offer the astronomer's interpretations of the *canali* he discovered. Some of his exchanges with Percival Lowell are collected by Alessandro Manara and Franca Chlistovsky in 'Giovanni Virginio Schiaparelli, Percival Lowell. Scambi epistolari inediti (1896–1910)' (*Nuncius*, vol. XIX, 1, 2004, pp. 251–96). Abbott Lawrence Lowell's *Biography of Percival Lowell* (New York, Macmillan, 1935) gives another perspective on their collaboration. Percival Lowell's books *Mars* (Boston and New York, Houghton, Mifflin, 1895), *Mars and Its Canals* (New York, Macmillan, 1906) and *Mars as the Abode of Life* (New York, Macmillan, 1908) develop the idea of intelligent life on the planet, while Alfred Russel Wallace challenges it in his response to Lowell, *Is Mars Habitable?* (London, Macmillan, 1907). The debate around the canals is summarised in

Dancing on Ropes

William Sheehan's 'Giovanni Schiaparelli: Visions of a Colour Blind Astronomer' (*Journal of the British Astronomical Association*, vol. 107, 1, 1997, pp. 11–15). Elena Canadelli in '"Some Curious Drawings". Mars through Giovanni Schiaparelli's Eyes: Between Science and Fiction' (*Nuncius*, vol. XXIV, 2, 2009, pp. 439–64) provides further details about the astronomer's observations. Other miscellaneous facts can be found in Michael J. Crowe's *The Extraterrestrial Life Debate, 1750–1900* (Cambridge, CUP, 1986) and George Basalla's *Civilised Life in the Universe* (Oxford, OUP, 2006).

Ada Lovelace's translation of Luigi Menabrea's 'Notions sur la machine analytique de M. Charles Babbage', published as 'Sketch of the Analytical Engine Invented by Charles Babbage Esq. By L. F. Menabrea, of Turin, Officer of the Military Engineers, with Notes upon the Memoir by the Translator' (*Taylor's Scientific Memoirs*, vol. 3, 1843, pp. 666–731), speaks for itself. For a broader picture of her life and work, see *Ada: A Life and a Legacy* by Dorothy Stein (Cambridge, MA, MIT Press, 1985), *Ada, The Enchantress of Numbers* by Betty Toole (Moreton-in-Marsh, Strawberry Press, 1992) and *Ada Lovelace: The Making of a Computer Scientist* by Christopher Hollings, Ursula Martin and Adrian Rice (Oxford, Bodleian Library, 2018).

5 Treasures of the Tongue
Most of John Florio's oeuvre is available online, including his celebrated translation of Montaigne, *The Essayes* (https://warburg.sas.ac.uk/pdf/ebh610b2456140A.pdf), and the dictionary *A Worlde of Wordes* (https://archive.org/details/worldeofwordesorooflor). Frances A. Yates' detailed analysis of these and his other works, *John Florio: The Life of an Italian in Shakespeare's England* (Cambridge, CUP, 1934), is complemented by F. O. Matthiessen's *Translation, an Elizabethan Art* (Cambridge, MA, Harvard University Press, 1931). John Dryden's writings are available at https://www.gutenberg.org/files/54361/54361-h/54361-h.htm.

A number of historical examples this chapter draws on, including the story of Adriaan Koerbagh, are taken from *Cultural Translation in Early Modern Europe*, a collection edited by Peter Burke and R. Po-chia Hsia (Cambridge, CUP, 2007). For Umberto Eco's *Experiences in Translation*, see notes to Chapter 2.

6 The Sublime Porte

The letters from Alexander Mavrocordato, chief dragoman to the Imperial Divan, are kept in the SOAS library among the Paget papers. His career is traced by Nestor Camariano in *Alexandre Mavrocordato, le grand drogman: son activite diplomatique, 1673–1709* (Thessaloniki, Institute for Balkan Studies, 1970). Other sources of information about Mavrocordato and his fellow dragomans include: Dimitrie Cantemir, *The History of the Growth and Decay of the Othman Empire*, translated by N. Tindal (London, 1734); Philip Mansel, *Constantinople: City of the World's Desire 1453–1924* (London, John Murray, 1995); Christine M. Philliou, *Biography of an Empire: Governing Ottomans in an Age of Revolution* (Berkeley and London, University of California Press, 2011); and Damien Janos, 'Panaiotis Nicousios and Alexander Mavrocordatos: The Rise of the Phanariots and the Office of Grand Dragoman in the Ottoman Administration in the Second Half of the Seventeenth Century' (*Archivum Ottomanicum*, vol. 23, 2005–06, pp. 177–96).

The Venetian language institutions are the subject of E. Natalie Rothman's study 'Interpreting Dragomans: Boundaries and Crossings in the Early Modern Mediterranean' (*Comparative Studies in Society and History*, vol. 51, 4, 2009, pp. 771–800). The examples of dragomans' own writings are borrowed from Tijana Krstic, 'Of Translation and Empire: Sixteenth-Century Ottoman Interpreters as Renaissance Go-Betweens', in C. Woodhead (ed.), *The Ottoman World* (London, Routledge, 2011, pp. 133–40). Aykut Gürçağlar's 'The Dragoman Who Commissioned His Own Portrait', in Zeynep Inankur et al. (eds), *The Poetics and Politics of Place: Ottoman Istanbul and British Orientalism* (Istanbul, Suna and Inan Kirac Foundation Pera Museum, 2010, pp. 211–17), offers a glimpse of dragomans' attire. The merits and drawbacks of Ottoman interpreters are discussed by Bernard Lewis in *From Babel to Dragomans:*

Interpreting the Middle East (London and New York, OUP, 2004) and
by Alexander H. de Groot in 'Dragomans' Careers: Change of Status
in Some Families Connected with the British and Dutch Embassies in
Istanbul 1785–1829', in Alastair Hamilton, Alexander de Groot and
Maurits van den Boogert (eds), *Friends and Rivals in the East: Studies
in Anglo-Dutch Relations in the Levant from the Seventeenth to the
Early Nineteenth Century* (Leiden, Brill, 2000, pp. 223–46).

7 Infidelities
The transcripts of the parliamentary hearing this chapter is based
on appear in *The Whole Proceedings on the Trial of Her Majesty,
Caroline Amelia Elizabeth, Queen of England, for 'Adulterous Inter-
course' with Bartolomeo Bergami: With Notes and Comments* and
*The Important and Eventful Trial of Queen Caroline, Consort of
George IV for 'Adulterous Intercourse' with Bartolomeo Bergami*
(London, John Fairburn, 1820). There is more to be found in *Satiri-
cal Songs, and Miscellaneous Papers, Connected with the Trial of
Queen Caroline* (London, G. Smeeton, 1820). A modern perspective
is given by Roger Fulford in *The Trial of Queen Caroline* (London,
B. T. Batsford, 1967). Ruth Morris analyses the trial from the lin-
guistic point of view in 'The Gum Syndrome: Predicaments in Court
Interpreting' (*Forensic Linguistics: The International Journal of
Speech, Language and the Law*, vol. 6, 2, 1999, pp. 1–29).

David Bellos' observation is from *Is That a Fish in Your Ear?* (see
notes to Chapter 2). Brian Friel's play *Translations* was first published
by Faber and Faber in 1981.

8 Precision Was Not a Strong Point of Hitler's
The memoirs that provide the bulk of this chapter's historical mate-
rial are: Eugen Dollmann, *The Interpreter: Memoirs of Doktor
Eugen Dollmann*, translated by J. Maxwell Brownjohn (London,
Hutchinson, 1967); Paul Schmidt, *Hitler's Interpreter*, translated by
Alan Sutton (Stroud, The History Press, 2016); Arthur Herbert Birse,
Memoirs of an Interpreter (London, Joseph, 1967); and Charles
Bohlen, *Witness to History: 1929–1969* (New York, W. W. Norton,

1973). A scholarly study of translating for dictators, complete with the Hendaye episode, can be found in Jesús Baigorri-Jalón's *From Paris to Nuremberg: The Birth of Conference Interpreting*, translated by Holly Mikkelson and Barry Slaughter Olsen (Amsterdam, Benjamins Translation Library, 2014). The first part of Hannah Arendt's 'Eichmann in Jerusalem' appeared in the *New Yorker* on 8 February 1963.

9 Little Nothing
Richard Sonnenfeldt's memoir, *Witness to Nuremberg: The Many Lives of the Man Who Translated at the Nazi War Trials* (New York, Arcade, 2006), is full of illuminating stories. The testimonies of the interpreters Alfred Steer and Peter Uiberall, among others, can be found in *Eyewitnesses at Nuremberg*, edited by Hilary Gaskin (London, Arms and Armour, 1990). Their colleague Siegfried Ramler recollects the past in 'Origins and Challenges of Simultaneous Interpretation: The Nuremberg Trial Experience', published in Deanna L. Hammond (ed.), *Languages at Crossroads* (Medford, NJ, Learned Information, 1988, pp. 437–40). A broader picture of the first Nuremberg trial, including the introduction of the simultaneous interpretation system, is painted by Ann and John Tusa in *The Nuremberg Trial* (London, Macmillan, 1983). Francesca Gaiba's *The Origins of Simultaneous Interpretation: The Nuremberg Trial* (Ottawa, University of Ottawa Press, 1998) covers the topic in great detail.

10 The Last Two Dragomans
Andrew Ryan's memoir, *The Last of the Dragomans* (London, G. Bles, 1951), edited by Reader Bullard, was published after the author's death in 1949. *The Last Dragoman: Swedish Orientalist Johannes Kolmodin as Scholar, Activist and Diplomat*, edited by Elizabeth Ozdalga (London, I. B. Tauris, 2005), documents the activities of the Swedish legation in Constantinople. The emergence of the Young Turks and the resulting government crisis are described in William Mitchell Ramsay's *The Revolution in Constantinople and*

Turkey (London, Hodder and Stoughton, 1909). Charles Doughty-Wylie's dispatches from Adana are kept in the Foreign Office archives (consular reports 48 and 83, 1909). Peter Balakian in *The Burning Tigris: The Armenian Genocide and America's Response* (New York, HarperCollins, 2003) analyses the Ottoman massacres in depth. The prewar failures of British diplomacy in Turkey are touched upon in Philip Mansel's *Constantinople* (see notes to Chapter 6).

11 As Oriental as Possible

Rubaiyat of Omar Khayyam, edited by Christopher Decker (Charlottesville, VA, University of Virginia Press, 2008), is one of many critical editions of Edward Fitzgerald's magnum opus. The circumstances in which it was created are touched upon in *Letters of Edward FitzGerald* (London, Macmillan, 1901) and described more fully in A. C. Benson's *English Men of Letters: Edward FitzGerald* (London, Macmillan, 1905) and Thomas Wright's *The Life of Edward FitzGerald* (London, Grant Richards, 1904).

Richard Burton's *Nights* can be found online at http://www.burtoniana.org/, along with a number of biographical sources, including *The Life of Sir Richard Burton* by Thomas Wright (London, Everett, 1906). Robert Irwin's *The Arabian Nights: A Companion* (London, Allen Lane, 1994) provides a commentary on different translations of the tales. Colette Colligan discusses the early reception of Burton's work in '"Esoteric Pornography": Sir Richard Burton's *Arabian Nights* and the Origins of Pornography' (*Victorian Review*, vol. 28, 2, 2002, pp. 31–64). The first instalment of Yasmine Seale's translation of the *Nights* is *Aladdin* (New York, Liveright, 2018).

Poetry translations are discussed in great depth by J. M. Cohen in *English Translators and Translations* (London, British Council, 1962) and by Matthew Reynolds in *The Poetry of Translation: From Chaucer and Petrarch to Homer and Logue* (Oxford, OUP, 2011). Octavio Paz's essay 'Translation: Literature and Letters', translated by Irene del Corral, appears in Rainer Schulte, John Biguenet (eds), *Theories of Translation: An Anthology of Essays from Dryden to Derrida* (Chicago, University of Chicago Press, 1992, pp. 152–62).

Notes on Sources

For Eliot Weinberger's 'Anonymous Sources' and John Dryden's preface to Ovid's *Epistles*, see notes to Introduction. Emily Wilson reflects on translation in a letter to the *LRB* (vol. 40, 9, 2018).

12 Fifty Per Cent of Borges

Norman Thomas di Giovanni's memories of Borges are the subject of his books *The Lesson of the Master: On Borges and His Work* (London, Continuum, 2003) and *Georgie and Elsa: Jorge Luis Borges and His Wife: The Untold Story* (London, Friday Project, 2014). Their joint translations, sadly, are now mostly out of print: *The Aleph and Other Stories 1933–1969* (Boston, MA, Dutton, 1979), *Doctor Brodie's Report* (London and New York, Penguin, 1992) and *The Book of Imaginary Beings* (New York, Vintage, 2002). Lawrence Venuti considers different approaches to literary translation in *The Translator's Invisibility: A History of Translation* (London and New York, Routledge, 1995), citing numerous examples. For Eliot Weinberger's 'Anonymous Sources', see notes to Introduction.

13 Word-worship

St Jerome's writings are the subject of several essays included in *Translation – Theory and Practice: A Historical Reader*, edited by Daniel Weissbort and Astradur Eysteinsson (Oxford, OUP, 2006). Anne Enright exposes Jerome's views on women in her essay 'The Genesis of Blame' (*LRB*, vol. 40, 5, 2018). Jane Barr's balanced analysis, 'The Vulgate Genesis and St. Jerome's Attitudes to Women', is included in Julia Bolton Holloway, Joan Bechtold and Constance S. Wright (eds), *Equally in God's Image: Women in the Middle Ages* (New York, Peter Lang, 1990, pp. 122–28).

Eugene A. Nida recounts his experience as a Bible translation consultant in *Fascinated by Languages* (Amsterdam and Philadelphia, John Benjamins, 2003). Matteo Ricci's approach to translation is summarised by R. Po-chia Hsia in 'The Catholic Mission and Translations in China, 1583–1700', appearing in *Cultural Translation in Early Modern Europe* (see notes to Chapter 5; pp. 39–51). The anecdote about Adriaan Koerbagh is taken from the same collection.

Further facts about Ricci can be found in Jonathan D. Spence's *The Memory Palace of Matteo Ricci* (London and Boston, Faber and Faber, 1985) and Mary Laven's *Mission to China: Matteo Ricci and the Jesuit Encounter with the East* (London, Faber and Faber, 2011).

14 Journalation
Most of this chapter's material is taken from various periodicals and private communications. The opening story is told in Maria Lúcia Pallares-Burke's '*The Spectator*, or the Metamorphoses of the Periodical: A Study in Cultural Translation' (in *Cultural Translation in Early Modern Europe*; see notes to Chapter 5; pp. 142–60). The Iran-related examples are cited by Robert Holland in 'News Translation', included in C. Millán-Varela and F. Bartrina (eds), *The Routledge Handbook of Translation Studies* (London, Routledge, 2013, pp. 332–46). Roberto A. Valdeón's 'Fifteen Years of Journalistic Translation Research and More' (*Perspectives: Studies in Translatology*, vol. 23, 4, 2015, pp. 634–62) contains a historical overview of news in translation. Andrew Bromfield's version of Victor Pelevin's novel, published in the UK as *Babylon* (London, Faber and Faber, 2001), serves as a practical guide to translating puns.

15 Dealing with the Natives
The Dilessi case is analysed in detail in Romilly Jenkins' *The Dilessi Murders* (Plymouth, Longmans, 1961). *Notes on the Recent Murders by Brigands in Greece* by Ioannes Gennadius (London, Cartwright, 1870) offers a contemporary account of the events told from a Greek perspective. Charles Tuckerman's *Brigandage in Greece*, reprinted from *Papers Related to the Foreign Relations of the United States* (London, 1871), is another commentary written shortly after the murders. Britain's reaction to the case and the liberties taken by Tuckerman's Greek translator are examined by Rodanthi Tzanelli in 'Unclaimed Colonies: Anglo–Greek Identities through the Prism of the Dilessi/Marathon Murders (1870)' (*Journal of Historical Sociology*, vol. 15, 2, 2002, 169–91).

The story of Solomon Negima is the focus of Chapter 6 of

Archaeologists, Tourists, Interpreters: Exploring Egypt and the Near East in the Late 19th – Early 20th Centuries by Rachel Mairs and Maya Muratov (London, Bloomsbury, 2015).

16 Rectify the Names

A. Henry Savage Landor collected his reports on the Boxer Rebellion in *China and the Allies* (New York, Charles Scribner's Sons, 1901). His Russian colleague Dmitry Yanchevetsky did the same in *U sten nedvizhnago Kitaya*, first published in 1903 and forthcoming in my translation as *By Never-Changing Cathay's Walls* (Amherst, MA, Amherst College Press). Earlier relations between China and the West are covered by William Gascoyne-Cecil in *Changing China* (New York, D. Appleton, 1912). Paul A. Cohen in *China and Christianity: The Missionary Movement and the Growth of Chinese Antiforeignism, 1860–1870* (Cambridge, MA, Harvard University Press, 1963) provides a scholarly view of the 1860 Sino-French Convention. *The Peking Gazette: A Reader in Nineteenth-Century Chinese History*, compiled by Lane J. Harris (Leiden and Boston, Brill, 2018), is a rich source of news stories. Joseph Estherick's *The Origins of the Boxer Uprising* (Berkeley and LA, CA, University of California Press, 1987) offers a detailed analysis of China's domestic affairs and interactions with the outside world in the late nineteenth – early twentieth century. Other academic studies on the topic include David J. Silbey's *The Boxer Rebellion and the Great Game in China: A History* (New York, Farrar, Straus and Giroux, 2013) and Peter Harrington's *Peking 1900: The Boxer Rebellion* (Oxford, Osprey, 2013).

Some of the present-day stories were privately communicated by former military linguistic contractors. The rest comes from media reportage and from *The Interpreters* (2018), a documentary directed by Andres Caballero and Sofian Khan, aired on the American channel PBS in 2019.

17 The Obligation of the Competent Authorities

This chapter is mainly based on a piece I wrote for the *LRB* in February 2017 (https://www.lrb.co.uk/blog/2017/february/shambles-in-court).

The other cases I cite have been reported in the British and North American media. Jonathan Downie talks of his professional experience in *Being a Successful Interpreter* (London, Routledge, 2016); some of his articles can be found at https://lifeinlincs.wordpress.com/author/integritylanguages. The English text of the 2018 Brexit white paper 'The Future Relationship between the United Kingdom and the European Union' is available at www.gov.uk/government/publications. Jean-Claude Juncker's commentary on his use of the word *nébuleux* can be viewed at https://www.bbc.co.uk/news/av/uk-politics-46572863/juncker-explains-nebulous-remark. Robert Walkden's letter (*LRB*, vol. 40, 22, 2018) deserves to be read in full.

18 Alogical Elements
The three versions of Mark Twain's story appear in *The Jumping Frog: In English, Then in French, Then Clawed Back into a Civilized Language Once More by Patient, Unremunerated Toil* (Harvard, Harper & Brothers, 1903). Most of the historical and technical information summarised in this chapter comes from Thierry Poibeau's very readable *Machine Translation* (Cambridge, MA and London, MIT Press, 2017). *Deep Learning* by Ian Goodfellow, Yoshua Bengio and Aaron Courville (Cambridge, MA, MIT Press, 2016) offers a comprehensive survey of AI. Frédéric Kaplan's blog can be accessed at https://fkaplan.wordpress.com, and Mark Liberman's at https://languagelog.ldc.upenn.edu/nll. Derek Schilling's lipogram 'Translation as Total Social Fact and Scholarly Pursuit' appears in *Translating Constrained Literature* (see notes to Chapter 2; pp. 841–45).

Acknowledgements

This book would never have existed without the encouragement and help of my colleagues and friends who took an interest in it. I was fortunate to have many brilliant translators, writers, editors and readers by my side, and my sincere gratitude goes to all of them. Ed Lake, who first thought of the project and persuaded me that I could do it, was a great editor to work with. The text was much improved by Hugh Davis' judicious copy-editing. My writing was propelled along by comments and suggestions made by those who read early drafts: Chloe Aridjis, Houman Barekat, Boris Dralyuk, Dennis Duncan, Bryn Geffert, Mark Polizzotti, Lorna Scott Fox, Yasmine Seale, Nicholas Spice, Andrew Stevens and Tom Wright. Thomas Jones published what was to become one of the chapters in the *London Review of Books*, having expertly edited the piece. Much of the book was written in libraries and archives, so let me extend my thanks to the invariably helpful staff of the British Library and the SOAS Library, whose work was crucial to the success of mine. I am also indebted to specialists who facilitated my research by pointing me in the direction of relevant sources: Andres Caballero, Sergei Chernov, Hamid Ismailov, Homa Katouzian, Noboru Koyama, So Mayer, Varya Nuttall and Donald Rayfield. Finally, I was fortunate to communicate with some of my protagonists, who proved fascinating interviewees, and I am grateful to these people – Norman Thomas di Giovanni, Jonathan Downie, Atar Hadari, Ivan Melkumjan, Stephen Pearl, Thierry Poibeau, Raz Mohammad Popal, Victor Prokofiev, Hiromi Sakai and Edna Weale – for their time and their stories.

Index

A

Ackroyd, Peter 169–70
Adana 123
Addison, Joseph 172, 173
The Adolescent (Dostoevsky)
 169
advertising 181–3
Afanasenko, Peter 29
Afghanistan 37, 38, 204–6
Ahmadinejad, Mahmoud
 177–8
Aitken, Captain Ed 205
Akalovsky, Alex 18
al-Jamaa al-Islamiya 175–6
al-Zawahiri, Ayman 175
Aladdin 140
Alberti, Girolamo 84–5
The Aleph and Other Stories
 (Borges) 148
Alexander the Great 80–1, 99
Alice's Adventures in
 Wonderland (Carroll) 149
Alone Through Syria (Miller)
 188
American Revolution 180
Analytical Engine 58–61, 63,
 233

Anemoyannis, Alexander
 184–6, 188
Anna Karenina (Tolstoy) 140–1
'Anonymous Sources'
 (Weinberger) 5, 133, 134–6,
 155
Antoniadi, Eugène Michel 55–6
The Arabian Nights 137–42
Arendt, Hannah 107
Aristarchi, Stavrachi 84
At Freddie's (Fitzgerald) 32
Atatürk, Mustafa Kemal 125,
 127
Automatic Language
 Processing Advisory
 Committee 223
Azerbaijan 46

B

Babbage, Charles 57–8, 59–61,
 63, 233
Babylon (Pelevin) 181–2
The Bacchae (Euripides) 142
back-translation 220–2
Bar-Hillel, Yehoshua 223, 231
Barnard, Edward Emerson 53
Barr, Jane 162

BBC Radio 4 177–8
BBC World Service 176–7
Begum, Iqbal 208–9
Beijing (Pekin) 195–7, 201–2
Bellos, David 30, 95
Bengio, Yoshua 229
Benson, A. C. 133
Bergami, Bartolomeo 87–90
Berlusconi, Silvio 22–6
Bible 158–64, 165–9, 170, 171, 227
Binet, Laurent 31–2
Bird, Kai 19
Birkett, Norman 114
Birse, Arthur 102, 103–4, 105, 106
Blackadder 93
blackmail 189
Bohlen, Charles 102–3, 104, 105
Bokhara 33–7, 40–1, 44–5
Bolsonaro, Jair 2
The Book of Imaginary Beings (Borges) 148
book titles 180–1
Borges, Elsa 148, 151–2
Borges, Jorge Luis 140, 142, 145–57
'Borges and Myself' (Borges) 154–5, 156
Boxer Rebellion 193–9, 201–4
Brexit 216–17
Britain
    Afghan interpreters 204–6
    Brexit 216–17

Great Game 33–45
and Greece 188–9
and Ottoman empire 120, 121–5
public service translation 208–12, 215–18
Bromfield, Andrew 181–2
Brougham, Henry 88, 89, 90–1
Bruno, Giordano 65
Brysac, Shareen Blair 34
Burgess, Anthony 43
Burgess, Edward 45
Burmese language 231–2
Burnes, Lieutenant Alexander 40–2
Burton, Richard 137–42
By Never-Changing Cathay's Walls (Yanchevetsky) 193–4, 195–6, 197–9, 201, 203, 204
Byron, Lord 59, 63

C
Camariano, Nestor 77, 78
Cambini, Andrea 71
Canada 213, 226
Cantemir, Dimitrie 77, 78, 79
Capita 210
Caroline, Queen 87–92, 94–5, 96
Carroll, Lewis 149
Castro, Fidel 19
Cerulli, Vincenzo 55–6
Chamberlain, Neville 98, 99, 107
Chandler, Robert 72

Index

China
  Boxer Rebellion 193–9,
    201–4
  Christianity 164–6
  Second Opium War 199–201
China and the Allies (Savage
  Landor) 193–4, 195, 196,
  197, 201–2, 203–4
Chinese language 194, 199, 201
chuchotage 111
Churchill, Winston 102, 104,
  105
Cicero 81
Cicogna, Doge Pasquale 84
Cixi, Empress-Dowager 195
Clinton, Bill 29–30
CNN 177–8
Cohen, Benedetto 88, 89, 90
Cohen, J. M. 131
Cohen, Paul A. 200
Cold War 8–21
Colligan, Colette 138
comprehension evaluation
  221–2
Confucius 198
Conolly, Captain Arthur 33,
  34, 36, 37–8
consecutive interpreting 111
court and police interpreting
  Britain 208–12
  cultural glossing 92
  discourse markers 116–17
  forms of address 46–7
  Italy 213
  legalese 3, 68
  the medium and the message
    92–3
  mistakes 190–1
  non-verbal messages 94
  Nuremberg trials 109–19
  oath 92
  Ottoman empire 121–2
  quality and costs 209–14, 218
  Queen Caroline's trial 87–92,
    94–5, 96
  swearing 93
  technology 234–5
  trust 190
Courville, Aaron 229
Cowell, Edward 131, 132
Cuban missile crisis 19–21
Curzon, Lord 128

D
D'Ablancourt, Nicholas 137
Daladier, Édouard 98
Dalrymple, Lord 187
Dante 63
De Gaulle, President 175
de Groot, Alexander 83–4
De Morgan, Augustus 59
de Nores, Giacomo 84–5
De senectute (Cicero) 81
Decottignies, Thierry 181
deep learning 226, 228
Deep Learning (Goodfellow,
  Bengio and Courville) 229
DeepL 229
Defoe, Daniel 34
Delacroix, Jacques-Vincent 173

Delamarre, Père 200
Denmark 11, 213
di Giovanni, Norman Thomas
    145–57
dialects 72
dictators 97–108
dictionaries 65–7, 165
Difference Engine 63
Dilessi murders 184–6, 188
disarmament 19
discourse markers 116–17
Dixon, George 12
Doctor Brodie's Report
    (Borges) 148
Dollmann, Eugen 97–8,
    99–102, 104–5
domestication 129, 135–7,
    170–1
Donovan, General William
    'Wild Bill' 109
Dostert, Colonel Léon 112
Dostoevsky, Fyodor 169
Doughty-Wylie, Major Charles
    123
Downie, Jonathan 215–16, 218
dragomans 74–86, 120–30
    Alberti 84–5
    de Nores 84–5
    Kolmodin 125–9
    Mahmud 80–1
    Mavrocordato, A. 75–8, 79,
        86
    Murad 81
    Phanariots and Levantines
        75–80, 83–4

Ryan 120–5, 126, 128–30
    as tourist guides 184–6,
        187–8, 192
    Yunus 80
Dryden, John 6–7, 69, 70,
    142–3

E
Eco, Umberto 31, 71, 72–3
Eichmann, Adolf 107
Einstein, Albert 57
Electrolux 182–3
Eliot, T. S. 70
Elogio de la sombra (Borges)
    147–8
English language
    as intermediary language
        229–30
    King James Bible 167–9
    vocabulary 66
Enright, Anne 161–2
The Essayes (Montaigne) 68–71
Estherick, Joseph 202, 204
*Et ce sont les chats qui
    tombèrent* (McCarthy) 181
Eugene Onegin (Pushkin) 141
Euripides 142
Europarl 229
European Convention on
    Human Rights 210, 215
European Parliament 213
European Union
    Brexit 216–17
    document translation 226,
        229

Index

'Everything and Nothing'
  (Borges) 148–9
Experiences in Translation
  (Eco) 31, 71, 72–3
extending a metaphor 10–11,
  230
*Extension du domaine de la
  lutte* (Houellebecq) 181
Eyewitnesses at Nuremberg
  (Gaskin) 113

F
Facebook 231–2
false friends 50, 175
Fath Ali Shah 42–3, 44
Ferrante, Elena 155–6
Ferriol, Charles de 78
Filene–Finlay system 112
First World War 123–4
Firste Fruites (Florio) 64
Firth, John Rupert 225
Fitzgerald, Edward 131–4, 135
Fitzgerald, Penelope 32
Flammarion, Camille 49, 51, 56
Florio, John 64–6, 68–71
Flournoy, Théodore 49–50
Foot, Michael 180
foreignisation 129, 135–7,
  170–1
Foucault's Pendulum (Eco) 31,
  72
France
  jeunes de langues 120
  and NATO 175
  Opium Wars 199–201

Francis, Pope 168
Franco, Francisco 107–8
Friel, Brian 95–6
Frigyes, Karinthy 31

G
Gaiba, Francesca 114
Galland, Antoine 139–40
Gascoyne-Cecil, William 199–
  200
Gaskin, Hilary 113
Generation 'Π' (Pelevin) 181–2
'The Genesis of Blame'
  (Enright) 161–2
Gennadius, Ioannes 185–6
George IV 87–8, 91–2
Georgie and Elsa (di Giovanni)
  151–2
German language
  ja 116–17
  'shithole countries'
    translation 2
  word order 116
Germany 213
  Nuremberg trials 109–19
Goldstein, Ann 156
Goodfellow, Ian 229
Google 228
Google Translate 158, 230, 232
Göring, Hermann 110, 113,
  114–15, 117
Gottsched, Louise 172
Great Game 33–45
The Great Game (Hopkirk) 34,
  40

Greece 184–6, 188–9
Green, Nathaniel 53
Grey, Lord 95
Griboedov, Alexander 42–4
Gros, Baron 200–1
*Guide for One's Turning
    Towards God* (Murad Bey)
    81

H
Hadari, Atar 169
Hammond, Paul 181
Handke, Peter 181
Hawskmoor (Ackroyd) 169–70
Hayter, George 95
Hayter, William 12–13
headlines 180
Heidegger, Martin 71
Henry, O. 134
Herder, Johann Gottfried
    136–7
Hess, Rudolf 111
Historiae Philippicae
    (Pompeius Trogus) 80
History of Hungary (Mahmud
    Bey) 80–1
Hitler, Adolf 97, 98–101, 102,
    107–8
Holland, Robert 177, 178–9
Hollings, Christopher 62
Home Office 213
Homo Zapiens (Pelevin) 181–2
Hopkirk, Peter 34, 40
Houellebecq, Michel 181
Hsia, R. Po-chia 165

Hull, Cordell 104
humour 22–7, 29–32
    Bellos 30
    Berlusconi 22–6
    Eco 31
    Khrushchev 11, 15, 16
    machine translation 232
    Yeltsin and Clinton 29–30
Humphrey, Hubert 11
Hungarian language
    leiterjakab 176
    Winnie the Pooh 30–1, 232

I
idioms 10–11, 31–2
    Khrushchev 8–10, 13–14,
        16–17
    machine translation 232
    Nixon 8–9
    see also proverbs
impartiality 92, 178–9
In Praise of Darkness (Borges)
    148
insourcing 218
interpreting
    Afghanistan and Iraq 204–7
    basic principles 92–4
    computer-assisted 234–5
    dictators 97–108
    errors 190–1
    future of profession 129
    wars 193–207
    see also court and police
        interpreting; simultaneous
        interpreting

Index

Iran 2–3, 177–8
Iraq 206
Ireland 95–6, 189
Irwin, Robert 138
Is That a Fish in Your Ear?
    (Bellos) 30, 95
Ismailov, Hamid 176–7
Italian language
    Florio 64–6
    Martian *canali* 48–56
    new realism 71
    Ottoman empire 74–5
Italy 22–7, 213

J

Jackson, Robert H. 117
Japan 1–2, 196, 204
Jasim, Imad Abbas 206
Jelinek, Frederick 227
Jenkins, Romilly 184, 185,
    186
Jerome, St 159–63, 170
jokes *see* humour
journalators 174
journalism 172–80
The Jumping Frog (Twain)
    220–1, 232
Juncker, Jean-Claude 217

K

Kabul 41–2
Kaplan, Frédéric 230
Karsten, Charles 91
Kelly, L. G. 160
Kennedy, John F. 17, 20

Khayyam, Omar 131–4, 135,
    137
Khiva 38–40
Khomeini, Ayatollah 178
Khrushchev, Nikita 8–10,
    11–21
King James Bible 167–9
Klebnikov, George 112
Kodama, María 154
Koerbagh, Adriaan 67, 167
Kolmanter, Georg William 90
Kolmodin, Johannes 125–9
Kress, Barbara 90–1
Kuzma's mother 10

L

Lady Chatterley's Lover
    (Lawrence) 142
Lama, Colonel Kumar 211
Landau, Moshe 107
language of thought 4, 230
LanguageLine Solutions 212
The Last Dragoman (Ozdalga)
    125–9
Lausanne, Conference of 128,
    130
Lawrence, D. H. 142
legal interpreting *see* court and
    police interpreting
legalese 3, 68
The Leisure of Philotheus
    (Mavrocordato, N.) 79–80
The Lesson of the Master (di
    Giovanni) 145–7, 148–9, 151,
    153, 155

Levantines 75, 83
Lewis, Bernard 75, 83
Leys, Simon 198
Li Hungchang 199
Lianke, Yan 208
Liberman, Mark 232
Life: A User's Manual (Perec) 30
literary translation
    The Arabian Nights 137–42
    book titles 180–1
    Borges and di Giovanni
        145–57
    dialects 72
    domestication and
        foreignisation 135–7
    Montaigne and Florio 68–71
    Pelevin and Bromfield 181–2
    poetry 131–5, 142–4
    quality 208
    Rubaiyat 131–4, 135
Liu 197–8, 199
localisation 174, 175, 178,
    181–3
Lockyer, J. Norman 53
Lolita (Nabokov) 171
Lovelace, Ada 58–63, 233
Lowell, Abbot Lawrence 55
Lowell, Percival 49, 54–5
Lowell, Robert 143

M
McCarthy, Tom 181
McCloy, John J. 19
machine translation
    and Bible 158–9

challenges of 230–2
computer-assisted tools 219
developments 222–9
evaluation of 221–2, 233–4
interpreting 234–5
pivot languages 229–30
Macron, Emmanuel 50
Mahmud Bey 80–1
Mairs, Rachel 187
Majocchi, Theodore 88–9, 91
Manheim, Ralph 181
Mansel, Philip 74, 79, 86
Mardrus, J. C. 142
Mars 48–56
Martin, Ursula 62
Mattarella, Sergio 94
Matthiessen, F. O. 70
Mavrocordato, Alexander
    75–8, 79, 86
Mavrocordato, Nicholas 79–80,
    86
Maxwell Fyfe, David 117–18
May, Theresa 180, 217
Melkumjan, Ivan 22–9
Menabrea, Luigi Federico 57–8,
    59–60, 233
mentalese 4, 230
The Merchant of Venice
    (Shakespeare) 122
Mèritens, Baron de 200
Meyer, Karl E. 34
military interpreters 204–7
Miller, Ellen E. 188
Ministry of Justice (MoJ)
    210–11

Index

'The Misery and Splendour of
Translation' (Ortega y
Gasset) 4
missionaries 162–6, 167–8, 200,
202
Monroe, Marilyn 15
Montaigne, Michel de 68–71
Mounin, Georges 134
Muncaster, Lord 184, 186
Munich Conference 97–8
Munthe, Mr 203
Murad II, Sultan 81
Murad III, Sultan 84
Murad Bey 81
Muratov, Maya 187
Muravyov, Captain Nikolay
38–40
Mussolini, Benito 97, 98, 99,
101, 102
Myanmar 231–2

N

Nabokov, Vladimir 72, 140–1,
149, 170–1
Nadar 176
Nasrullah, Emir of Bokhara
33, 35, 36–7, 44–5
National Register of Public
Service Interpreters 209
natural language processing
222–6, 228
Negima, Solomon 187–8
neural networks 225–6, 228
New Yorker 146, 147, 148, 151
newspapers see periodicals

Nicholas I, Tsar of Russia 44
Nida, Eugene A. 163–4, 167–8,
169
Nikousios, Panagiotis 76
Nixon, Richard 8–10, 14
Northern Ireland 182
Nuremberg trials 101, 109–19

O

Obama, Barack 24–5
Ohlendorf, Otto 118
Opium Wars 199–201
Orange 182
The Origins of Simultaneous
Interpretation (Gaiba) 114
Ortega y Gasset, José 4
Ottoman empire 74–86, 120–30
Oulipo 30
outsourcing 209–12, 218
Ozdalga, Elizabeth 126

P

Paget, William 77–8
Pascoli, Giovanni 99
Pavlov, Vladimir 102, 104,
105–6
Payne, John 137–8
Paz, Octavio 134–5
Pearl, Stephen 73
Pekin (Beijing) 195–7, 201–2
Pelevin, Victor 181–2
Perec, Georges 30
periodicals 172–6, 180
Persia 42–4
Phanariots 75–80, 83–4

Philo of Alexandria 159
'Pierre Menard, Author of *Don Quixote*' (Borges) 150–1
pivot languages 229–30
Plana, Giovanni 58
poetry 131–5, 142–4
Poibeau, Thierry 227–8, 229, 231, 233
Poirot, Louis de 165
polysemy 50, 230–1
Pompeius Trogus 80
Popal, Raz Mohammed 206
Porter, James 83
Potsdam Proclamation 1–2
Pottinger, Lieutenant Eldred 38
proverbs
  Florio 65
  see also idioms
Pushkin, Alexander 141, 171, 193
Putin, Vladimir 25–6
Pygmalion 228

R
Raja, Anita 156
Raleigh, Sir Walter 65
Ramler, Siegfried 114
Red T 207
Remainder (McCarthy) 181
Ricci, Matteo 164, 165–6
Rice, Adrian 62
Richard, Timothy 202
Robinson Crusoe (Defoe) 34
Rohingya Muslims 231–2
Roosevelt, Franklin D. 102

Rossetti, Dante Gabriel 131
Rothman, E. Natalie 75, 84–5
Rubaiyat (Khayyam) 131–4, 135, 137
Russia
  anti-government protests 179–80
  Great Game 34–5, 36, 38–40, 42–4
  see also USSR
Russian language
  dyrka and *otverstie* 57
  karantin and *blokada* 20
  Kuzma's mother 10
  loanwords 171
  otkrestit'sya 176
  predstavlyat' 179–80
  sputnik 8
  toska 72
  vypivshi 190–1
Ryan, Andrew 121–5, 128–30

S
Sakai, Hiromi 216
Savage Landor, A Henry 193–4, 195, 196, 197, 201–2, 203–4
Schacht, Hjalmar 110, 118
Schiaparelli, Giovanni Virginio 48–56
Schilling, Derek 30, 235
Schleiermacher, Friedrich 136
Schmidt, Paul 98–9, 100, 101–2, 105, 107
Seale, Yasmine 140
Second Frutes (Florio) 65

Index

Second World War
  Nuremberg trials 101, 109–19
  Potsdam Proclamation 1–2
  Tehran Conference 102–3
  Yalta Conference 104–5
  see also Hitler, Adolf;
    Mussolini, Benito
Selassie, Emperor Haile 128
Septuagint 159–63, 166
Serrano Súñer, Ramón 107–8
Shakespeare, William 70–1, 122
Shannon, Claude 222
Shapiro, Norman 149
Sheehan, William 49–50, 56
'shithole countries' 2
Shute, John 71
simultaneous interpreting
  111–19
Slugg, J. T. 48–9
Sonnenfeldt, Richard 109–11,
  113
A Sorrow Beyond Dreams
  (Handke) 181
Spain 107–8, 213
Spectator 172–3
Speer, Albert 110, 118
Spineto, Marquis de 88, 89, 90,
  95, 96
Stalin, Joseph 102–3, 104, 105,
  106
Starnone, Domenico 156
Steele, Richard 172, 173
Steer, Alfred 112, 113
Stein, Dorothy 62
Stevenson, Robert Louis 156

Stoddart, Colonel Charles 33,
  34, 36–7
Sugiyama, Akira 196
Sukhodrev, Viktor 10, 12, 13,
  16–17, 18–19
Süleyman, Sultan 80–1
summits 102–6
Susskind, David 16–17
Suzuki, Kantaro 1
swear words 93, 232

T
Taiwan 2
Taubman, William 8–9, 12
TED talks 227
Teffi 171
Tehran 42–4
Tehran Conference 102–3
The Tempest (Shakespeare)
  70–1
thebigword 210–12
Theroux, Paul 155
Thomas, Joseph Llewellyn 188
The Thousand and One Nights
  140
Tientsin (Tianjin) 195–6,
  203–4
Tiepolo, Antonio 82
Times 14, 124, 180
Tindal, N. 77
Today (BBC Radio 4) 177–8
Togo, Shigenori 1
Tolstoy, Leo 140–1
Toole, Betty 62
tourist guides 184–8

Tournament of Shadows
  (Meyer and Brysac) 34
transediting 174
translation
  domestication and
    foreignisation 129, 135–7,
    170–1
  as general notion 235–6
  quality and costs 208–14,
    218–19
  as trade 5
  and trust 190–2
  as utopian exercise 4–5
  see also interpreting; literary
    translation; machine
    translation
Translations (Friel) 95–6
'Translator' (Teffi) 171
The Translator's Invisibility
  (Venuti) 149
The Trial of Queen Caroline
  (Hayter) 95
Troyanovsky, Oleg 12, 17
Trump, Donald 2, 94, 180
trust 184–6, 190–2
Trypani, C. (Athanasios
  Trypanis) 123
Tuckerman, Charles 188–9
Turkey 122–30
Twain, Mark 220–1, 232, 236
Tzanelli, Rodanthi 189

U
Uiberall, Peter 115–17, 118–19
United Kingdom *see* Britain

United Nations (UN) 18, 19,
  73, 85, 177, 178, 226, 231
United States (US)
  Afghan and Iraqi interpreters
    206
  Cold War 8–21
  public service translation
    212, 214
USSR
  Cold War 8–21
  Second World War 102–6
  see also Russia

V
Venice 75, 80, 82, 84, 120
Venuti, Lawrence 149
Vittorini, Elio 71
Voltaire 173
'The Vulgate Genesis and St.
  Jerome's Attitudes to
  Women' (Barr) 162

W
Walkden, Robert 218–19
Wallenberg, Gustaf 126–7
war 207
  Afghanistan and Iraq 204–7
  Boxer Rebellion 193–9, 201–4
The War of the Worlds (Wells)
  49
Warner, Charles Dudley 187
Weaver, Warren 222, 230
Weaver, William 31
Weinberger, Eliot 5, 133,
  134–6, 155

Index

Wells, H. G. 49
Whatever (Houellebecq) 181
Wikipedia 226
Wilson, Emily 143–4
Wilson, Horace 107
Winnie the Pooh (Milne) 31, 232
Woe from Wit (Griboedov) 43
Wolff, Joseph 33–6, 41, 44–5
word embeddings 225–6
Wright, Thomas 133–4, 137–8
Wunschloses Unglück (Handke) 181

Y

Yalta Conference 104–5
Yanchevetsky, Dmitry 193–4, 195–6, 197–9, 201, 203, 204
Yates, Frances A. 65, 69, 70–1
Yeltsin, Boris 29–30
Young Turk revolution 122–3
Yunus Bey 80

Z

Zorin, Valerian 19